William Dickinson

Cumbriana

Fragments of Cumbrian Life

William Dickinson

Cumbriana
Fragments of Cumbrian Life

ISBN/EAN: 9783743349971

Manufactured in Europe, USA, Canada, Australia, Japa

Cover: Foto ©ninafisch / pixelio.de

Manufactured and distributed by brebook publishing software (www.brebook.com)

William Dickinson

Cumbriana

CUMBRIANA.

CUMBRIANA

OR

FRAGMENTS OF CUMBRIAN LIFE

By the Compiler of the
"GLOSSARY OF CUMBERLAND WORDS AND PHRASES"

SECOND EDITION
REVISED AND ENLARGED

LONDON
WHITTAKER & CO AVE MARIA LANE
WHITEHAVEN CALLANDER & DIXON MARKET PLACE
1876

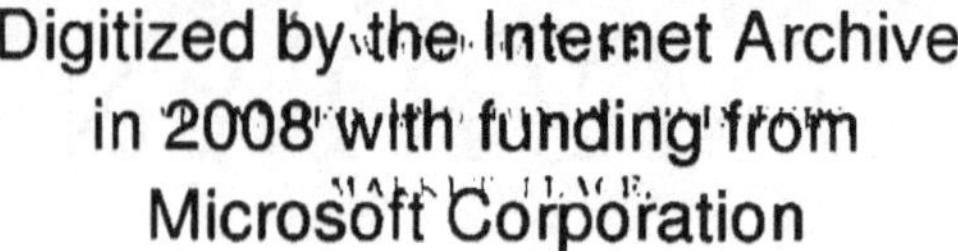

DEDICATED,

MRS. CRAIG GIBSON.

———

In memory of my fellow-labourer and acceptable contributor in attempting to perpetuate the Cumberland dialect in its purity, and of the old-standing friendship I had the happiness to enjoy during the life of the late Dr. Alexander Craig Gibson, this volume is dedicated to his amiable and much respected relict; as another, among many, memorials of his great skill in portraying the habits and feelings of the humbler classes of the people of this county and its borders; and of the admirable talent displayed in his "Laal Dinah Grayson," "Bobby Banks' Bodderment," and numerous other unapproachable effusions in our quaint and quiet dialect.

WM. DICKINSON.

PREFATORY NOTE.

Encouraged by the rapid sale of "Cumbriana," I am induced to issue a Second Edition, with the additions my friends have kindly supplied, and with due revision.

W.D.

INTRODUCTION.

AT the risk of overstocking the market, now when so many writers exercise their pens on my native dialect (and there are only few who do not try to make our broad dialect broader still), I again venture before the public in practically applying the contents of *The Glossary of the Words and Phrases of Cumberland.*

Trifling as the contents of this volume may seem to some, the collection has been made with a view to perpetuate a remembrance of local traditions, and of the manners and customs of old times, with occasional illustrations of character exhibited in the sayings and doings of the people of Cumberland, and occasionally of its immediate borders. An experience of more than threescore and ten years has made matters of this nature very familiar; and many old people will be able, from personal recollection, to confirm the correctness of most of what is introduced.

It is not to be expected that the whole contents of the volume will be found entertaining to every one who may chance to read it, for tastes vary; but it is hoped that all may find something pleasing in it, and that none may find anything of an objectionable character.

Some of the anecdotes may be interesting from their connection with the names of persons living, or with localities. Some may lose a portion of their interest to the rising generations in the lapse of time, but all will aid in preserving a record of local legends and unwritten tales which are fast passing into oblivion ; and they may also tend to enliven the hearth of many a family in the dulness of a long winter's evening. If used in moderation, the reading may last over many weeks, and need interfere with no moral, household, or other duties in the rehearsal. Some three or four of the anecdotes have appeared in the local papers, and are inserted here because they essentially belong to the county and are worthy of revival. Some anecdotes may lose their point after the existence of the generation during which they took their rise ; and that circumstance should be taken into account in reading a few of the following.

There is a certain connection between the tale and the teller, or the originator, of an anecdote, which heightens the interest ; and if this link be broken by the absence or death of the person most concerned, and the reader or listener does not happen to have been acquainted with the peculiarities or drollery of the party, the anecdote suffers in proportion ; and many will suffer from being read, instead of being delivered by the originator with his own emphasis and action.

Some will be found of genuine wit. Many are ridiculous blunders, or simplicity personified ; but all will aid in recording the manners and customs, or in furnishing illustrations of character pertaining to the present, as well as to times gone by.

More anecdotes and amusing speeches have had their origin among the simple-hearted and the lowly of the slow-speaking Cumbrians, than have arisen from the more elevated classes. From the one may be reckoned the outflowing of the feelings of the heart, while the other may be, in a great measure, the result of education and research. The one is a sly humour or innocent simplicity, the other may be the offspring of wit or of higher learning.

Almost every village could contribute a good quota of anecdote; and many lone houses have been the repositories of amusing stories and legends, illustrative of rural life and manners. These, through the alterations in the style of living, and in the improved and constantly improving systems of education, with a continual widening of intercourse among all classes, to which the extension of railways largely contributes —these have, in some measure driven out, or have assisted to quell as vulgar, the habit of repeating anecdotes; and thus, much of the domestic history of the county has been for ever lost. This collection may afford the means of acquainting the people of one end of the county with the sayings and doings of the inhabitants of the other. To those who have mingled much in the different grades of Cumbrian society, it need not be said that we are a quiet spoken people. And the few who have not been dwellers with us, and who may have patience to wade through this fragmentary production, will find it true that, unless under great excitement, we are not of the race that is wont to set the lakes on fire. An occasional burst of forcible language will occur, under strong influences; but the ordinary tenor of speech is of a retiring character.

It has not been without some effort and research that this collection has been brought together. Some can, in the exuberance of their memory, relate anecdote after anecdote, who cannot be prevailed upon to commit them to paper; and amid such abundance there is no little difficulty in recollecting and selecting, and writing in the racy style of a good narrator, such ones as may be acceptable to a reader; and doubtless many worthy of record are entirely lost in this way.

The following are part of the jottings made from time to time, as opportunity offered; many, if not all the actors have crossed that bourne whence none return.

I gratefully acknowledge the valuable contributions of the late Dr. A. C. Gibson, Mr. Heskett, Mr. H. A. Fletcher, Mr. Jefferson, of Preston Hows, and other friends.

W. D.

THORNCROFT, WORKINGTON,
    26th April, 1875.

CUMBRIANA.

" As life requires repose from serious employment, and this repose may be enlivened by amusement, there seems to be a virtue relative to the intercourse of men in their hours of relaxation and merriment, regulating both the matter and the manner of their relaxation."—Aristotle.

UNPUBLISHED RECORDS.

RALPH DOUGLAS'S ADVENTURE ON THE ICE.

In the last quarter of the eighteenth century Ralph Douglas was an athletic young man, living with his parents at Woodend, in Thornthwaite, and was fond of shooting, skating, &c. One winter's day he set off with his gun and skated across the lake to have a day's shooting in Bassenthwaite; he amused himself till dusk, when he returned by the nearest line over the ice from Bawness towards home, and being an excellent skater was careering away in great enjoyment when he felt the ice bend under him. Thinking that, if he attempted to turn, the ice would give way, he concluded it was best to go on as quietly and quickly as possible, and to endeavour to get upon stronger ice. After a few strokes he found the ice still weaker, and that a dish or hollow was formed under him as he proceeded, and he felt he was always at the bottom of it. Being a good swimmer he never lost confidence, but continued on till the ice did break and in he went, gun and all.

He kept hold of the gun with one hand and managed to swim with the other hand to the edge of the ice, and to lift his gun upon it. The ice breaking as he advanced, he pushed his gun upon it before him ; and partly swimming, and partly holding on by the edges till it broke, he contrived to advance, after several breakings, to where the ice was strong enough to bear him. Raising himself on his elbows, by a sudden and venturous spring he got on the sound ice once more, after travelling in the water more than a hundred yards in a keen frosty evening. But his troubles were not at an end, for by the bending of the edge of the ice when he was in the act of mounting it, his favourite gun slipped off and sank to the bottom. Not liking to make another plunge, although a good diver, he made the best of his way home, where a party of young people were assembling, by invitation, for a dance ; and without giving them any attention, or thinking of anything but of saving his gun, he ascended to the hayloft. Knowing the depth of water in which his gun lay, he selected a dry pole from the loft and tied it by the middle to a rope, and the rope to a stone ; then hastening back, threw all into the lake together, as near to his gun as possible, and had the satisfaction of seeing the pole float on the water over the place. He then went home and enjoyed himself with the party, not mentioning his adventure to anyone.

The frost continued a few days, but did not freeze hard enough to permit of his going to his pole. Confident in his expedient, he waited till the thaw came : and then, in a boat, rowed to where he expected his pole-buoy, but found he had miscalculated, and that the ice, on breaking up and being driven before the wind, had cut the cable which anchored his buoy. The pole had floated down the lake ; the rope had sunk ; and the favourite gun still rests at the bottom of lake Bassenthwaite.

I'LL TRY THEE, DICK.

In the year 1800, Joseph Waite, of Brownrigg, in the Abbey Holme, ordered his sons to yoke his horse " Dick " to the cart, and to load it with well-dressed wheat.

When the usual load of six Cumberland bushels was put on, he told them to put on more, and more still; saying with each sack, " I'll try thee, Dick ! " His sons thought their father had gone mad, for he ordered them to put on till twenty bushels of good wheat were on the cart, still saying, " I'll try thee, Dick ! " He started with Dick and his load, repeating as he went " I'll try thee. Dick," till he finally delivered it at the Abbey Mill and received sixty guineas for his one-horse cart-load, or three guineas per Carlisle bushel ! Dick had less difficulty and much praise in returning with his load of money.

HAY CASTLE AND DRUNKEN DICKINSON.

On the authority of Thomas Litt, of Distington, in 1838 a man of four score, I have it that Hay Castle and much landed property near it, with all the Manor of Distington, belonged, within his memory, to a person named " drunken " Dickinson, and had been in the family for many generations.

Dickinson was a very tall man, and very outward in conduct. Through his and his immediate ancestor's extravagance the family became reduced in circumstances, and, for a livelihood, Dickinson bound himself apprentice to the great grandfather of the late Thomas Hartley, Esq., of Gillfoot, a merchant and shipowner. The manor and most of the lands were sold in the meantime to the then owners of Moresby Hall, who afterwards sold them to the Lowthers. Dickinson continued very idle and dissolute; and, during a drunken fit, after the expiration of his apprenticeship, he sold the Hay Castle and land to some person who took advantage of his intoxication and bought the whole for a mere fraction of its value.

Mr. Hartley, hearing of this, interested himself in the case, rescued the property, and restored it to the owner, subsequently purchasing the reversionary interest for an annuity of sixty pounds during Dickinson's life. He, Dickinson, still continued his habits, and by some unaccountable means took a strong dislike to Mr. Hartley, employing every means to annoy and abuse him ; and on one occasion, having thrashed his best friend. was committed to gaol for six months. After his liberation he again attacked Mr. Hartley, almost killed him, and was a second time imprisoned for a longer term. Being still in receipt of his annuity he held on drinking to such an excess, after coming out of gaol, that it soon ended in his death; and the reversion came entire into Mr. Hartley's hands.

The ruins of the old castle still stand on the north side of the mill ; and tradition says large vaults with groined arches may be found there, but covered with soil and rubbish.

DUELLING.

A gentleman, who had frequent access to the documents belonging to the archives of Workington Hall, stated that, in old times, during an assize meeting at Carlisle, a Curwen and a Howard of Corby quarrelled ; and one called the other a " tyke." A challenge and duel on the sands ensued, when the Curwen shot the Howard.

LAMPLUGH CLUB.*

CAN ya remember owt o' " Lampla' Club " when it was i' full voag, aboot 1808?

Aa was at yan o' ther girt yearly club days at t' Cross, an' can tell ya summat aboot it.   It's still hodden o't second Friday o' Joon, an' that year a reet het day it was.   It was Wilson o' Mowerkin's‡ turn to be President, and a grand leukan fellow he was as he marcht ta church an' back ageann, wid a blue sash ower his shooders, and a girt flag flappen abeun his heed.   A gay lock o' fwok hed giddert up i' time ta gang to t' church, an' away we struttit.   A band o' music went furst, an' than t' President, like sum girt general at t' heed av an army ; bit a querish army he hed to follow him !   T' preest, oald Mr. Gregson, marcht next tull aim, an' then a few couples o' t' oaldest men int' club : and than ivry kind went, ov o' sworts, an' sizes, an' ages ; bit a lot o' t' bettermer swort went afoor t' rest.   Lampla' Church was as full as it cud cram, for sum 'at com in leatt hed ta stand o' t' time, an' two or three bits o' lasses fentit an' hed ta be bworn oot.   It's weel it was nea warse, for it was parlish sweltry.   When t' singers began, sum o' t' music men streukk in wa ther girt gruntan horns an' things, an' playt base.   Aa hardly thowt it whyte reet, bit it was varra nice, an' it meadd me o' thirl sumtimes.

T' oald man gev us a canny laal sarman, an' aa dar say a reet gud an ; and nea doot he wad git his ginny for't, at oald Lord Lampla' left in his will, ta be gien to t' preest for preachan that day as lang as t' club hods tagidder.   Sek crushing theer was amang t' lads ta git oot ! bit t' President meadd tham o' fo' back an'

<hr>

*The incidents herein related are true, the dates of a few minor ones excepted.
‡ Mockerkin.

keep theer pleasses efter him. When we gat to t'
Cross theer was mair an' mair cumman ivry noo an'
than, an' fwok squeezt in to t' dinner teables till theer
was hardly room to lift a fork. They dinnert on hofe
o' t' efterneun, an' t' band playt, bit t' main fun
duddent begin till t' edge o' t' ibnin.

Fwok keept cumman in still fray o' parts—

> " Lampla' an' Loweswater, lang men an' lean.
> " Ho-s, roags, an' theeves, fray Branthet an' Dean,"*

an' menny a yan 'at wad hardly hev sek anudder
holiday till t' next club day mebby. Beath o' t'
hooses† was far ower laal to hod a quarter o' them,
an' fwok hed to stand aboot int' lonnin, or lig ageann
t' dykes, an' lissen t' band playan, or chatter away
amang thersells. Till o' t' dinneren was ower theer
wazzant a chance o' gittin owt ta drink oot o' doors,
an' sum went an' drank at Lund spoot, while yan or
two brayzent fellows fray Harras Moor squeezt in an'
brang oot a quart in ayder hand, for thersells an' sek
like ; an' mebby reet aneuff—if they nobbet payt
for't !

On efter dinner a bit. when fwok hed gitten a glass
or two round, t' President began to tell t' club fwok
hoo t' club matters steudd, and hoo mickel mair they
hed this year int' iron kist, an' than theer was a cheer,
an' t' oot deur fwok wondert what was ta cum next.

Than he telt them hoo menny new members had
entert this year, an' he sed ther consarns was flurrishin
famishly, an' ther was anudder hurray ! An' then he
sed he whopt ivry body wad join, an' t' club wad seunn
be as strang as t' bank ov Ingland ; an' to be shoor,
that dud bring oot a hurrah ! an' t' lads oot side teukt
up an' meadd o' ring ageann.

Than t' hoose folk gat mair help, an' they set furms

* Traditional Rhyme.
† There were two Inns at Lumplugh Cross at the time.

an' oald barrells oot ageann t' hoose side, an' on be' t' dykes ; an' fwok drew into knots o' ther oan kind, an' fell to crackan an' chatteran like a hundred wizzels in a steann wo. Oald Carter was theer fray t' mill, and he'd teann gud kearr to git into fettle seunn on, an' he capert in an' oot an' chattert like a teamm pyet, amang fwok he'd niver seen afoor. He gat helpt up on a plank 'at was laid cross two barrels, an' wad co' a seall.

An' just when he was gaan to strike off a lot "goin, goin," sum unlucky elf gev t' barrels a shuv, and doon he com like a sleatter. An' when he was fairly dun ower for owt else, he cud still rwor oot, "go, Billy, go," as if he was fleean away astride ov his oald gallapan nag.

'T" crak gat varra thrang noo, an' t' fell-deall lads talkt aboot ther cur dogs, an' t' best way to cure t' scab, an' telt how menny sheep they'd hed smoort i' t' girt Martinmas snow. Branthet chaps hed gitten Fisher ov Innerdale brig amang them, an' he keept them o' laughan wid his droll stwories aboot cockfeytin ; an' than he gat a match meadd for a main o' cocks ageann Easter. They treatit him, an' he led them on a fine peazz.

Harras Moor fellows was a kind o' hofe fratchan wi' Dissenton fwok aboot ther bull-dogs an' tarriers, bit they'd been darkan an' lissenan at t' seamm time, an' when they hard a word aboot a cockfeyt, they wad hev a finger in it teah. Bit Fisher saw what was gaan to be up, an' he wazzent lang till he hed them o' feytan togidder, an' o' was towry-lowry ! He was a rare eg-battle, bit he teuk gid care to keep at ootside his-sell.

When this scruffel was on, t' Whillimer lions cuddent be whyet, an' they com forrat an' sed they war enny o' them riddy for enny body, an' Symy Lock hed a bit ov a toozel wid sum o' them.

An' rare wark theer wad ha' been if Will Litt *
heddent sprang in amang them an' sed they suddent
feyt, an' he whangt them aboot like as many geslins;
bit he duddent git them fairly partit till sum o' them
gat gay bleuddy feasses.   T' meast o' them was willin'
to giv way ta him, for they o' knew it was neah single
handat job to cum crossways o' him, an' it o' settelt
doon ageann.

Them in t' hoose hed gitten gayly croozy be this
time, and famish cracks they hed.

Willy Pearson was leattish o' cumman, an' he popt
his heed in at deur, an' sez, " Winge, what hoo preuvv
ye o'? " and sek a laugh it raizt !

Oald Jobby,* o' Smeathat, crakt o' pooers about his
white bitch, Countess, an' two or three mair hounds
he hed ; an' he telt yan ov his fox-hunting stwories,
hoo he tally-ho't a fox ya Sunday † mwornin, just as
day brak, oot ov a borran o' steanns, abeunn Flootern
tarn, i' Herdas end ; an' hoo it teukk ower be t'
Cleugh-gill, an' t' hoonds viewt him sa hard, 'at he
teukt' Broadwater, an' swam cross t' hee end ont, an'
t' dogs went roond an' gat on t' drag, an' up t' Side
wood.   Hoo he ran hevvy a while, as weel he med
when he was o' wet, and they whisselt him up be t'
Iron Crag, an' be t' Silver Cwove, an' than throo t'
Pillar, an' a gay rough bit o' grund it is !   Hoo he
shakt them off a bit theer, an' they at him ageann, an'
meadd o' ring amang t' rocks.   Hoo they ran him
roond be Black Sale, an' Lizza hee faulds, and clam
oot be t' Scarf Gap, an' on to t' Wo' heed, an' thay
beeldit am ondert' Brock Steann, an' he was seaff
aneuff theer !   Fwok o' lissent to sek a huntin teall,
an' when it was ower thay buzzt and talkt yan amang
anudder, like bees in a het day.

* Author of " Wrestliana," &c.
* Mr. Joseph Bowman, of Smaithwaite.
† Sunday morning was then a common hunting time for the fox.

Will Pearson, o' Bannockrow, telt a gay good stwory aboot his runnin t' trail ov a brock frayt fairy-whols * tull aboot Eskat woods, wid his five white dogs; an' thay startit t' brock theer, an' Jossy Steel man streukt dykin ax intat brock's buttock; bit it mannisht ta git intat whol efter o' an' wad likely dee theer.

Deyell,† o' Stocka Ho', an' Jothan Branthet, talkt aboot gedderan tithe; an' Jo Deall sed theer cud be nowt sa good as Lampla puddin'.‡

Tom Brown, an' William Frear, an' oald Billy Graham, and Banker Billy,§ wid his wig and pigtail, gat tagidder, an' talkt lang aboot aljibra,—bit thay gat o' t' crack to thersells; an' sum o' them wondert if Johnny Ware wad put owt in t' "*Packet*" next week, aboot sec deeins as they hed theer.

Harrison, o' Watter Yat, thowt the "*virginity* o' man was cun till a parlish pass, when fwok cud lock t' wheels ov a wood-waggon to hinder't o' runnin amain— an' he remembert time when three woo wheels was gangan in his oan hoose, an' noo theer was two marvel chimla pieces an' what nut!"

Jwony Braythat squeekt and meadd rymes ivry noo an' than, an' meadd o' fwok laugh.

Saul, o' t' Ho', wad talk aboot nowt bit Lampla' hokey bulls, an' sec-like, and he seunn went off heamm.

Willy Fisher, wid his hair o' plettit roond, smeukt cleet leaves an' annaseeds, an' talkt aboot t' best way o' makkin mote; an' a deel o' tham wondert what sec feutt-bo lake they wad hev at Leeps boddam next Easter Sunday.

Jwon White, o' t' Hollins. was in for shuttan snipes, an' skooderan them doon i' t' Scalla || springs i' hard

---

* Limestone caves near Millgill-head.　　† Dalzell.
‡ Lamplugh pudding consisted of biscuits or buns steeped till soft in hot ale, with seasoning and spirits according to taste.
§ The late Mr. W. Dickinson, Sen., of Kidburngill.　|| Scallow.

weather; bit sum o' them telt am he sud ha' been
pooan his sheep oot o' t' snow drifts astead of shuttan
snipes, an' he slinkt away oot.

Mattha Jackson bragt aboot findin an eagle liggan
deed, at Murton-brow-heed, when he was a bit ov a
lad; an' it was t' last 'at hed been seen i' t' country.
He sed it hed claws as thick as his thooms, an' thay
war neah laal ans! Mattha shot in wid a stwory
aboot his trailan a car-wheel up to Knockmurton pike
an' settan 't off doon t' screes. It went like a mill-o'-
fire, an' leapp fray crag to crag, an' was smasht o' to
flinders afoor it gat doon into Cogra Moss.

Clark Anthony winkt an' girn't and set fcasses, an'
sang—

> " My wife is dead, and I am free,"
> " Seah far tha weel soor apple tree ;"

an' menny a rare sang was sung beside, til t' loft was
wantit for t' dancers. An' than sek a kick-up! T'
lasses an' lads war seunn o' out on t' fleurr tagidder,
an' dansan pell-mell, fit ta brek t' loft doon. A deal
o' t' elder set began ta sydel away when t' fiddles
streuk up, an' sum o' t' rest began ta git rayder ower
full an' gat ta janglin like owt.

Jacob Fox brayt a Workiton chap till he was o'
bleud an' batter ower, an' then he chopt up a drinkin
glass, an' eat it ivry snap. Neah wunder he was o'
bleud an' o'! Gayly leatt on next mwornin some o'
them fand Jacob pooan brackins to lig doon on i'
Murton lonnin.

Thay refuse't ta let Kit Marshall hev enny mair to
drink, an' pot am oot, an' off he went heamm in his
tantrums, an' was seunn back wid his ax ower his
shooder, an' began to hag his way throo t' deur, an'
swearr he was nobben carven his cwot ov arms on't,—
bit efter sek wark as that we'ed better say laal mair
aboot it. It was noo gittan on ta daybrek, an' dansy

King* ast if enny o' t' lads wad set am towerts Pard-
sah† as he was rayder short seetit, an' med git inta t'
becks. Tom Wilson was riddy for owt' at leukt like
fun, an' he wad steer Dansy heamm. When thay gat
to Cross-yats beck, Tom thowt it wazzent seaff for
beath ta venter ower t' sleatt brig at a time, an' thay
sud tak t' watter. It wad be towerts a yard deep at t'
hee side, an Tom pot am next that side, an' telt him
ta hod weel up. When they war fairly in t' deepest
on't, Tom mannisht ta stummer an' fo', an' bring t'
maister wid am, —an' beath hed ta crowl oot, like two
hofe droont rattens. Tom set am on a bit, an' than
cum back ta t' Cross, wet as he was ; bit he care't nowt
aboot that if he nobbet gat a bit o' spwort raizt. An'
seah endit that club day, an menny anudder sec like
beath afoor an' sen.

FEMALE COURAGE.

FOR courage and prompt contrivance in a case of
emergency, the following, told by a son of the actress,
has not often been surpassed. About 1850, on a fine
summer day, when the family were out and busy with
haymaking, three undisguised tramps went to a lone
farm house near Egremont, where only the old lady
was at home. They were very importunate for relief,
and pressed to be admitted into the house ; but the
old woman, who was stripped to her work and very
busy, desired them to stay outside till she brought
something for them. She quickly opened the door
partly, and put out the muzzle of a gun, threatening
to shoot, and they thinking from her dishabille that
she was a maniac, took to their heels and ran off, not
knowing that the gun was empty.

* Mr. King, a noted teacher of dancing.   † Pardshaw.

THE "CRACKS" OF AN ORE-CARTER'S WIFE.

Cum sit thee ways doon, and give us thee crack,
Aav been rayder badly and pain't a' me back;
A crack does yan good, an' aav less to deah noo
Sen t' horses was selt, an' aav neah hay to poo.

Oor Jemmy ses t' horses hes dun us laal good,
Takkin o' in account it's no wonder they sud;
For they eat sek a heap o' good things, barn, aa lay,
Thoo waddent beleev't if aa talkt for a day.

I't' dark winter mwornins' about three o'clock,
He shootit o't' lads ta git up, an' be gock !
He nivver cud lig a bit langer his sel,
For fear t' lads sud leave owt undun an' nit tell.

An' what cud aa deah when he was afeutt,
Bit up an' makt' poddish, while he went ta teutt
Amang t' horses an' git them ther crowdy an' meal,
For hoo cud they work if they warrent fed weel?

Than away thay wad hurry to Cleator for ore,
Wi' sum hay in a sek an' ther best leg afore;
Thay com back o' sweat an' o' dust twice a day,
An' t' white horse as reed as if daub't wi' reed clay.

An' t' lads, to be shoor, sek seets they com heamm,
Wi' sek cleaz, an' sek feasses, it was a fair sheamm;
An' than thay meadd t' blankets far warse nor git oot,
For thay leukt for o' t' warld like webs o' reed cloot.

Yan med wesh, barn, an' scrub till yan's fingers was sair,
An nivver wad t' things o' yan's house be clean mair;
T' varra hair o' yan's heed gat as reed as a fox,
An' it spoils o' my caps 'at's lockt up in a box.

Bit noo sen thayv oppent oot t' railway to't' Birks,
Weev partit wi t' horses an' cars, an' two stirks;
Teahh lad's gitten hiert, an' aav less ta dee,
An' tudder, nowt suits am but ganging to t' see.

What changes it's mead in our Hensigem street!
An' asteed o' reed muck we'll hev't clean as a peat;
For weev Innerdale watter as cheap as oald rags,
An' we'el now see laal mair o' t' oald cars an' oald nags.

'Twas just tudder day 'at yan fell doon i't street,
'Twad ha' pittit thy heart, barn, ta leukk on an' see't;
Hoo it greannt as it laid till they reetit it up,
An' they yokt it ageann and laid at it wi't' whup.

Oor Jemmy, he sez, if he ivver gits poor,
Thay'll be settin am up for a mileston hees shoor;
Bit he laughs when he sez't, for he's summat laid bye,
An' he'll still mak a leevin as seaff as he'll try.

Beddelmer-gill Feull, April, 1856.

THE LEGEND OF MOCKERKIN* TARN.

The Tarn is on the roadside from Cockermouth to Lamplugh. Its extent is about a dozen acres ; and it is said to occupy the site of the ancient village of Mockerkin.

SIR MOCHAR, the dwarf, was a valiant knight,
  And he dwelt in a noble old hall ;
He had forty stout yeomen well arm'd for the fight,
  All ready to answer his call.

His hall was a castlet o'er top't by a tower,
  Around it a moat wide and deep ;
A drawbridge and gateway evinced his power,
  With dungeon below, and strong keep.

A sturdy old knight was Sir Mochar the dwarf,
  Both active and self-willed was he ;
Courageous and fierce too as ever donn'd scarf,
  Or hung up poor carle on tree.

With features sun-stained, and countenance grim,
  His teeth all uneven and yellow ;
His hair and his beard all grizzled—not prim,
  Himself a repulsive old fellow.

His shoulders were broad and his frame so strong,
  His stature but four feet three ;
His legs were short, and his arms were long,
  And he sat on his horse like a flea.

The long-handled axe was his favourite brand,
  He could chop off a limb like a woodman ;
The stroke of his weapon came easy to hand,
  Oh ! he was a fierce—not a good man.

* *Kin* is a diminutive term ; hence little Mochar's tarn, or the modern Mockerkin tarn.

His coal-black charger shone bright as his axe,
    And of courage as high as his own ;
A pair so determined could seldom be match'd,
    They could daunt nigh to death with their frown.

And all that Sir Mochar the dwarf undertook,
    In battle, in foray, or chase ;
It was done in the saddle.   His charger black Rook,
    With Sir Mochar was still in his place.

The dark deeds of evil were Mochar's delight,
    His horse could enjoy them as well ;
Whatever deed crossed the mind of the knight,
    By instinct his horse it could tell.

And when he was called to the war by the king,
    With his battle axe slung by his side ;
His forty bold yeomen with axe, bow, and sling,
    And Rook in the height of his pride.

With the pageant of war so delighted was he,
    At the prospect to kill and to slay ;
His heart would beat quick, and he'd chuckle with
      glee,
    And Rook would like feeling display.

None knew where black Rook was bought, neither yet
      where
    He was bred, nor his pedigree told ;
Some said and believed he had dropt from the air,
    And all wonder'd he did not wax old.

The knight had lost teeth—his hair iron-grey,
    And he grew more morose as he ag'd ;
Whatever he said he would never unsay,
    Right or wrong if he once it engag'd.

Black Rook shone like jet, and was active and strong,
   Without a grey hair on his hide ;
He was swift as the wind, and endurëd it long,
   When his Master appointed to ride.

And when in pursuit of the boar or the deer,
   With twenty fierce hounds in full cry,
Black Rook he would yell and Sir Mochar would cheer,
   Their delight in the chase was so high.

No boar. neither deer, could escape the fleet pack,
   With Rook and Sir Mochar in chase ;
For Rook never tired with Mochar on back,
   And each always kept in his place.

No distance annoy'd them, nor speed cut their wind,
   Nor up-hill nor down-hill flagg'd they ;
Nor halted nor swerv'd in the course from the find,
   Till boar or stag turnëd at bay.

And then would Sir Mochar alight from his steed,
   With bright hunting blade in his hand ;
And would strike with such nerve that he never had
     need,
   The stroke to repeat with his brand.

And then the strong Dwarf to Hall Mochar would
     wend,
   On the saddle before him his prey ;
But how it got there, or who did help lend,
   No man but Sir Mochar could say.

Some thought he was wizard enough in himself,
   Some thought his horse Rook would lie down ;
Till the carcase was slung by the aid of an elf,
   Or by strong gust of wind it was blown

To the front of the rider and there placëd sure,
  And some thought black Rook it could swing
From the ground with his teeth, and make it secure,
  As if it were bound with a string.

However 'twas done, it was always done well,
  And quickly to homeward they'd veer;
The huntsmen and yeomen seem'd under a spell,
  So far they'd been left in the rear.

He had followers many, but friends he had few,
  Neither wife nor yet children had he;
His men were sent out their oft search to renew,
  Till they brought him fair damsels in—three.

From hearth-stones of comfort these fair ones were
    torn,
  And consenting or not 'twas the same;
For he was their thane; on his lands they were born,
  They must go at the sound of his name.

And home they were brought him, as others before,
  Unhappy and sorrowful all;
To 'scape in his absence determined full sore,
  Whenever that time should befal.

Aware of his doings in times not remote,
  They dread his intentions of harm;
The sorrow to others he'd formerly wrought,
  Was sufficient to cause them alarm.

Of wrong he'd no thought, no compunction had he,
  No regrets ever crossëd his mind;
That his deeds were of evil he never could see,
  Nor thought his base actions unkind.

C

To his sins quite oblivious ; to errors so blind ;
  Unknown to all virtues or grace ;
No enjoyments had he of a praiseworthy kind,
  Except in the wars or the chase.

He delighted in rapine, in plunder, in blood,
  In revel and riot as well ;
And oft when the larder grew bare to the wood,*
  His yeomen to horse would compel.

Then up mounted he, and away went the band,
  Determined to harry the North ;
The best sheep or kine they could find on the land,
  To homeward they'd hurry them forth.

Enwrapt in goat skins were hard bannocks—(their fare
  During forays) and strapt on the back,
And oftentimes meagre and small was their share,
  —In meal-ark † at home not a snack.

No eye had Sir Mochar nor yet had his men,
  For aught save the plunder in view ;
The beauties of nature were outside the ken
  Of both he and his hard-hearted crew.

The small crops of bigg and oats found on their route,
  Served their horses for food as they went ;
The owners they thought would not find the thieves out,
  Nor look to the reivers for rent.

In one of these raids, so successful were they
  In lifting a score of good kine ;
And in getting them safely and quickly away,
  Before the day on them did shine.

* Shelves.
† The meal-chest, where meal, oat-bread, and sue: were usually kept.

And over the Border, and round Solway moss,
    Over which not the boldest durst ride ;
Lest his horse and he sink—irretrievable loss,
    As sure as if drowned in the tide.

And over the moors, and through the fierce streams,
    Where bridges or roads were not found ;
And through the foul swamp where the wild-fire
     gleams,
    And o'er many an old battle-ground.

Escaping pursuit to Hall Mochar they wend,
    All hungry and tired, man and beast ;
Quick orders are issued that first they intend,
    To slay and make ready a feast.

The fleshers are summoned the fattest to slay,
    Ever ready to come at his call ;
The long oaken table must make its display,
    Green rushes must carpet the hall.

Strong ale from the cellars was soon in request,
    Sir Mochar ordained it to be;
The maidens were ordered to don in their best,
    That night he would spend in high glee.

He'd accomplished his object, replenished his store,
    Had harried the fair glen of Nith ;
He spoiled the Scots, whom no goodwill he bore,
    To them, or their kin, or their kith.

They had forded the Annan and fierce rolling Esk,
    The deep winding Eden they swam ;
They had crossed the Derwent in glen picturesque,
    And all came in safely but Sam.

Now, Sam was a henchman, with countenance bright,
   Of merry good nature and free ;
Sir Mochar had eyed him at morn and at night,
   With jealousy firëd was he.

The maidens encaged in that gloomy old hall,
   Some innocent smiles would bestow ;
On the well-favoured youth, who was also in thrall,
   So Sir Mochar resolved he should go.

Then mounted behind a stout yeoman was he,
   And off to the raid he was sent ;
He was neither forewarned of what was to be,
   Nor aware of Sir Mochar's intent.

The yeoman had orders—(forgot is his name,)
   To unhorse the poor youth in the flood ;
And in crossing the Eden, that river of fame,
   With the yeoman 'twas well understood,

That his horse was to curvette, and caper, and rear,
   That the youth might be slipt off behind ;
So when the mid stream they had swam to or near,
   All the Dwarf said was done to his mind.

For this yeoman got into the midst of the troop,
   The cattle all swimming before ;
When his horse 'gan to plunge, and the yeoman to stoop,
   As if he would help the lad more.

But he seized the youth's ankle with vigour replete,
   And swinging him quickly around ;
Hitched him into the stream, and beneath the horse-feet
   He was kickëd, and trampled, and drowned.

———

Sir Mochar grew merry and so did his men,
   And fast flew the gibe and the joke;
And round went the can and the drinking horn—then
   Sir Mochar attention bespoke.

He told of his deeds in the chase and the wars,
   Of the numbers he'd struck to the earth;
He boasted his misdeeds and showëd his scars,
   Then made them his subjects of mirth.

He told what he had done, and what yet he would do,
   When the beeves he had stolën were eat;
He'd again cross the Border to shew what he could do,
   And never would dream of being beat.

He dwelt on his deeds and more boisterous grew,
   He thumpt with his fist on the table;
And swore at his yeomen their horns to renew,
   For drinking would no man disable.

And still as he spoke he took time to refresh,
   And direct can and horn to go round;
He'd never be baulked, he swore by all flesh
   He'd have all he wished above ground.

And quick went the horn, and fresh orders sent out,
   For the maidens to bring in more ale—
Three cans at a time, capacious and stout,
   And they to appear without fail.

He had wine in his cellars and brandy from France,
   And the maids should all drink of the best;
They should sing of his deeds, with his yeomen should
   If only they came fitly drest.   [dance,

" So call in the maidens and bring up the wine,"
   " And haste ye, I'll brook no delay;"

" To revel in freedom let all now incline,"
  " Or else, like the dogs, slink away."

" And hark ye, make room for the maidens I say',"
  A woodcutter came to report ;
He had seen the three wenches steal softly away,
  In the dark, while the rest were at sport.

Then up rose Sir Mochar in fury and rage—
  Struck his silver cup flat on the board ;
He cursëd the maidens and bann'd the dead page,
  And roarëd in vengeful discord.

Some minutes before and the hall had resounded
  With jollity, drunkenness, mirth ;
It now rang with vile imprecations unbounded,
  To all which Sir Mochar gave birth.

He shouted—" To horse ye dark villains and ride ;"
  " Take the pack and divide it in three ;"
"Scour the country at speed, and if the maids hide,"
  " Bring them hither.   I'll teach them to flee ! "

They saddled their horses, all tired as they were,
  And rode on the search in the dark ;
The dogs were unkennelled and snuffëd the air,
  Where the maidens had not left their mark.

They scoured the woods, and they skirted the mire,
  They beat round the bush and the tree ;
They durst not delay nor too often enquire,
  Though they wishëd the maidens were free.

Sir Mochar had thoughts that his men might neglect
  To do his commands—or allow
The maids to escape ; or in some way protect,
  Or show favour he did not know how.

So he mounted black Rook and rode furiously forth,
  His axe slung his shoulders behind ;
Determined to ransack east, west, south, and north,
  Resolved his maidens to find.

He heard the dogs bay in three separate arts,
  As each maiden to homeward was aiming,
And fleeing in terror to different parts,
  And aid from above all were claiming.

The dogs were too true, and stuck close to their trail,
  The men were obliged to hark forward ;
For fear their stern master should suddenly hail
  In the rear of them, southward or norward.

He did, and o'ertook them in Hodyoad ghyl,
  As one man was clutching the victim ;
When up rode Sir Mochar and swore he would kill
  Any one who dared thwart or restrict him.

And up went his axe to the stretch of his arm,
  And down quick as thought on the maid ;
Her blood spirted up in his face, red and warm,
  And a corse she was instantly laid.

A grey-headed man looked up at Sir Mochar,
  And said, " Sir, you'll rue this when sober,"
He then in his arms attempted to lock her,
  When Mochar, as sure as October,

Laid him dead at his feet. The maid was his daughter,
  And both in grim death were now laid ;
The father had hopes if he join'd them and sought her,
  He might save her from harm—so he prayed.

Sir Mochar enraged at himself for this deed,
  Made Lamplugh echo his dread curses ;

He vow'd he would save the fled twain if the speed
 Of black Rook would but make him their nurses.

So homeward he rode in his fury ; a hound
 Was again fiercely laid on the scent ;
The trail of the hunt the dog readily found,
 He furiously following, went.

Crossing Black-beck with speed—over Pardshaw-crag
 Heard the dogs in the dark keenly cry ; [dash'd—
Through the edge of Moss Ring he flounder'd and splash'd,
 Then found the White Causeway's path dry.

Then onward he hurried to Eaglesfield crag,
 But there he arriv'd too late ;
For the ban-dogs had seized the maiden, to drag
 Her down to the earth to her fate.

And just as Sir Mochar rode up to the scene,
 Her short dying shriek rent the air ;
The dogs had her throttled, with savageness keen,
 Before he could bid them beware.

One moment he looked at his dogs as they tore
 At the throat of the victim, her hair
Was unloosed and lay spreading and drinking her gore,
 As it reeked from the throat of the fair.

Then up went his axe and with unfailing stroke
 He clave a dog's skull—'twas his best ;
He mangled and maulëd some others, and broke
 The ribs and the backs of the rest.

And there they lay howling and writhing in pain,
 And rolling the victim upon ;
While he 'gan to curse and to blaspheme again,
 For success on that night he had none.

He turned black Rook to homeward once more,
   And bitterly spurred his flanks;
Rook bounded and snorted, and swiftly he bore
   Sir Mochar to other vile pranks.

Rook swift and untiring, soon brought him to home,
   Where he learn'd the course of the third
Of his maidens, whose aim to the east was to roam,
   And to flee his foul house like a bird.

To the eastward he followed in bitter remorse,
   The fugitive hoping to save;
But four of his yeomen approach'd with the corse
   Of the maid from a watery grave.

She had heard the deep bay of the dogs on her track,
   And she fled in all haste in the dark;
The briers and thorns tore her dress from her back,
   And on her fair skin left their mark.

Towards Loweswater lake she fled bleeding and sore,
   Rushing fast down the hill in her fear;
The dogs close behind when she stept on the shore—
   The horsemen alarmingly near.

She stood for a moment—turned round on her foes—
   Gave a shriek that echoed o'er the lake;
Then headlong she plunged—brought her life to a close,
   And baulk'd the fell hounds of their take.

For a moment he thought o'er the ills of that day,
   And the evils befalling the night;
And saw that in all he had made the chief play,
   And that all had been done by his might.

Disappointed he swore that none of their kin,
   Or his yeomen, should ever again
Break bread or take shelter, his castle within,
   While it on the earth should remain.

Now frantic with rage he spurr'd home with a will,
   And finding his warder asleep ;
Blaspheming he swore every man he would kill,
   If his castle sank twenty miles deep.

No sooner he said than a terrific peal
   Of thunder the foundations shook ;
The lightnings gleam'd. and the turrets did reel,
   And the knight and his steed black Rook,

With castle and all sank fearfully deep,
   The waters rush'd up and around ;
And closed above them and laid them to sleep—
   No more were they seen on the ground.

Thus perish'd Sir Mochar the dwarf in his sins—
   A forfeit his lands to the crown ;
And thence the possession of Multon begins,
   And Percies of ancient renown.

The stones of the tower may still be discerned,
   When the tarn is tranquil and clear ;
About twenty feet deep, by those who are learned,
   And have eyes of the wizard or seer.

On Michaelmas night if the stars are not bright,
   Nor the mist on the water too dense—
No matter how windy or stormy that night
   If th' observer possess a due sense

Of the power of his sight, and put faith in it all,
  He may catch a mysterious sight
Of a something slow-floating, emerge from the tall
  Reeds and rushes, more dark than the night.

And slowly and softly the tarn three times
  So quietly voyaging round ;
And then with a sough of the wind's soft chimes,
  Disappear with a lurch and a bound.

This phantom is thought to resemble black Rook,
  On whom his grim master bestrides ;
And all may pronounce, who on it may look,
  It's like nought in this world besides.

On fine Sunday mornings in summer they say,
  Church bells may be heard ringing clear ;
By all who believe in this legend and lay,
  And the sound always thrills them with fear.

And those whom the sins of Sir Mochar dragg'd down
  (Who not of his sinning partook ;)
Wear each a white robe and a golden crown,
  With a bishop's pastoral crook.

They dwell in a palace of crystal below,
  Of hundreds of fathoms so deep ;
And this is the whole that we mortals may know
  Till we rise from our last long sleep.

W. D.

Workington, 1875.

BRANKS AND SONKS.

A GENTLEMAN farmer, residing near Penrith, relates that in one of his journeys to the fairs in the north of Scotland, about 1830, he travelled by coach and sat alongside of the late Mr. Thomas Tweddle, of Askerton Castle; on remarking that their pace was slow Mr. Tweddle said, " Hoot man ! sen Ey meynd, we used to tak yen o' the naigs fray the pasture, and just clap the branks on his head an' the sonks on his back, an' away we went. An' thou kens that was a gey bit slower, an' we cudna de ony better i' thir days."

Branks were a kind of bridles with hempen head-stalls without bits, and Sonks were turf saddles.

Fancy the discomfort of riding two or three hundred miles with such accoutrements and no stirrups; or perhaps only rope stirrups, if any !

CARRYING IT OUT.

A DUEL took place between Sir James Lowther and Sir Frederick Vane. when Sir James shot his antagonist through the foot. The Rev. Henry Lowther's father had been second to Sir James and was his heir, and was not a little surprised when Sir James called on him, some two years after the duel, to request him to be ready to second him again, as he meant to have another shot at the villain, and that he had only been waiting till the wounded foot was healed. Mr. Lowther demurred and finally declined, saying Sir James had already had satisfaction. Sir James turned away in a huff, and made a will leaving the whole property to William, another branch of the family, the father of the present (1869) Earl of Lonsdale.

WILLY LAMB.

IN 1843 I heard various anecdotes of William Lamb, the late owner and occupier of Fell End farm in Ennerdale, and amongst them were the following :—

One Thursday morning Willy was on his way, slow and easy, to Whitehaven market with his butter for sale; when near Hensingham he observed two boys playing at marbles, and heard them dispute about a buck-rabbit. " Buck-rabbet, buck-rabbet," says Willy, " Darret! I want a buck-rabbet."

The boys were willing to sell him the rabbit, but not unless he waited the conclusion of their important game. He sat on horseback, with his basket of butter on his arm, a patient and seemingly interested spectator, until the play was finished, when he went with the boys to their mother's house in Hensingham to view the rabbit. The mother scolded the boys for not having bought butter for her, instead of playing at marbles till the market was over.

Willy pleaded for them, saying the market could not be over when his butter was not there at all ; and after long altercation they agreed to exchange the rabbit for a part of the butter; when he finding he had really " missed his market " turned his horse and rode home with his bargain and the remains of his butter.

Though the farm he occupied was his own, the house was so old and bad that the only place in it free from rain-drop, on a wet day, was under the large beam across the old-fashioned open fire place.

One very stormy day a neighbour found Willie toiling at the churn, and the rest of the family all assembled under the beam as the only place they could stand dry in.

He was so very indolent as to leave his potatoes in the ground all the winter and take up a supply as wanted; but the snow laid so long one winter that Willy was obliged to purchase a supply at a sale, till the thaw came, and he could lift his own. Sometimes, when spring arrived and Willy had potatoes to spare but still in the ground, he would turn them up with the plough, and after adding a little manure, would quietly turn them in again for another season's crop.

His improvidence, with the aid of a costly lawsuit against Moses Nicholson, whose bull threw Willy over a hedge, reduced his means till he was obliged to sell his estate, after building a new dwelling on it, and scarcely having time to finish it. Times were not brisk, and he had some difficulty in disposing of his estate : but having succeeded, he went home rejoicing, and ordered his wife to prepare something good for supper, as he had at last got his land sold, for he had long been plagued with it. His wife was sorry rather than glad, and unwilling to make a feast; having nothing better than ordinary fare in the house he was not to be put off in this way. saying, he was always fond of good eating ; and bade his wife kill the young grey goose, as she had only sat a fortnight, and would make a nice roast. Accordingly the poor goose was killed, *skinned*, and roasted, and Willy enjoyed his feast on the sale of the only property he ever had.

Willy was parish clerk at Ennerdale for many years, and prided himself greatly on his vocal performances as a psalmist ; and when he felt the pinching of want he laid great blame on his parents, who, he said, would not buy him a fiddle, he who had so fine an ear for music ! Being always of opinion that his ruin was to be imputed to the want of the fiddle. He was fond of hunting, and in his better days kept two or three hounds to join the pack of the late Mr. Henry Westray, of Eskat, Bow-bearer to the Earl of Lonsdale. One of these, a black bitch called " Shifty," was his especial favourite, and enjoyed a cushion in his arm-chair as her bed ; when he was so far reduced as to find it needful to apply for parochial relief, he was several times repulsed until he consented to part with his hound.

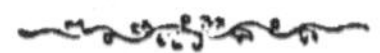

PARISH PARLIAMENT IN OLD DAYS.

IN a field called Deer-garth, on the Armboth Estate in Wythburn, is a large grey stone having a sloping flat top. Around this stone, called the " Girse Howe Stone," Manorial Courts and public meetings of the parishioners were formerly held, the attendants resting their backs against the stone, or sitting or standing around, according to convenience and the state of the weather.

ABSOLUTION.

FROM an ancient manuscript register of the Prior of Wetheral it appears, that Robert Highmore, Lord of Dewaldeth, had taken a mare " of the goods of John " of Torpenhow had got the mortuary, wherefore he " " was excommunicated;—and having asked absolution " " and restored the mare to Sir Robert Ellargill vicar of " " Torpenhow, and in remembrance given the six best " " oakes in his wood to the vicar, the bishop of Carlisle " " absolved him."

WRECKING.

A VESSEL belonging to Captain Abraham Bell, of Whitehaven, was wrecked on the Drigg coast some years ago, and his brother and a friend went to take charge of the wreck. A deep snow was on the ground, so that they easily traced part of the plundered goods to the neighbouring houses, and recovered it. The late Mr. Thompson, of Sandford, assisted the care-takers in the recovery, and also in the use of sticks and whips in driving off the more audacious plunderers.

At the distance of a mile, or more, Mr. Anthony Bell saw a person riding leisurely along on horseback, landwards from the shore. At two or three score yards behind this person the snow appeared to be moving—the jumping motion of the snow keeping at the same distance behind the horse; on surveying the procession with a glass, he at once suspected it was some one conveying away part of the ship's belongings. Taking horses, and going a circuitous route, they came close upon the rider, (a blacksmith of the neighbourhood), who had borrowed ropes and a horse, and, with pipe in mouth, was composedly dragging the ship's mast away. Surprised in the act, he dismounted and cut the ropes, and as quickly leapt on the horse and galloped off, leaving the plunder to its proper owners.

STRANGE IF TRUE.

IT has been reported that Sir——— bought a field, and stipulated with the vendor that payment was to be made when the first crop was taken off. The calculating purchaser had the field sown with acorns, and the first crop would be oak timber.

BATTLE WITH A BULL.

IT is but seldom that an encounter takes place between a man and a bull, and more seldom that the battle ends in victory to the man. For once the fact can be recorded as an instance of cool courage not often heard of in rural communities.

In the very early part of the nineteenth century, Mr. John Watson, of South Mosses, in the parish of Arlecdon, had a big bull of the longhorned breed, which was very much inclined to "fend" for himself by ranging wherever he liked, and was also evil-disposed towards mankind.

One sunny summer day, when people were busy in their hayfields, Mr. Watson saw his bull trespassing in a neighbour's pasture, and set off to drive it out, leaving his hat and coat in the hayfield. He kept a little rough-coated brown cur, which alone had any safe control over the bull. The dog had not gone to the hayfield with its master, but was basking at home in readiness for an accustomed call to duty. Hastening towards the bull, the master kept whistling and loudly calling for "Mop" as he went—that call, being well known by the bull, was often sufficient to induce him to return sulkily crooning to his own pasture.

Mr. Watson took a hayfork with him as a walking stick, and to use as occasion might require. He got into the field where the bull was before the dog came ; and immediately as the angry animal saw him, it made to him in a round trot, increasing in speed as it came nearer. The dog being yet too far off, no help near, and no time to be lost, he had presence of mind to place the end of the fork-shaft against the base of the stiffest *bull-toppin** within reach, and, pointing the

* The reed-like grass *Aira cæspititoa.*

D

grains of the fork in the direction of the coming attack, stood with it poised in his hand between his knees so that he could raise the points or lower them to where they were most likely to take effect. The faithful dog was making its best speed, and reached, snapped at, and bit the heel of the bull as it made its final rush at its master, who met, with all the coolness of a hero, or the courage of despair, the brutal assault, and guided the prongs so judiciously as to pierce the frontal bone of the bull a little above its eyes, and to spring a little to one side, lest the impetus of its run should force the animal upon him. The sudden attack by the dog caused the bull to swerve and turn round, with the pitchfork sticking in its skull and half the broken shaft hanging to it; and, while the dog kept chasing and biting the heels of the bull, the owner got away in safety.

The bull I saw many times after with the two wounds of the hayfork above its eyes, and its manners were considerably improved by the collision.

Once on breaking bounds on a hot day, previous to the above, this white bull missed his footing and plunged into a very miry sowe, and floundered about in it, sinking deeper and deeper till he was all covered except his head and horns. At last he found a foot-hold, and by a strong effort managed to scramble out, greatly quieted down. The peaty mud dried on his hide and converted the white into a dusky black bull. He wore the mantle during several dry days, but on rain coming it gradually left him, and he was himself again, and as riotous as ever.

WILL O' THE WISP.

In my younger days, before much progress had been made in draining the marshy lands and bogs of West Cumberland, I often heard of Will o' the Wisp having been seen in still or mild nights, hovering and dancing over the wet and low-lying districts.

Previous to that draining period, the ague had been a prevalent disease in the neighbourhood of moist localities. Happily, this malady has entirely left us; and its usual companion, the *ignis fatuus*, is rarely, if ever, now seen, since the evident cause has been in a great measure removed.

Travelling homewards on a mild and moist evening in late autumn, over an undrained route on the highest part of Dean Common, I was fortunate enough to have a convincing proof of the occasional existence of the phenomenon of Will's Wisp. I was on horseback, and the horse I rode was only partially dried after a slight shower; without thinking of such a subject I was agreeably surprised by a pale greenish flash of light approaching the mane of the horse from a few inches' distance, and instantly receding and disappearing in the darkness. This occurred in the same playful manner a few times, when the light grew rather more vivid, and at last it settled on the mane before me—quivering and jumping with the trotting motion of the horse. It was at times so transparent that I could easily distinguish the black mane through it. At other times the light was dense enough to obscure the object beneath it. After going a few score yards at a smart trot and admiring the unusual visitant, I ran my hands up the mane, when the phosphorescent light disappeared for a moment, and again settled as before. This was experimentally repeated a few times, and no sensation of heat felt, when the beautiful light capriciously divided, and a portion attached itself to the ends of my black silken neckerchief. I tried if this portion would disappear by stroking with the hand, and it did so, and reappeared two or three times, when both illuminations gradually vanished, and I felt some regret for having disturbed my singular and pleasing companion. Probably the pace the horse was going might have some effect in severing the appearance from me. Since that night, now more than forty years ago, I have never been favoured with any similar sight, though often exposed in the same way, and often thinking of the circumstance.

FORESTALLING CORN.

IT was stated in 1860, that J. B———, of C——— in the Abbey Holme, a wealthy man, had then sixty stacks of grain standing in a field of about five roods in extent, and they had been decaying there thirty or forty years. A very near neighbour estimates that sixty other stacks of grain, in various stages of decay, may be seen on other parts of the farm. While an elder brother of the owner was living, a cart was laden with wheat for Wigton market, and some difference as to the price to be asked occurring to prevent its being taken away on the day intended, it has since stood so long, that the owner has had the cart-wheels three times painted to prevent decay. In the granaries numbers of stacks stand filled with grain, and they have stood there so long that if handled or touched they would almost to a certainty fall to pieces. About 1840, a good sized ash tree was seen growing through one of the stacks.

COBBLER'S BILL RENDERED.

Whitehaven, 18—

Mr. St——l.

To John Larney, Dr.

			s.	d.
Nov. 16	To	clogged up, Miss....................	o	2
Dec. 14	,,	mended up, Miss..................	1	3½
Jan. 13	,,	toe topped, Master................	o	3
April 1	,,	turned up, clogged up, and mended, the Maid...........	1	7¾
May 1	,,	lined, bound, and put a patch on, Madam....................	o	6
,, 10	,,	soling, the Maid....................	o	8½
,, 14	,,	topping, Madam....................	o	6
,, 15	,,	putting a patch....................	o	2½
,, 16	,,	stretching and easing, little Master	o	2
		£o	5	5¼

Settled,

John Larney.

MILITARY DISCIPLINE.

WHEN, seventy years ago, England was threatened with invasion by the French, the Cumberland volunteers, under the command of J. C. Curwen, Esq., were assembled at Workington for drill. The drill-ground was then on the fine green level of threescore acres between St. Michael's Tower and the sea, which, since that time, has carried about fifty acres of it away. After two or three weeks' training, Adjutant Dawson came to inspect and test the efficiency of the volunteers. Captain John Hetherington's Branthwaite company were put through the ordinary exercise and passed

with approbation. They were then examined as to
the order of their arms and accoutrements, when Brown
Bess with her flint locks was found sadly awanting.
The adjutant was so incensed that he d——d them
and ordered them to the "right about," facing the sea
at high water. The company was formed of farmers'
sons and farm servants : tall, strapping, well-looking
fellows with their sergeant, Will Pearson, a noble looking man, known to and liked by all. The next order
was "march," and they stumped to the water's edge
without a recal. Not knowing what was to follow,
the men eyed the serjeant, who liked sport and saw
the dilemma, and he in an undertone said, "Gang in,
lads, he'll not drown ye."

In they slowly marched ; some much amused, others
not relishing the bath, but all ready to obey orders.

Until over knee-deep they got on pretty well ; but
as the slope continued and the slippery stones increased in number and bulk they found greater difficulty, and many got ducked. Some few dropped their
guns in the deep water and many a dive took place
for recovery ; but the water being clear, all were eventually found. The sergeant, a tall grenadier, kept
quietly encouraging his men. The adjutant on shore,
enjoying a hearty laugh at their discipline and determination, when he saw them nearly up to their necks
called a "halt" to "right about." Welcome was the
command, and a scramble was made for the shore ;
but before it was reached Pearson had them formed
in regular order, and the adjutant with all due solem-
nity complimented the men as they stood in the
water, and said that although they had hitherto been
known as the dirty company, he hoped they were now
perfectly clean and would remain so ; and as to their
courage, they were fit to face the French or the devil
with Pearson at their head.

DR. GIBSON'S ANECDOTES.

DR. A. C. GIBSON having kindly handed to me the manuscript of his amusing lectures on the Folk-lore of the lake district, with permission to publish, it is with no little pleasure I avail myself of his liberal kindness, and duly acknowledge his ability as the best living writer of songs and other productions, in the Cumberland, Westmoreland, and Furness dialects. His anecdotes and traits of character must entertain every one ; and much instruction may be gathered from his lively descriptions.

His inimitable " Joe and the Geologist" and " Bobby Bank's Bodderment " are sufficient to place him at the top of the first rank in that department ; and his various historical pamphlets, and other writings in connection with the Cheshire and Lancashire Historical Society, induce us to wish he had written much more.

Let him speak.

MOST of the specimens of humour that I have given so far, may be said to be nothing more than demonstrations of oddity or absurdity, and, were I to stop here, it might be held that though the people, whose amusing qualities I am endeavouring to elucidate, do possess the faculty of saying and doing what may excite laughter by its grotesqueness, its eccentricity, or its mere folly, they are not gifted with the attribute of wit, or originality, clever sayings, happy repartees, sly sarcasms, or smart satires. I believe, however, that I can draw,

from the other end of my memory's wallet, a few recollections that may prove them to be no more destitute
of the power of making witty remarks, than they are of
the habit of saying what is merely funny or ludicrous.
Of aptness of repartee, for instance, I think the following a tolerable example.

Those who were in the habit of riding or driving
through the lake district some years ago, may remember that at the turnpike gate between Grasmere and
Dunmail raise, the toll used to be taken by a good
looking young matron, to whom it was a pleasure to
pay the pence, were it only for the sake of her bright,
black eyes. One summer morning, a party of young
men, on a walking excursion to Keswick, were approaching this gate, when one of the company, who
had some pretensions to the character of a wag, stept
briskly out before the others to the open door of the
toll-house, and called out, "What have these fellows
to pay?" The pretty toll-taker hurried out and seeing
nothing but a group of pedestrians, replied sharply,
" Nowte !" "Nowte," said the wit, staring up at the
table of rates, "what, I see there's a charge for asses."
"Yes," said she, readily, "but there's nin for feuls, sooa
thoo may gang on."

Of pointed innuendo I remember two or three specimens which I think worth preserving.

In the Lancashire part of Lake-land, three generations of congenital or hereditary doctors have lived and
thriven, all following other occupations, but enjoying
considerable repute amongst their rustic neighbours
for skill in curing the diseases of both man and beast.
The first of the family who took up the healing trade,
(an eccentric, but shrewd old fellow of whom many
queer stories are told,) chanced to be at the little inn
at Lowick bridge, near Ulverston, soon after he had
announced his intention of practising surgery as an ad-

ditional branch of business, and there encountered a neighbour who, from his notorious habit of speaking in a bitter, ill-natured style, was known by the sobriquet of Reeden't, (that is cross-grained,) Coward. He immediately accosted the self-qualified medico with, "What I hear thu's gā'n to tak up doctorin'." "Why," said the old Jack of all trades, for such he was, "what than? What hest'e got to say ageán it?" "Nay, nowte mich," said Reeden't Coward, "only mind thou docters nowte but fooak." "What for that," demanded the doctor. "Why, for this," said Coward, "thou sees beeasts cost brass."

Of the same stamp is another, which occurred at the same snug little house of entertainment.

An old doctor of the neighbourhood, not self-qualified like the last-mentioned, but exceedingly pungent and rough, not to say coarse in his ordinary speech, often called at Lowick Bridge when making his rounds, for a glass of ale; and, on one such occasion, was asked by the landlord what he thought of the ale he was drinking. "Well, not much," was his frank reply. "It should be summat extra," said the landlord, "I hed t' moat o' t' way fray Scotland." "Fray Scotland, hed ye'?" said the doctor, "than nixt time ye' brew, I think yo'd better git yer moat at heam an' fetch t' watter fray Scotland!"

Another story with some of the medical elements in it, was told me long ago in a different part of the lake country.

A farmer at Lorton sent to some distance for a cow doctor to visit one of his cattle. Some time afterwards the doctor met his client "in' t' market i' Cockerm'uth street," and enquired after his patient. "O," said the farmer, "she's finely—she mendit reet away, efter that stuff ye' gev her—she's finely, an' I o' much obleeged tull ye." "It's ower lal," said the doctor, scratching his head, "Its ower lal. I will wŭrk as cheap as any body—bit *much obleeged tull ye'* wôn't dee !"

Another story, again from the south, is still more pointed—and I give it here.

On a dark Candlemas evening, a druggist from Ulverston, driving down a road, shaded with wood, about fifteen miles from home, came upon a heap of road material which had been thrown, very improperly, from a gravel pit over the roadway, so as to leave but little room for carriages to pass. The consequence was that the gig was upset with such violence that its occupant was pitched a considerable distance into the wood, sustaining some damage, particularly to his clothes. The parish surveyor, a small landed proprietor of the old school, through whose carelessness the accident occurred, soon afterwards received a demand for the payment of damages done to vehicle, harness, and wearing apparel, the heaviest item in the account being a new great coat, which was said to be utterly spoiled. The whole amounted to what I remember considering the very moderate sum of £13, for which the surveyor, after taking advice and ascertaining his liabilities, gave a bill at three months ; cunningly, but, of course, erroneously supposing that, as his term of office would expire before the bill came to maturity, his liability would be transferred to his successor. However, he soon found out his mistake, and, to his huge indignation, had to provide for the bill from his own private funds. Still smarting under the remembrance of his loss, he went the following Candlemas to Ulverston, and strolling up the main street, when near the Sun Inn, he spied his enemy, as he deemed him, standing at his own shop door on the opposite side, and called out, "Well, ha'e ye been gitten' a new cooat leeatly ?" and, receiving an affirmative answer, continued, " And whatten parish ha'e ye been in this year ? " Taking out his revenge by insinuating that the unfortunate druggist was in the habit of clothing himself at the cost of the parish officers round about.

Mere sharpness of reply often takes an amusing turn, though there be nothing essentially witty or humorous in the construction of the said reply. Thus: an elderly man who had wrought hard all his life at the slate quarries in the beautiful and secluded little valley of Gillerthwaite, astonished his neighbours one week end by informing them, rather suddenly, that he had made up his mind to go and see London. His acquaintances, to whose minds the idea of a journey to London presented an incomprehensible amount of difficulty and peril, said all that could be thought of to dissuade him from carrying out so foolhardy a project ; and one of them asked him in a tone which showed that the objection conveyed in the query was considered unanswerable, " What's putten Lunnon into yer soft āld heed ? He'a ye any frinds i' Lunnon?" " No," said the determined old traveller, " I gitten ne'a frinds theear yit ; but," giving a jingling slap to his breeches' pocket, " I's gā'n ut teeak a frind wi' me!"

A tolerably stinging reproof is sometimes administered in the vernacular of the dales by the out-speaking natives, in a manner that merits illustration, and the following may, I think, be recorded as a fair example :—

A late landlord of the Salutation Inn, at Ambleside, was standing in front of his house, engaged with some other veterans of the neighbourhood, in discussing their several ages. The subject of their conversation attracted the attention of a young nobleman staying at the hotel, who was afterwards distinguished by his prominence in some of the freaks supposed to be rather common at that date amongst the junior aristocracy.   His lordship lounged up to the little conclave, and, referring to their discussion, drawled out, " I say, Stalkah, what shall I be like when I'm an old fellow of 70 or 80 ? "   Mine host, not having much respect for a lord who was a lord and little more, replied, with more curtness than courtesy, " Why, thou's a young feeul now, an' thou'll be an āld feeul than."

The Quakers of Cumberland and Westmoreland, in the generation now almost passed away, not having, when young, the educational advantages possessed by their children in the great scholastic establishments belonging to the Society at Wigton, Ackworth, and elsewhere, were plainer in their speech and more simple in their habits, probably in consequence of having less scholarship.   But though their minds were less cultivated, or possibly *because* they were so, they were more quaint, more unlike ordinary people, less conventional, and therefore more interesting than their descendants, who are now conforming more and more to the ways of the world—while the strict integrity, the universal conformity to the rules of life prescribed by their religion, the regard for truth and fair dealing that I found to prevail with those members of the body amongst whom for a time my lot was cast, and with whose ways of life and habits of thought I had sufficient opportunity of becoming intimately acquainted, have left upon my memory an impression of esteem and respect that time will hardly efface.   It is, therefore, not intended as a reproach, much less a sneer, that I here relate a circumstance exemplifying the curious ignorance of the meaning of even ordinary words, which at that time, say five and twenty years ago, was not uncommon amongst the senior agricultural Friends in Cumberland.

I was walking at night with a Quaker farmer up the meadows skirting the Marron, where that pretty little stream separates the parishes of Lamplugh and Dean, and our conversation turned upon some doggerel rhymes which had appeared in a Whitehaven newspaper, and were said to be founded upon a story about an old gentleman having shot his own great coat hanging in his orchard at night, under the impression that the coat was a thief. This doggerel had borne the title of "A Lamplugh Legend," and I was condemning the publication of it as an unwarrantable invasion of the privacy of domestic life, and an impertinent attempt to throw ridicule upon a respectable neighbour, when my companion said, "O! there was nowte amiss in it only calling the man such a name." "Name," said I, "what name was he called?" "Why, *legend*," said the unlettered Friend, "I think it was a varry wrong thing, whatever thou may think, to call any man such a name as that." "Legend!" I exclaimed, "it's the story itself, and not the old gentleman it's told of, that was called a legend; and, very likely, it was called so to show that even the writer himself thought it mightn't be true." "Nay, nay!" said he, with what I thought was a touch of the proverbial obstinacy of his sect, "How can a story be an evil spirit? for that's what legend means." "Nonsense," said I, "it simply means an old story that nobody would vouch to be true." "Ah!" said he, "thou's welcome to thy own opinion about it; but when I was at Cockermouth, t'other day, I ass't a man from Embleton, a varry knowledgable man too, an' he said legend means the devil's brother or any evil spirit; an' thou cannot say it was right to give such a name till an old man an' t' father of a family." I was silenced, of course, and it was some days before the solution of this odd definition of a very common word dawned upon me, but when it did I had no doubt that my worthy neighbour and his Embleton oracle had confounded *legend* with *legion*, and that the latter had drawn his interpretation of the word from that passage in the New Testament where a devil is made to say, " Our name is *Legion*," and so on.

Many anecdotes have been told of the ready wit and quiet humour of this respectable sect, but I think the following has hardly been surpassed.

Two elderly Friends, both members of the congregation that assembles at the ancient meeting-house near Pardshaw, were imbued with a very unquakerlike mutual hatred and hostility, and not only quarrelled bitterly when they met, but missed few opportunities of reviling each other behind their backs. One of them, talking of his detested neighbour in the usual strain, was checked by another Friend, saying, " Thou shouldn't speek i' that way of him ! Thou knows he's yan o' t' pillars o' our meeting." " Ey," was the reply, " but there's different mak's o' pillars ; there's a kind they co' caterpillars—he's yan o' them ! "

Of the odd indirect manner of conveying a reproof, or expressing dissatisfaction, said to be characteristic of this Society, a tolerably amusing specimen has been reported to me as having occurred at Kendal.—A well-known member of the Society of Friends resident in that most Quakerly of towns, employed a man at day's wages to delve his garden. On looking in towards evening to ascertain progress, the Friend was rather disgusted to see the very small space of ground that had been turned over during the day, and addressed the workman thus :—

" Thou *must* be a strong man." " Nay," said the gardener, with becoming modesty, " I's nit sa strang as I used to be." " I don't know what thou hast been," said his employer, " but I think thou must be a very strong man still, I don't believe there's a man in Kendal but thyself, that could squeeze so long a day's work into so little room."

It is not often that Quakers are led into the indiscretion of railing against other sects ; and it is not common with them to allow themselves to be carried by the heat of disputation to such unwarrantable lengths as were reached in the following instance. A Quaker gentleman, of Ulverston, or the vicinity, dining with a party of neighbours at the ordinary, at the Sun Inn there, was baited rather unduly on certain church questions, respecting which he was known to hold very strong opinions ; the discussion gradually increasing in warmth and freedom, culminated in a hot dispute upon the character and conduct of church ministers in general, on which the Quaker expressed a very decided opinion, and justified it by adducing the instance of a clergyman of Low Furness, who, not long before, had been convicted of forgery at the Lancaster assizes, and condemned to transportation. "Well, but surely," remonstrated some of the company, "surely you don't bring a convicted criminal forward as a fair sample of our clergy?" "Yes, I do," said the Friend, doggedly, "Yes, I do—I consider him to be a very fair average parson!"

It is well-known that in the early days of Quakerism its proselytes and disciples were not the unobtrusive and peaceful religionists that their descendants of our times must be admitted to be, but offered much more than a merely passive resistance to the claims and pretensions of the Established Church, and often brought trouble upon themselves by entering the churches, interrupting the services, and disturbing the congregations. One very laughable instance of these over jealous demonstrations, in which the intruding Friend was signally discomfited, is given, in a note, in Nicolson and Burn's History.

At the date of the story, nearly two hundred years ago, the clergyman at Shap, whose name was Dalton, was what is locally called *peed*,—that is, blind of one eye.   He had gone to preach for a neighbour parson, called Fothergill, in the chapel of Ravenstonedale, and, when in the middle of the service, was interrupted by the entrance of one of the primitive Friends, who, not knowing that the pulpit was occupied by a stranger, planted himself in the centre aisle, and called out, " Come down, thou fause Fuddergill ! "   The clergyman, without any signs of annoyance, quietly asked, " Wheea telt thee 'at I was fause Fuddergill ? " and the reply was, " The spirit within me tells me what thou is—so come down ! "   " Then," said the priest, " the spirit within the' is a lying spirit,—for ivery body here knows 'at I's Peed Dawton fray Shap ! "

A book was published some time ago, on the signs of public-houses.   It has attracted considerable attention and excited much interest in most literary circles, especially amongst those who are more or less devoted to subjects of social archæology.   Our district would afford some curious materials for such a book, and there are one or two stories of signs which happen to serve my present purpose, as this :—

A man at Wigton, having taken a public-house, was desirous of setting up an attractive and appropriate sign, and, with that view, consulted a friend who happened to possess a little classical learning.   The friend suggested Bacchus as something both suitable and attractive.   Now I remember one of the Whitehaven papers taking an amateur concert-singer to task for refining the name of the jolly god into Bake-hus, thus :—

> " Bring in Bak-hus, all divine,
> And fill the bowl with rosy wine."

The Wigton sign-seeker would have reversed this mispronunciation, for the only Bacchus he was acquainted with suggested something widely different

from either rosy gods or rosy wine ; and he remonstrated with his classical adviser to this effect,—
" Bacchus ! Bacchus !!—T' sign for that wad be a
yubben mooth, an' mebbee a leeaf or two—but I's
wantin a sign for a *public*-hoose, nit a bak-hus !"

But a better joke than this is told of a sign at
Ambleside.

When Dr. Watson, the celebrated Bishop of
Llandaff, came to reside at Calgarth, on Windermere,
he purchased several small properties in that part of
the country ; amongst others, an old established
public-house at Ambleside, which, like several that I
recollect, was well and widely known by the sign of
the Black Cock—generally abbreviated by the country
people, amongst whom it was popular, into the second
syllable. When the property became the Bishop's,
the host, wishing to propitiate his new superior, proposed to substitute his most reverend head for the
sable fowl that had crowed silently over the door for
unknown generations. Dr. Watson, in contravention
of the example set him by Sir Roger de Coverley,
readily accepted the proposed compliment, and very
soon a rude but unmistakable portrait of the prelate,
with shovel hat and episcopal wig, took the place of
the old and homely device, somewhat to the disgust
of the customers ; and, what was a more serious
matter, the landlord of an upstart opposition house
adopted and set up the superseded sign, and the
bishop's tenant found himself between the horns of
an awkward dilemma : either that he must resume
the popular designation of his hotel, and so, in all
probability, give offence where he was anxious to
please, or, otherwise, see some of his customers go
to the rival house, under the influence of the name
they loved for its very antiquity. He, however, met
the difficulty with notable ingenuity—for very soon

another board appeared, immediately under the bishop's likeness, inscribed, " This is the Old Cock," it is to be hoped with all the success it merited.

In the invention of exaggerations and impossibilities, our Yankee cousins have long held undisputed pre-eminence ; but I have heard in the lake-country, one or two of this class of facetiœ which, although perhaps inferior in raciness to many of their American prototypes, possess a very satisfactory degree of extravagance.

I remember the respectable tenant farmer of Crakeplace Hall, apropos of a newspaper account of some enormous vegetable production that I had related to him—turning to, and, with all possible gravity, telling me the following :—

" O, that was nowte tull a crop o' turmets 'at was grown abeùn twenty year sen bee Clem. Mossop o' Prior Skeàl, nār Co'der Brig.　Its gūddish grūnd theer, and what wid that, and heavy mūckin an' wide thinnin oot, he rais't sec turmets as niver was heerd tell on ayder afooar or sen—they wer' sa big.　Fwoke com fray o' parts to leùk at them ; an' aboot Martinmas a young bull fairly eat his way intul yan on them, as a moose may'd intul a cheese, an beàd theer.　They thowt t' beast was lost till a while efter Kersmas, when he woak't oot on't a gay bit fatter ner he went in. Clem. was sa plees't 't he hed t' skell o' t' turmet carriet yām, an' meàd them put some lang sticks across't for pūrches, an' it meàd a famish hen hull—t' hens o' sat in't at neet—while next winter, an' than it soffen't an' fell togidder efter a hard frost."

An exaggeration, worthy of America, occurred in a reply made by a guide on Coniston Old Man, to a gentleman who asked him if the mists were thick there. " Thick ? ey ! They're sūmtimes that thick 'at ye may'd drive a peg intult mist an' hing up yer hat on't."

An Ambleside guide being on Fairfield, with a tourist, was asked by him if he thought the hills grew larger as they grew older, and, by way of paying him back in what he thought his own spurious coin. replied, "Growe? To be suer they growe! I've heard my fadder say 'at he mindit when Loughrigg Fell theear wasn't mich bigger nor his hat."

Our dale people lack the imagination that is required to emulate the Irishman in the manufacture of that species of jokes called bulls. The only real native Cumbrian bull that I remember at present was perpetrated by the public bellman at Penrith, who perambulated the streets with his bell one market day, proclaiming the loss of an empty sack with a cheese in it.

Sheer impudence often passes for wit in the lake district, as well as elsewhere. Indeed, most of us will find as much amusement in hearing quoted a reply or a taunt, when humour depends upon ready audacity, as from the choicest specimens of ready wit. Of this reprehensible class of jokes the following may suffice as a specimen, and also of the sort of impudence that amuses the people of the dales. A very old lady, a near relative of a late Member of Parliament for West Cumberland, was lately taking a walk in the lane behind her residence, not far from Windermere, when she met a little ragged urchin whom she did not recognize as belonging to the neighbourhood. My venerable friend (I may well say venerable. for she was then within two or three years of a hundred) was of an inquiring turn of mind—and she accosted the boy in somewhat authoritative tone with the question, "Who's little boy are you?" and the young scamp replied, in the Scottish fashion, with another question, thus—"Wha's ald woman are yee?"

Of readiness in reply, I think the following a tolerable sample.   A lame old man named William Bowness used to travel about the southern part of the lake district in a deep-sided cart that had been so made to accommodate the calves which it was his business to purchase in the dales, and carry off to sell to the butchers.   From following this traffic for many years, and from being rarely seen without a calf or two beside him in the cart, he was known much better by the name of Coaf Willie than by his own proper patronymic—indeed I had known him for some years before I discovered his rightful name.   Old Coaf Willie was one day driving past the smithy that stands by the beautiful little stream called Yewdale Beck, and close to the bridge that connects the two Conistons.   The smith, looking out of his shoeing shed, called locally a teeo-fo, that is a to-fall or lean-to, and observing that Willie's cart was empty, cried out, "Willie! Whar't t' coaf?" and Willie, touching his pony with the whip, answered coolly, "In't teeo-fo!"

I remember once being a good deal amused by the chaff that was kept up amongst some country lads, who chanced to be fellow passengers with me in a third-class carriage on the Kendal and Windermere Railway.   At the Stavely Station, one, who seemed more of a wag than the others, imitated the sharp blast of the starting whistle and exclaimed, "Now my lads!—Anudder feed o' corn * an' off we go!"   And a more matter-of-fact sort of fellow, who seemed to prefer something more substantial to chaff, said, very gravely, "We' gitten nowte to chowe corn wi'."   "We dunnat chowe it," said the first, "we swally it yall!" Whether by corn he meant to typify the passengers or the money of the proprietors, I was not able to discover.

An artist friend of mine, who resides at the pictur-

* The corn was evidently the coal supplied to the engine furnace.—*Ed*.

esque village of Sawrey, has a servant named Miles—
a very handy fellow, and very useful to his master in
mounting canvasses, making stretching frames for
pictures, and other such jobs.   On one occasion Miles
essayed a more ambitious achievement, and made a
new stock to his gun.   Rather proud of his handi-
work, he carried it to the principal place of resort in
the village—the shoemaker's shop—·and, exhibiting it
to the master, exclaimed, " Theear ! what think ye o'
that, Joe ? "   After examining it carefully all over, he
returned it to the maker, saying drily, " Well, Miley,
nut to *be* a gun-stock, it's as like a gun-stock as owte I
iver seed i' me life ! "

The following has been told to me by an intelligent
dalesman, as proving that some of the tourists who
over-run the country are in nowise intellectually
superior to the country people themselves :—Two
young men of the tourist class were sitting in the
coffee-room of the Royal Oak, at Keswick, when one
was overheard inquiring of the other, " Which do you
think the finest—Derwentwater or Keswick Lake ? "
" Why," said his friend, " I should say they were
synonymous."   " Well," rejoined the querist, " so they
are, no doubt, but I think Derwentwater by far the
most synonymous of the two ! "

Instances of misapprehension of the meanings of
unaccustomed words and phrases are often quoted in
the district.   One of the best of them was told of a
wealthy yeoman, well known in West Cumberland,
who was sent when a youth to Green Row to finish a
not very complete education, and being asked in class
what is a verb active, replied, " a lish an." The same
gentleman, when somewhat elderly, was dining at
Cockermouth Castle, and having inadvertently filled
his mouth with artichoke, husky leaves and all, he
put it out, and threw it over the table between the

guests opposite into the fire beyond, exclaiming as he did so, "Good Lord, what stuff gentlefolks does eat!"

An imperfect version of the following has appeared in the local papers; it has often been told as an odd illustration of the simplicity and ignorance of the agricultural class :—A worthy farmer in Furness having bought a weather-glass, from which he expected accurate information on the present as well as the future state of the weather, was considerably disgusted to find that during the persistence of a spell of very wet weather the pointer still kept inclining up towards fair; and at last on a pouring morning, seeing that the barometer was indicating fine weather more decidedly than ever, the farmer, quite out of patience, pulled it down from its nail, carried it out into the rain, and addressed the delinquent machine with, " Istà a leear or istà nūt a leear? Thow girt clot-heead! Wilt'a believe they awn ee'n ?"

I could extend this list of trifles very considerably did time permit, and if such extension were desired ; but I think I have cited enough to accomplish the purpose with which I proposed to set out. No doubt many of my little specimen stories may be considered insignificant and vulgar ; but if that were said I should reply that an aggregation of trifles may constitute a very important whole, that to a real lover of his kind or the earnest student of human nature, nothing can be insignificant which tends to make him more familiar with, or to enhance his interest in, any previously little-known class of his fellow-men. As to vulgarity, I should hardly trouble myself to repel that imputation. I have, long ago, come to the conclusion that nothing can be offensively vulgar to a really generous spirit that does not comprise indelicacy or affectation, both of which, I trust, I have succeeded in avoiding while running my line of lake country anecdotes off the reel of my memory.

It is not so easy to say much about the lakes or the people that dwell near them, without coming into contact with the great poet whose long residence there was, according to Miss Martineau, " the crowning honour of the district." It is remarkable, therefore, that although Wordsworth professed to draw much of his inspiration and many of his subjects from the daily life of the humble and unlettered people around him, he has altogether failed in interesting them in his writings. The dales' men care and know literally nothing about the poetry in which their fortunes and their failures, their virtues and their vanities, seem to the educated and trained lovers of that class of literature to be so beautifully, if tediously, and sometimes painfully portrayed.

In the course of a conversation, which, in the presence of a literary friend, I was once holding with two respectable 'statesmen in Langdale, I was told that the worthy dame we have just parted with was, after many years of mutual kindness and services, taken to live at Rydal by "Yan Mr. Wadswūrth—t' maister o' t' Stamp Office." My friend was rather startled at this irreverent manner of treating the name and calling of the great moral poet, whom, knowing only through his works, he had been accustomed to revere as one far above any of the ordinary offices of life ; and desired me to enquire as to their knowledge or estimate of Wordsworth as a poet, and I asked if they'd ever heard that Mr. Wordsworth made poetry. " O yes ! they believed he was a fūrst rate hand at that mak' o' wark." But this was said in a tone indicating that they thought little of his position as a poet in comparison with his dignity as chief distributer of stamps ; I then asked if they'd ever read any of his poems. "No! they couldn't say they had!"

My lamented friend the late William Fell, surgeon, of Ambleside, had a memory well stored with anecdotes connected with the romantic, and, as regards the people and primitive district, in which he worked so long and so usefully; and had *he*, in some such position as I now occupy, to relate those in the manner in which it delighted him to tell them to his friends, he would have been heard, I fancy, with a degree of pleasure and satisfaction that I can hardly hope to excite. One of the most striking of these incidents, so related by Mr. Fell, was that of his coming upon the poet—his illustrious neighbour and life-long friend, seated under Hammerscar, spouting, gesticulating, and apostrophizing the Aurora Borealis, which with unusual splendour, was shooting and glancing over the lofty summits of Seat Sandle and Helvellyn. It was a treat to hear Mr. Fell describe this encounter, but then he was an educated man with well-cultivated tastes and appreciative sympathies, and his less intellectual neighbours, in humble life, regarded such outbursts of poetic enthusiasm with widely different feelings. One instance of the odd misconstruction they put upon these demonstrations, which I think is worthy of record, was told me by a well-known and talented portrait painter, who, while executing commissions at Ambleside, used to find his temporary studio made use of as a favourite lounging place by the men of leisure thereabout. Amongst the most welcome of these loungers was the late Hartley Coleridge, who then, and down to the time of his death, resided at the Nab-Cottage on Rydal Water. Making his wonted appearance at my friend's painting room one morning, Hartley was accosted with the common salutation of "Well, Mr. Coleridge, what's your news this morning?" and replied, "Your enquiry reminds me of the answer I've just had to the same. As I was walking down I came upon a poor man from Rydal, breaking stones, and like you I said, 'Good morning, John, what news have you this morning?' and John answered, 'Why nowte varry particlar, only āld Wadswūrth's brocken lowce ageen?' You must know," proceeded Coleridge, "that the Poet Laureate's muse is not always in a propitious mood; and occasionally, when he is in the throes of composition, he goes about the lanes boo-oo-oo-ing away—and the country people believe that what are really fits of inspiration are paroxysms of insanity." This is curiously borne out by a similar anecdote that appeared many years ago in Chambers' Journal, in a short but well written series of papers on the lake country. The writer, as well as I recollect, said, that while resting in a cottage at Rydal, he asked the chatty old mistress of the house if Wordsworth made himself neighbourly amongst them, and she replied, "Well, he sumtimes gaùs booin' his pottery about t' rooads an' t' fields an' taks na nooatish o' neàbody; but at udder times he'll say, 'Good morning, Dolly,' as sensible as oyder you or me!" These anecdotes are interesting, as giving us a glimpse of the manner in which a great master worked at his craft. It is well known that Wordsworth took more than usual pains and trouble in elaborating and finishing his productions after they were composed, and it is very probable that these frequent mutterings and mouthings, which the people about very naturally took for indications of mental aberration, were outward signs of the process of polishing and refining which his compositions, already worked off, were undergoing in the mind of their author.

Another of these stories, and then we'll try another

subject.—When the poet died, which he did at a ripe age. a lady neighbour told the news to an old man working in her garden.   After muttering a few ordinary expressions of concern and regret, the old fellow suddenly brightened up and said, " But what than— t' mistress is a gay cliverish kind of a body—I reckon she'll be carrying on t' business."

It is not often we see cause to regret any consequence of the general diffusion of education.   Indeed, it would hardly be true to say that such cause *can* be seen, save, perhaps, in some very exceptional case. In the central and southern lake country, however, the now common possession of the accomplishments of reading and writing, has rendered unnecessary the existence of an interesting small class of public servants—for, now that the farmers and small 'statesfolk. or at least some of the younger members of each of their households, are able to write their own letters of business, friendship, or love ; the scriveners, or deed and letter-writers, lately an important and curious social institution in the dales have disappeared.

Readers of lake literature will remember that one of the multifarious, perhaps incongruous. occupations, by which the Rev. Robert Walker, of Seathwaite,— " He by shepherd swains called Wonderful," contrived to eke out his narrow income, was that of writing letters and other documents for his illiterate neighbours ; and this work, according to his most distinguished biographer, accumulated so upon his hands at Candlemas, when all settlements are made in that part of the country, that he often wrought at his desk the whole night through : and, no doubt, had his mind not been so much occupied by other matters (not the least important of which was scraping money together), Wonderful Walker might have preserved the recollections of some remarkable events in the private histories even of his primitive flock.

One of the last and most respectable of these general scribes in the Windermere district was called Nicholson —husband of the very popular old lady who, for many years after his decease, managed the post office at Ambleside. His experience has been represented to me as being rich in odd incidents and amusing developments of character and feeling. One of them, as related by himself, is sufficiently short and sufficiently racy for my present purpose, and so I give it. He had been sent for to draw out the will of a dying 'statesman in Langdale ; and the account he gave of the proceedings as reported to me was this :—" It was plain eneeuf 'at ther' was nèa time ut looase, sooa, I gat out my writin' gear an swattit mè be t' bed, to tak' down what he hed to tell mè. Well, it seem't till me 'at he want't to leeave sum'at till iverybody akin tull him. Ther' was fifty pūnd till this an, an' fortv pūnd till that an, an' thirty pūnd till sūmbody else— till I thowte he'd gitten gaily nār to t' far end o' what he hed ut leeave—but ther' was niver a wūrd about owte for't wife, an' when he stop't I says, ' But hevn't yè forgitten sumbody?' ' Nay,' says he, ' Ther' nin I forgitten, I think.' ' Yes, yes!' says I, ' yè for-gitten t' mistress!' He rèar't his-sel up i' t' bed when I said that, wi meear stren'th nor I thowte was left in him, an' t' wūrds com hist out like, through his bare teeth, as he said, ' Forgit her? Nay, never! I've hed a sairy time on't wid her!' An' o' 'at I cud get him ut due." continued the worthy scribe, " was to leeave her a melder o' meeal."

A predecessor of Mr. Nicholson in the same office, and in the same locality, was a man named Arthur Mackerthwaite, and as one of his professional ex-periences, the following outrageous story is told.

On a market day he was accosted by a countryman who, in language strong and idiomatic, said he wanted him to write a letter for him to a person of whom he had ordered a pig, and who had sent one home without a tail, a deficiency that he seemed to think was of some importance. They adjourned to a public-house, ordered in glasses and writing materials, and Mackerthwaite commenced operations by asking what he was to tell the delinquent. "Tell him?" said his client, whom the question threw into a fume, "Od hang him for a snowk-snarrel an' a ghebber in a market 'at gangs o' up an' down a town an' niver pays a shot—Od hang him!—tell him owder to send mè a pig 'at hes a tail, or send me a tail for thisan 'at he hes sent." This as I have said is outrageous in its absurdity, but it is scarcely more so than was the impatient reference to his failing sight that was made by a veteran hunter, whom I knew long ago. He formed one of a group who gathered on the side of a deep hollow, in the fells, and all save him had the rare good luck of a fine view of the finish of a hunt on the opposite hill-side. His companions detailed to him, as well as they were able, the events that rapidly followed each other in this, the most exciting portion of the chase, in the view of which his defective eyes baffled all his efforts to participate. At last, fairly maddened by their hurried and eager account of what was going on within their range of vision, he cried out, "Hang thor āld een o' mine, I wish they wer' nobbut out o' togidder, I believe I wod see better through t' hooals."

This brings me to the subject of Mountain Fox Hunting, a sport eagerly followed by nearly all the men residing amongst the fells. The fox there is not carefully preserved and cherished as in some parts, to become the chief actor in a favourite sport, but is pursued to destruction as the most mischievous of all

vermin—is allowed no law, and shewn as little mercy.
The perseverance of his enemies is often wonderful.
I have known a fox go to earth in a spot where the
mixed rock and gravel rendered the process of un-
earthing very difficult, if not, as is often the case,
altogether impossible. His pursuers worked in relays
at this stronghold for more than six and thirty hours,
when they reached and despatched him : then they
carried the carcase, dangling from a pole, to the nearest
public-house, to drink his arval—which means a
funeral libation, paid for in such cases by the township where the capture occurs.

The nature of the country renders riding to hounds
an impossibility in the central and southern parts of
the fell district, and for those accustomed to the
facilities, or the merely stimulating difficulties, of a
good hunting country, it is not easy to appreciate the
pleasures of Mountain Fox Hunting, or the keenness
with which it is followed, or the fervour with which it
is enjoyed.

Apropos of this subject, I found in the *Kendal
Mercury*, the other day, a report of one of these fell
hunts, the writer of which seems equally *au fait* to
their peculiarities, and to the grandiloquent in paragraph making; and as it seems more pat to my purpose than anything I could do myself, I take leave to
appropriate it.

CONISTONE.

SPLENDID FOX CHASE.—Actuated by an eager desire
to recover their late severe beatings, and inspired with
the sublime conviction that Dame Fortune, according
to her reputed custom, would in due course of events

"favour the brave," the Conistone foxhounds had a Kennel meet on Saturday last. Strange though it may appear, a kennel hunt means nothing else than the top of Conistone Old Man. It was a glorious winter morning, such a one as is not easily forgot. The snow, it is true, was thick on the hills, but withal, sweet, calm, and sunshiny. There is music up the steep breast of the grand "Old Hill," or we would tell of ever-shifting scenery, of fine panoramic views of hills, and fells, and tarns, and lakes. for twenty miles around. Roaring and raving through pass and glen went the echoing cry of hounds and hunters, as a brave old "duffer" scaled the heights above the Copper Mines and over Wetherlam. The snow was evidently too deep in the hills for reynard's pleasure, and he forsook the wild mountains for the beautiful scenery of Tilberthwaite, where banks of ferns, streams deep and still, suggestive of well-fed trout, or swift and bright. making pleasant music over their pebbly courses, abound. After crossing the "beck" at Tilberthwaite, for awhile the scent was indifferent, owing to reynard's wet jacket, but it soon improved, and the hounds, chanting like a "choir of martial monks," pressed him on into Yewdale. where yews yet grow that probably furnished bows for the archers of "lang syne," that made the strings twang in many a hard-contested field. After leaving the rude romantic valley, the hounds and fox had it all to themselves, except now and then an encouraging cheer from farm or cot as they passed swiftly along, for all the hunters were left far behind on the hills above Conistone. On—on. went pursuers and pursued over Holme Fell and Iron Kell, then swept like a flight of wild birds over the outlaying plains between Pull Scaur and Latterbarrow, making the village of Outgate re-echo, and the grey towers of Wray Castle ring with aërial harmony. For neither brake nor borren did reynard turn aside, but from find to finish pursued a straightforward course, the hounds going all the time without " let or hindrance " at a high pressure speed, rolling forth billows of harmonious music through the echoing hills. In an open field on the shore of Windermere, at Bellgrange, witnessed only by a solitary ploughman, foxey was pulled down. The impetuous cry of the furious pack resounded over the lake in every imaginable gush and trill of melody, which, had it not been heard, would scarcely have seemed possible to be of earthly heritage. Like old soldiers after the battle with their remarkable incidents, it is related that the Conistone hunters, though they none of them saw anything of the hunt but the opening burst in the early morning—are telling in great glee all the " ins and outs " of the chase, and showing " how fields are won."

I was conversing once with a gentleman who had kept a pack of hounds and hunted the High Furness country for very many years, in fact until the approach of age and its infirmities warned him that it was time to give it up. My old friend was a fine specimen of the better class of yeomanry of the district, and could talk as it chanced to suit his company, either in the local dialect or in common English. On the occasion I refer to, he was describing a chase when his pack had raised a fox in the woods of Graythwaite, near the foot of Windermere—ran him directly up the western shore of the lake, past Ambleside, over Kirkstone, into Patterdale, and back over the fells into Rydal. where they ran into him. " And how much of this fine run did you see?" I asked. " Why, we saw the beginning on't," was his reply, " we followed as hard as we could on to t' top o' Kirkstone, when we met a man 'at had seen both fox and dogs down in Patterdale." " Well, then," said I, " I always thought it was a joke against you, but I find it's quite true, that you think you've had a fine day's sport if you meet any-body that tells you he has *seen* the fox."   " Confound ye," cried the veteran, " ye're not a bit better nor old Tommy Barron, of Bowness, 'at used to say we mayed crack as we liked about our hunting, an' our shottin, an' fishin, an sic-like, but he never hed any sport at com up to crossing t' watter tull Furness Fells of a het afterneeun, an' 'killin hag-worms."   And having got the laugh on his side, the old sportsman was satis-fied.

One prominent feature in the character of the dales' folk, and one which I should much regret to see mo-dified or impaired to any serious extent, is their fru-gality in living, and chariness of incurring any unusual expense.   This principle involves a large amount of meritorious self-denial and renunciation, generally cheerful and unaffected, of even very moderate luxuries and enjoyments.   It is, therefore, worthy of respect, and I should be unwilling to be thought capable of turning any reasonable manifestation of it into ridicule.   Occasionally, however, it developes itself in a manner that affords amusement to any spectator who, from having resided in towns or from other circumstances, has not been accustomed to the rigidly plain and homely style of living practised in the dales.   Indeed, familiar as I was for years with the daily life and domestic habits of these worthy people, their anxious and unconcealed avoidance of even a very moderate and commonplace expenditure often came upon me with an irresistibly laughable effect, especially when accompanied by a disposition that even amongst them was unusually penurious and pinching, as in the following instance :—

A farmer, in very comfortable circumstances and re-spectably connected, being ill, his appetite, very much to his own disgust, became dainty and difficult to please; and one day casting about for something he could fancy, he at length asked me if a bit of cheese would do him any harm. Now the principal merit of the cheese made by the wives in his vicinity—which, as its makers boast, is "clear beath o' dirt and butter" —is its extreme slowness of digestion—its property, as they also say, of staying by yè—and this, of course, was out of the question as a *bonne bouche* for a delicate stomach. But, anxious to indulge his fancy for any food not grossly improper, I told him that a bit of cheese of better quality than that made by themselves would do little harm. "Oh," said the sick farmer, "ye mean gud Lankister cheese?" "Yes," I replied, "good cheese, such as you may buy at the grocers' shops." His face immediately assumed an expression showing that he had made up his mind to do something tremendous, and, striking his hand upon the bed, he exclaimed, "I'll send for a quarter of a pūnd on't."

This true story rather reminds us of that which, I daresay, you have all heard, of the country lad, at Cockermouth fair, wishing to treat his sweetheart to a ribbon, and learning that some she fancied was two-pence a yard, cried out, "Cùm than—we'll nūt be shabby for yance—whang her off a quarter of a yard on't."

The most general, and perhaps the most strongly marked manifestations of this unwillingness to part with money, however, are those exhibited in the country people's dread and abhorrence of anything that tends to increase the poor rates. It is not too much to say that the duty of keeping the rates down is part of their religion, for, generally speaking, they have no religious feeling half so strong, and no moral principle to which they are half so devoted. I never incurred so much popular displeasure, or was subjected to so much hard language, as once when, inadvertently, I took a lodging for a sick stranger woman, without reflecting that the place I had her brought to was not in the same parish as that where her illness began, without anticipating indeed that she was likely to apply for parochial relief at all. She did so apply, however, and in doing so brought a storm about my ears which I am sure I shall never forget.

The most *outré* incident arising from this inordinate horror of even an individually imperceptible increase of rate that I have heard of, occurred in the same township some time before I made the blunder just noticed. A 'statesman of considerable means, but of sordid habits and exceptionally coarse manners, one morning, not far from his house and near to the boundary of the township in which he was rated, came upon a worn-out tramp lying by the roadside, and evidently dying. Knowing that if the man died there, *his* township would probably be put to the expense of finding a coffin and a grave for him, the wealthy rate-protector hurried home for a horse and cart, and, assisted by his sons, carried the miserable wayfarer over the boundary into the next township, and laid him down there to die, which he speedily did, his death being accelerated, in all probability, by the removal. This sharp trick had no greater success than it deserved. The transportation had been seen by certain of the ratepayers to whose shoulders the burthen was sought to be transferred, and the result was that our acute old friend, to escape consequences still less pleasant, had to bury the stranger at his own proper cost. For this he never forgave him, but continued to curse his memory so long as he continued to live. The sight of the tramp's grave, or even of the churchyard where he lay, always as he left the public-house that adjoins it, would excite his ire to active demonstration. He would grin and shake his fist at it, and, addressing the unconscious offender that slept beneath, would say with a powerful oath, " Thou ligs theear snūg aneeuf, but it steeud me in a bonnie pennie to put thè theear."

The peculiarities of the dialect, and the manner in which they are made to appear, have not unfrequently a very odd effect. Two anecdotes extracted from a paper of mine on " The Ethnology of the Lakes," published several years ago in the *Transactions of the Historic Society of Lancashire and Cheshire*, have recently gone the rounds of the newspapers ; and I now recur to them as aptly illustrating this particular phase of the ludicrous. The first was an imperfect account of an adventure of my own, which happened in this wise :—

I was walking up the pleasant little village of Branthwaite, and came upon an old lady villager pottering over something or other in the gutter near her house. Wishing to propitiate her, I remarked that there had been a good deal of rain in the night, for the river was swollen. " We co' it a beck," said she very snappishly, and turning her back upon me, called out to her grand-daughter, " to bring oot t' scrapple." And I, with some deference of tone, asked simply, " What may a scrapple be ? " when the girl came out with a small coal-rake, to which the old dame pointed, saying, " Whè, that's what a scrapple may be !" And as I moved away, rather sheepishly, I heard her call across the road to a neighbour, " I doon't know whoar t' doctor's been browte up, he co's t' beck a river, an' doesn't know what a scrapple is."

In the other story, a boatman on Ullswater, in reply to the rather foolish enquiry, as he no doubt considered it, made by a gentleman he was rowing, "Does it ever rain here?" said, "Why it douks and dozzles an' does, an' sùmtimes gi's a bit of a snifter, but it niver cūms iv any girt pell!"

Several amusing illustrations of the Cumbrian habit of abbreviating the definite article, THE, into its first letter have long been in circulation, and are often quoted by writers on the dialect. I think the best of these, however, has not yet been published, which is this :—

Two gentlemen, a resident in Whitehaven and a visitor, were walking on the old North Wall there, when the former asked a boy they met what ships had come in by the tide, then past the height. The lad's answer seemed to be this, "There was Tenry, an' Tebe an' Tant an' Tatlas an' Taurora," an apparently alliterative string of ships' names which rather mystified the stranger, to whom it had to be explained that this was their informant's, and indeed most of Whitehaven people's, way of pronouncing the names of vessels called the Henry, the Hebe, the Ant, the Atlas, and the Aurora, which were all well-known colliers at that time, say thirty years ago.

With regard to the curious manner in which the dialect varies in different parts of this county, it will be remembered that in the interesting essay prefacing his "Glossary of Cumberland Words and Phrases," my friend Mr. Dickinson, the best informed, the most accurate and most exhaustive of the lexicographers of our native speech, has divided the county into three portions—North-East, Central, and South-West. Now it is only in the middle district that pure, unsophisticated Cumbrian is spoken. In the South-west—"up i' Oopha an daown i' Millom"—the dialect is considerably mixed up with those of Lancashire and Westmoreland, which certainly do not improve it. In the North-east it is adulterated with Scotch : I say adulterated advisedly, for while pure Scotch and pure

Cumbrian are to me more delightful than any other spoken sounds, the mongrel speech compounded of both, as used on the immediate south of the Border, grates on my senses very disagreeably. The Southwest dialect, though inferior both in music and strength to the pure Norse-rooted vernacular of Central Cumberland, is not so unpleasant as the northern vitiation, and its difference, except in some idiomatic phrases, exists mainly in the pronunciation of the vowels and diphthongs ; but I think you must agree with me in preferring whoar to whār, or snow to snā, w'ole to hooal, heid to heead, feùl to feeul, and so on. These differences have sometimes been a source of amusement to me. I remember being interested in over-hearing a young miner from Borrowdale taxing his energies in trying to teach a native of Coniston, where the dialect is nearly that of Southwest Cumberland, to pronounce the word school in *his* fashion—Scheùl—all his efforts being ineffectual in getting anything from his pupil but *schœul.*

I was still more amused at the same place, when standing. one winter evening, in the spacious kitchen of the Black Bull Inn there, talking with the landlady —a gem without polish, but also without flaw—and our conversation was interrupted by a man poking his head in at the door and asking, "D' yè want any flooks, mistress?" "Any what?" inquired Mrs. Bell, "Flooks," repeated the man. "I mūn cūm an' see what yè gitten," said she, and went out. In about a minute she returned in a chafe, saying, "Būrn t' fellow wi' his flooks—He toaks sa fine yan doesn't knā' what he meeans." "What would you call them?" I asked. "Why fleeùks!" said she, "Yee wod be wār ner t' man girt like, an say flooanders, but to my fancy, fleeuk is meeast like his bisness." I inferred from this that my plain spoken hostess knew the fish-

cadger's meaning all along, and pretended ignorance
to punish his assumption of a refinement unbecoming
his occupation.

Of this notion, that the nature of the subject spoken
of should influence the character of the language
applied to it, the following is a rather amusing illustration. I was chatting with a gentleman, in Lamplugh,
who did not generally express himself in the dialect of
his neighbourhood. He was relating to me some incidents showing how much his premises were infested
with rats, and whenever he named them he called
them, in the country manner, rattens. His daughter,
who was present, at length remonstrated with him on
using a vulgarism which involved the trouble of using
also a superfluous syllable, and asked, " Why can't you
call them rats, papa ? " He, evidently thinking that
there was no occasion to be so particular with vermin,
replied rather scornfully, " Rattens is good enough for
them ! "

One peculiarity of speech prevails all over the lake
district, and, indeed, is by no means confined to it—
I refer to the habit of employing adjectives, without
any regard to their original signification, as exaggera-
tives or intensifiers of other adjectives of quite distinct
and often of very opposite meaning. Of this, we may
commonly hear such examples as a terrible fine day—
a cruel nice woman—a 'larming good crop ; and once,
as I was walking up the lane that leads from the
Cockermouth road past Skelsmer to Lamplugh Church,
I found the old blacksmith from Ullock leaning against
the hedge, and talking with a party of workmen engaged in hacking up the surface of the road prepara-
tory to relaying it. I remarked that they were making
a rough road of it in the meantime, and the smith
interposed, " Ey, I was just tellin them 'at they're
spoilin' a *heinous* gūd rwoad."

I remember hearing in the same rural parish a curious application of the very expressive word *tew*—which is generally used as a verb, meaning to harass or distress. I was sitting in the night-time by the fireside of a worthy unlettered methodist, who thinking it right to improve the occasion, broke out suddenly, and apropos of nothing, with, "I often think aboot Adam an' Eve; what a sad job it was 'at they sud ha' spoil't oor property as they dūd!" "Ey, ey!" assented an old female neighbour who was sharing our vigil, "Ey, ey! it was a sair tew that."

While in this locality I may mention that a joke, which within the last few years has had place in the *facetiæ* column of very many newspapers, was told to me long years before it appeared in print as having originated in Lamplugh. The people there have, or had a custom of saying that Lamplugh Cross is "eight miles from ivery spot and sixteen from Keswick." If one take the trouble to investigate this saying, the comprehensive expression, "ivery spot," will be found to limit its application to the five towns of Egremont, Whitehaven, Harrington, Workington, and Cockermouth. Near to this curious centre of civilization, the story went that a man, well known in the parish, and affected with an impediment of speech when hurried or excited, though at ordinary times he spoke well enough, was breaking stones at the roadside, when a traveller rode rapidly up and called out, "How far is it to Keswick?" Poor Tom essayed to give the information demanded, but after sus—sus—sussing for a long time, the rider waiting impatiently, and finding himself unable to bring out even the first syllable of the "sixteen mile," went upon another tack, and setting his breath free, roared out, "Hang the', gang on—thu'll be theear affoar I can tell the't."

This story reminds me of another, turning upon a

similar inquiry, and reflecting rather severely upon
the fair fame of a village, not quite like "ivery spot,"
eight miles from Lamplugh Cross :—A lady it is said
was approaching it from Whitehaven, and asked a boy
how far she was from Distington, when the ill-natured
whelp replied in terms which I would not like to re-
produce or to allude to farther than to say they did
not answer her inquiry. They however seemed to
answer her purpose, for she said politely, "Thank you,
my boy—I know I cannot be far from Distington
when I hear such language as that."

*   *   *   *

An aged and childless couple, who resided in Whitehaven—in one of the narrow thoroughfares which con-
nect Queen Street with Scotch Street—had dwelt together so long, in what Wordsworth, apostrophizing
Charles Lamb and his sister, very beautifully called
"dual loneliness," that they had ceased to regard or
to speak of themselves or each other as separate exist-
ences ; and instead of saying I or me, or my husband
or my wife, both had acquired a habit, when referring
to him or herself or each other, of saying, "yan on
us," and this habit was maintained till they had reached
extreme age ; when one sad morning the old man
awoke and found that she who had so long formed
part and parcel of his own life, was lying dead beside
him, having departed in the night, and that so peace-
fully as not to disturb the husband sleeping at her
side. On making this terrible discovery, the old man
rose, opened the window, and alarmed the neighbours,
who, shocked and sympathising as they were, could
hardly hide their amusement as he kept repeating,
"O dear, yan on us is deed—yan on us is deed !"

Almost painfully in contradistinction to this gro-
tesque, and yet very beautiful manifestation of perfect
conjugal union, is an incident which came under my

own observation in the southern part of the lake district, equally ludicrous but by no means equally pleasing. The proprietor of a pretty little estate on the banks of one of the finest of our lakes, had a wife whose temper was only surpassed in acerbity by that of her husband. He had the advantage, too, of being gifted with a vastly superior knack of making very ugly remarks. For many years anything like a kindly, or even a civil word had never passed between them. The matrimonial chain galled both sorely; and the cup of life, filled up with constant wrangling and strife, became more and more bitter as age crept upon them. The pitiable woman, when I knew them, was severely afflicted in body as well as in mind. She had lost her sight for some years, and one of her knees became affected by disease, rendering amputation of the limb necessary. This operation was performed, and the amiable husband evinced not the slightest interest in the proceedings which he knew were going on within doors, but went plodding stolidly about his ordinary work outside. As the surgeons were leaving the house, they met him bringing in the cows, and were accosted by him with, "Well, haè yè gitten her leg off?" "Yes." "Ah, t' hang yè," said he, "ye've began at t' wrang end!" And seeing the doctors look rather bewildered, he exclaimed in a tone that showed he meant it all, "I say yè begun at t' wrang end—yè sud teean her heead!"

The opinion on matrimony in general of this unworthy member of the worthy 'statesman class, may be gathered from another anecdote, which I had from the active and useful dissenting minister, who himself figures in it, and who has now, I believe, been for many years located in one of the coast towns of Cumberland. This gentleman served three chapels, several miles apart, on the Sundays, and held occa-

sional week-day services besides in another dale many
miles away. One of his meeting-houses occupied a
retired situation near to the residence of the cross-
grained old yeoman I have just been dealing with,
who compounded for sins he was inclined to by attending public worship there pretty regularly. The minister one day informed the congregation that he wished
to have collections made in aid of the Baptist Missionary Society. In this he was strenuously opposed by
our cantankerous friend, who, in reply to the state-
ment that the society contributed in an important
degree to the support of the chapels, and, therefore,
was entitled to *something* in return, exclaimed, "We
knā nowte about na missionary societies—ther' was
land left for t' suppoort o' thor chapels, an that's o'
'ats' want 't." "Nay, nay, Isaac," said the patient
pastor of this impracticable sheep, "ye cannot say
that twenty-five pounds a year is enough to keep your
minister and his wife and his pony." "Why," per-
sisted Isaac, "it's reet aneeuf ye' sud hev a pooany—
ye cud n't weel get throo yer wark wi'out it—but es
for t' wife, I dooant see what yè hed u't due wi' sick
fancies !"

The married state, in the uneducated particularly,
seems to develop extreme sentiments and sometimes
to call forth rather irrational demonstrations of feeling; and in the lake country, where the people are
not much in the habit of suppressing their feelings or
concealing their sentiments, they oftentimes crop out
in a manner that affords amusement to an observer.
An example of this in one, and that the most agreeable, direction, occurred in the boast made to a neighbour by a farmer's wife at Dean. "Ooar John," said
this fortunate wife, "ooar John niver contradictit me
iv his life. If I war to say 'at black-puddings grew
upon churry trees an' sossingers com ruddy meàd fray

t' moon, he wadn't say udderways ! Wadn't thoo nūt, John?" she continued, appealing triumphantly to her husband who was present. " Neea, my lass, I wadn't," was his response, "wadn't say udderways if thoo said I com ruddy meàd fray t' moon mysel' !"

This may be taken as an example of unreasoning harmony in married life, interblending the absurd with the affectionate ; but I have known the reverse of the matrimonial medal, equally unreasoning discordance, manifest itself in a form combining the absurd with the brutal.

Thus : a fellow in Westmoreland, given to staying out at night, came home once even later than usual, and finding his uncomplaining wife sitting up for him, began incontinently to beat her. The poor woman protested against such treatment when she hadn't said a word to provoke it, and the preposterous scoundrel exclaimed, " Neea ! thoa said nowte—I knā thou said nowte ; but th'u's a thinkin divel !" And so the poor wife was punished for the unexpressed thoughts which her husband knew his conduct must of necessity give rise to.

The following offers a simple and very homely example of the unselfish kindliness of married life—so pleasing to contemplate, and, as I am glad to attest, so far from rare in the class from which most of my illustrations are drawn.

An old man, who lived at the low end of Working-ton, was roused in the middle of the night from a sound sleep, fairly earned by a long day's work, I think in the Ropery, to be informed by his wife that she could not sleep a wink. I believe that most of us would have exhibited some little irritation under these circumstances ; but this fine old Trojan, giving his sleepy eyes a rub, and suiting the action to the word, said, " Can té nūt, my lass? Can té nūt ? Why then, let's sit up and hod a crack."

It is curious that as I recal each of these simple illustrations of humble domestic life to memory, another in strong contrast to it seems to force itself upon my recollection, as if to compel me to bear in mind that the good and pleasant in most of the relations of this life are often counterbalanced by something not quite so good, and much less pleasing; and so the cheerful self-abnegation of our old Workington friend appears to fix my attention upon an instance of stolid insensibility as much at variance with it as though the actors in each did not belong to the same species. This anecdote was told me many years ago by a lady neighbour, to the remembrance of whom a sad interest is now attached from her only son being one of the victims of that terrible casualty on the Matterhorn in 1865, by which, as may be remembered, three English gentlemen and a guide came to a fearful end.

The lady went one afternoon to see a poor neighbour who was on her death-bed. On reaching the cottage, the kind visitor found the dying woman's husband and daughter sitting in " the house." or outer apartment, regaling themselves with tea and apple-cake. Passing through to the inner room, she saw that the sick woman was in the act of dying—and dying alone—while those nearest to her were enjoying their meal quite apart. Naturally shocked, the lady hurried back, crying out, " John ! John ! your wife's dying." " Whya, whya, my lady !" said the insensate old animal—disposing with great deliberation of a huge mouthful of apple cake—" Whya, whya, my lady ! we mun hev our tea if she wur deead !"

CUMBERLAND ANECDOTES.

ILLUSTRATIONS OF CHARACTER
AND MANNER.

"Lo, here I bring you a bouquet of flowers, of which nothing is my own except the string which has bound them together."—*Montaigne.*

An attempt at classification is made in the following collection of anecdotes, but without any very definite arrangement being observed, though, perhaps, sufficient to aid in referring to any particular section of the following collection. There is no little difficulty in assorting the mass, and in placing each in its proper department. The shades mingle and confuse each other till selection is almost impossible, and a miscellaneous division is adopted as a receptacle for the rejected of the better ascertained classes. None are put forth as perfect, and taste and judgment differ so much, that what one may approve as witty another may stamp as of some other quality.

W.D.

ILLUSTRATIONS OF CHARACTER AND MANNER.

EY, EY, EY!

It is no uncommon thing in the country, where the interchange of ideas is of less frequency than in towns, for some people to be tickled with a word or phrase, and to use it in playfulness until it becomes an adopted child, and is grafted upon nearly every sentence or reply, till the conversation of such persons cannot proceed without it.

An instance of this kind occurred with the late Isaac Cartmell, of Smaithwaite, who was a Keswick butcher, doing a good business, and well respected. He was a quick talker, and had a habit of commencing a reply with, "Ey, ey, ey," on almost every occasion. A bet was made with a London traveller, that Isaac would assent to whatever the stranger said to him. Next day being market day, and Isaac at his stand, the commercial accosted him with, "Mr. Cartmell, they tell me you give short weight." The instant reply was, "Ey, ey, ey! who said seah? who said seah?"

MAK TO YER LIKIN.

On the introduction of tea into the northern counties, and while it was yet a great novelty, and, of course, a great treat, the proper mode of using it was not settled. Some boiled it and ate the leaves, throwing the decoction away. Others mixed the boiled leaves with fresh butter, and ate the mixture with bread, drinking the fluid. Other methods equally rational were essayed, but little relished, till some uniformity of custom began to obtain, and sugar and cream were found agreeable additions. A glass of rum poured into the last cup, and called a " laced cup," was invented to qualify the bitter ingredient, and was usually given as a treat to visitors.

Before the conventional custom of the present day was well established, we are told of a woman having invited a few friends to partake of a treat, without giving it a name.

When the guests were assembled round a table well furnished with bread, butter, cheese, and other tea requisites, she bade them welcome, and, without saying what was before them, she poured out each a cup of tea, and said, " Now than, mak to yer likin—mak to yer likin ; " and set them the example by helping herself to sugar and cream, and initiating them into the mysteries of sipping tea. This injunction being repeated with each round of cups, their curiosity was excited to know what they had partaken of, and one of them ventured to ask, saying, " You've gien us a good treat, and we like't it reet weel. Nin on us iver hard tell o' *mak to yer likin* befoor, and we wad like to know what it's meadd on ? " After indulging in a proud and hearty laugh, she told them it was " that new-fangled stuff they co't tea."

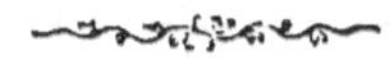

I DARR SAY.

When the late Christopher Parker, Esq., was high sheriff of Cumberland, he was invited to dine with a neighbouring yeoman of considerable wealth, who was not a little proud to entertain the high sheriff. The dinner was substantial, and full justice was done to it; and the host had sundry opportunities of introducing his by-word, but no wine appeared. When dinner was over, and ample time and sundry hints had been given, the sheriff spoke out and said, "Mr. Bell, I should like to taste your wine." "I darr say, I darr say,"—and no more notice was taken of it, and no effect was produced.

The saying, "I darr say," had a long run in the neighbourhood, and provoked many a laugh among those to whom the high sheriff and Franky Bell were known.

FANNY GRAHAM.

Among the labouring population it is not rare to find a brusque manner in combination with a hale frame, and more commonly among females; such was Fanny Graham. Fanny might not be a fair specimen of Cumberland stamina, but she certainly exhibits no symptom of the degeneracy of the race in respect of bodily powers.

When 93 years of age, she walked one morning from Lazonby to Plumpton, between four and five miles. The Rev. Mr. Harrison meeting her said, "I wonder, Fanny, you don't walk with a stick." "Shaff o' ye," says Fanny, "it's nought but pride o' ye. I rackon nought o' fwok walking wid a stick till they're up in years a bit."

As a whining contrast: a neighbouring old woman called to see her during the keen cold of the early part of January, 1871, when Fanny was about 97, and still fresh. Bewailing their hard fate she said, "O dear, Fanny, this hard weather 'ill finish beàth thee and me, I think." "Humph!" says Fanny, "a likely stwory indeed! Thou mun speak for thysel; I'll git through 't, I'll warrant me. Dee indeed! What's to make us dee, I wonder? We sartently can stand a bit cold like this."

Between the above-named two periods, Mr. Heskett met Fanny walking from Lazonby to Plumpton on an extremely wet day; and, on his return, met her again tramping along under a large cotton umbrella, which, in its then wet state, would be no little weight. She looked up and said, "It's rayder clashy." He assented to her remark for the rain was pouring down, and the roads were muddy and slippery enough to bother a much younger person.

Fanny died in February, 1873, in her 100th year.

DICK FARGYSON'S MAN.

THE late Richard Ferguson, Esq., of Harker Lodge, saw a boy holding a saddle pony in English Street, Carlisle, and asked the boy to whom it belonged— well knowing it was his own. "It's Mr. Blamire's," says the boy. "And who is Mr. Blamire?" "He's oald Dick Fargyson's man." "Here's sixpence for you, my boy"—and he walked on, very much amused.

A PUZZLER.

THE late John Christian Curwen, Esq., was such a hasty and careless writer that he sometimes had a

difficulty in deciphering his own hand-writing. A
tenant once handed him one of his own letters which
neither could make anything of, and did not say it
was his own.   Mr. C., after looking it over, handed
it back, saying, "What fool has written this? Take
it to my steward, Mr. Hoodless, he can read any
writing."

AN ENGLISH BULL.

WHEN the late J. C. Curwen, Esq., was in Parliament,
he held a great extent of land in his own occupation,
and had a large farming establishment.   During a
session, his land steward, Mr. Hoodless, wrote him
that one of the bulls had attacked and nearly killed a
labourer.   Feeling much anxiety for the safety and
welfare of his people, and being so busily engaged
that he was obliged to economise time, he hastily
wrote to the steward to "shoot that d——d bull."
Mr. Hoodless had often been sorely tried, but never
fairly beat, in reading letters from his master; but
this one of four words he was obliged to ask the
cashier, Mr. W. Swinburn, to read for him.   Again
defeated, he took the mystic scrawl to the solicitor,
Mr. B. Thompson, but he, like the others, was unable
to decipher the short command, and the letter was
put away.

A Parliamentary recess occurring a few weeks after,
Mr. Curwen came down to Workington Hall, and,
looking through his herd, discovered the wicked bull
still living, and angrily accosted his steward with,
"Why haven't you shot that d——d bull, Hoodless?"
"That's it, sir," said Hoodless, "now I can read your
letter," pulling it out of his pocket, and so restoring
his employer to good humour.

FIDDLING BY MAIN STRENGTH.

An energetic but very bad fiddler was asked if he played by note and answered, "No." "Do you play by ear?" "No." "Then, what do you play by?" "Main strength."

A QUALIFIED COMPLIMENT.

A Cumbrian having entered into the state of matrimony who did not entertain a high opinion of his new connections was asked by a friend what kind of a wife he had got. To which he replied, "A good an of her swort, but a mortal bad swort like reed herrin broth."

ADVICE PREPAID.

Willy Walker, of Hackthorp Hall, a Quaker farmer, had a lisp in his speech, and a good share of humour on suitable occasions.

He had an appointment to meet a person on business who was not punctual and kept Willy waiting at the public-house agreed upon. Whilst waiting an acquaintance dropped in, who asked him if he would accept a glass of anything. "Yes, I'll take a glass of rum and water, hot, with thee." The glasses were emptied, and Willy was asked to have another. The crack went on, and the glasses went off a second time. After a short delay, the man offered a third, which was accepted and likewise drunk off. In a little time the man grew impatient, and said that after paying for three rounds of glasses it was fairly Mr. Walker's turn

to treat. "I'll not treat thee, friend. Thou hast had
enough; and if thee has any more, thou wilt be to
take home in a cart."

JOE ABBOTT AND HIS TEACHER.

THE late Mr. John Slee, of Tirril, a Quaker, was a
clever mathematician and an excellent classical teacher,
and spread abroad numbers of well-educated grown-up
young men. Among his pupils Joseph Abbott, the
son of a neighbouring farmer, was conspicuous for his
readiness of speech and vigour of action, and for his
great inventive devilry.

Mr. Slee, having sold an overgrown calf to a butcher
who lived a short distance from Tirril, would essay the
delivery himself, by way of taking exercise. It had
long been remarked by the pupils that none of them
had ever known their master to either laugh or smile.
The frisky calf was haltered, and the couple sallied
forth during play-hour at mid-day. They were noticed
by the pupils, and Abbott resolved to create a little
sport with his demure master, who had evidently
enough to do, though a tall and strong man, to restrain
the gambols of the scampering animal. Abbott crept
to the end of a narrow lane just in time to give a loud
shout when the couple were passing, and off went the
calf helter-skelter, with tail erect, and dragging the
stern commander of the school in so violent a way
that he was obliged to let go his hold or be dragged
down in the dirt. The mischievous lad was soon
stealthily back among his schoolfellows, who with difficulty repressed their enjoyment of the sport, and pre-
tended not to notice their master as he tried to get to
the house without being observed. Joe was heartily

applauded, but was tauntingly told he need not appear in school again, and that he durst not.   " Yes, I dare," says he, " and I ll make the master laugh too, and that is what none of you ever could do."   Nothing daunted, he went in with the rest, and, assuming the broadest dialect, with all eyes on him, and all in silent attention, he walked up to near Mr. Slee with—" Noo, maister, hoo dud ye git away wi' t' cofe?"   Instantly a smile, as welcome as the sunlight, opened on Mr. Slee's countenance, and so electrified the pupils that they burst into a general laugh—and their master joined them.   " Now," said Joe, " that *was* a laugh !"

JOE ABBOTT AGAIN.

JOE would seem to have had more favour shown him than he was fairly entitled to, and the following in some measure explains the cause : he was a slow learner at school, and exercised his master's patience in a very trying manner.

In addition to teaching, Mr. Slee dealt in flax, lint, tow, &c., and supplied his neighbours with those articles when spinning-wheels were in fashion.   Once, when Joe had given more than ordinary trouble by doing bad lessons, as well as many little mischiefs in the school, Mr. Slee called him up, and after lecturing him said, " Joseph, I would have turned thee out of the school long ago, but I have a great respect for thy father."   Joe replied, " Ey ; he buys a varst o' tow on ye."

Once Joe had worked a whole week at a money question in Addition.   Every afternoon he took his slate up to the master, and each time it was wrong, and he was told to go back and try again.   On the

Friday he took great pains, and went up in great hopes he was right. Mr. Slee looking it over said, "It is twopence-halfpenny wrong yet, and thou must go back with it." "No, no," said Joe, putting his hand into his pocket, "I'll pay t' difference mysel. I've hed trouble enough with it."

Joe attained celebrity as a wrestler, but not as a scholar.

CO-OPERATIVE HELP.

THE late Mr. Joseph Sanderson occasionally took his recreation in a few days' quiet drinking, when he would collect a few willing companions to join him at his own expense. He used to recite his verses, sing songs of his own composing, and relate anecdotes to the admiring circle, and was always ready to pay them for their loss of time. These indulgences commonly ended with the week, and on the Saturday night he would dismiss his friends, saying he had no further occasion for them, and bid them good night. They took it in turns for one of them to stay behind to say, "We're varra mickle obleeged to you, Mr. Sanderson, and when do you think you'll want us again?"

THE RUM THIEF.

CAPTAIN Knubley kept a few couples of beagles at Wigton, with Tom Furnass as huntsman. One morning the dogs were cast off at Crosshill, where Mr. Tiffin joined them. Not finding a hare, they crossed over to Drayrig farm to try there. Old Mary, who enjoyed the cry of the hounds, invited them, in her unadorned welcome, to come in with, " Noo, hoo ur ye this mwornin ? Sit ye down, an' I'll fetch ye summat to drink." Tom and the dogs were outside, and Mary said, " Come in, Tom, and steek t' deur to keep t' dogs out." While the gentlemen were refreshing, she offered Tom the choice of a glass of spirits, or a bason of poddish with a bottle of ale as a wash-down. Tom chose the poddish and wash-down ; but, by mistake, Mary put down a bottle of rum instead of ale with the savoury mess. The gentlemen went out and waited for Tom, and, thinking he was long in coming, returned to see what detained him, asking if he was going to sit there all day. Tom says, " O Captain, it's stealin' me away." " What's stealing thee away ? " " Just come in and teàsst this." The captain at once detected the thief and said, " Thou old varment thou's supping rum to thy poddish." " Ey," says Tom, " an' it's gaan wi' ma varra fast." So it did, and Tom's hunting was fairly over for that day.

HARD WORK.

J—— D——, a local brother, was holding forth at the Market Cross in Egremont on a warm day. Energetic action and forcible delivery caused him to perspire very freely. Pausing, and wiping his head and face with a handkerchief, he said to his audience, " See ye how I's sweetan o' riddy ; but I's just gaan to begin wi' the divel, an' than ! " He had not words to express himself strongly enough, and the laughter of his hearers relieved him of the difficulty.

CONCEIT.

J—— E————, of Workington, fancied he had a
peculiar call to instruct the ignorant of the town on
the way to obtain a place in heaven; and, being of
opinion that his humble origin and calling were a
sufficient title to an equality with the gifted apostle,
he stated to his hearers that " Paul was a tent-maker,
and I's a blacksmith, and between us we'll dea parlish
things I's warrant ye."

THE Cumberland system of courting has been so often
and so truthfully described in so many of its phases,
that it is unnecessary here to add to what must be so
well known.   But one or two relative instances in
connection therewith may not be out of place.

THE FUN OF COURTING.

ABOUT 1790, Joseph Wright, of Frizington Parks, and
Jack Robinson, of Kinniside, were suitors for two
sisters of the Watson family, of South Mosses, and
agreed to go together one evening to try their luck
with the young ladies, and to carry out a freak of
Jack's prolific brain.   The dwelling-house at Mosses
was, like most farm-houses at that time, thatched, and
all the rooms were on the ground floor.   Much hospitality was practised at that day to all visitors; but in
this instance Joe was freely admitted, and Jack
thought it better to wait till most of the family
retired, as he was not much of a favourite with the
seniors.   He did his best to discover what went on

inside; and, as had been the case on former occasions, a fine piece of beef was brought out for Joe's refreshment. Jack had made some provision in anticipation of this, and mounted the roof as silently as possible, whilst Joe did his best at the beef and in occupying the attention of the family, though he could hardly restrain his laughter at the expected result. However, he succeeded so well that no remark was made, until some bits of straw fell from the thatch upon the table, which was noticed by a brother of the girls, and attributed by him and Joe Wright to rats in the thatch. For a short space suspicion was quelled, but quickly a long pole, armed with a hay crook, was pushed down, stuck into the beef, and up it went. The family stood amazed, watching the ascent of the beef, when, just as it was about to disappear through the roof, the hook tore out its hold, and down came the beef upon the broad pewter dish, and laid it, small stand table and all, prostrate on the clay floor. All rushed towards the door, but Joe Wright contrived to be first there; and while apparently struggling to open the door with his hands, was eagerly pressing it close with his foot, exclaiming that some one held it outside. The door was kept shut long enough for Jack to escape without discovery, but they made no matches with the family either that night or after.

A TROUBLE NO TROUBLE.

THERE used to be an old saying—

> "Needles and pins, needles and pins,
> When a man marries, his trouble begins."

We have learned that in one instance, in Loweswater, a man's troubles began before marriage. A yeoman was courting a young woman, and their practice differed somewhat from the usual Cumberland custom of that day, for they sat one on each side of the fire. Peter thought he advanced his cause best by walking over to the lady at intervals and kissing her ; and when the kissing idea came into his head he used to say, "Now, Betty, I must trouble you again." "O, no trouble at all, Peter !"

NIGHT COURTING.

However reprehensible this custom may be, the chance of its being suppressed is still remote. It was at one time universal, but happily is much modified of late years.

A farmer near Dean had his attention attracted by a gentle tapping at his bedroom window, a little after bedtime. At that period it was the custom in most cases, in the country, for the head of the family to sleep in the parlour, as the guardian of his household. On a repetition of the tapping, he looked through the window and saw who was there. He then went and whispered at his daughter's room-door, " Nanny, here's Willy ——, o' W——, wi' three lands. Git up, my lass, and let him in." Willy, with his three estates, was a coveted suitor, and had mistaken the window.

VERY BUSINESS-LIKE.

Courtship among a certain class of Cumbrians is invariably carried on clandestinely, apparently under the feeling that there is no fun in it unless pursued after dark and in secrecy. No such feeling, however, seems to have animated the blunt, honest *'statesman* who rode up to the house of the lady of his choice, and, the damsel herself having appeared at the door, said, " I just co't to tell thee that I ha' been thinkin' o' gittan weddit', and I thought thou was as like suitan' me as owt. Now, I's just gaan to t' market, and I'll co' as I coo back, and see what thou says about it." He gravely rode on, and on his return was accepted.

A less successful swain, who would not take a refusal, was reported by the lady's mother to have followed her daughter for twenty years, and for " twelve on them hoddenly ;"* he was only deterred from further prosecuting his suit by the at-length impatient father, who threatened that " if he catched him inside his foald yat agean " he " wad tak t' bill-heuk tul him, 'at wad he."

⁕⁕⁕⁕⁕

OVERDONE.

OTHER versions of this story are given, but the following was narrated to the writer by one who knew both the actors :—

A postman in the far west of the county overtook a butcher leading a calf by a cord tied round his own waist, and vainly endeavouring to induce the animal to cross a foot-bridge on the path. The butcher requested the postman to stand behind the calf and blow his horn when the calf was got into a favourable position. When the word was given to " Blaa, Jimmy, blaa !" a sudden and loud blast was given, and over leapt the calf into a deep moss-pool dragging the

---

* Without intermission.

butcher along with it. On recovering his feet, he turned to the astonished postman and roared out, "Thaaw fooal! thaaw!—that was far oor girt a blaa for a fat cofe."

A HIGH SHERIFF.

IN times long gone, the magistracy of the county was occasionally recruited by the appointment of an unpolished diamond, and few could support this character with more honesty than Mr. W——, of Penrith, best known as Justice W——. He was High Sheriff of Cumberland in ——, and according to custom, before the days of railway travelling, went to meet the Judge of Assize at Teman, on the border of Northumberland, and escort him to Carlisle. Instead of assisting the Judge into his carriage on receiving him from the charge of the Sheriff of the sister county, he quietly seated himself. One of the Sheriff's footmen hinted that he should have handed the Judge in first. He quickly slipped out at the opposite door, and came round to hand in the Judge, saying, " Now, Mr. Judge, get in and sit ye down; it's o' t' seamm thing who gits in furst." When seated, the long walking-stick of the Sheriff (so common in those days) was stuck up between them. The motion of the carriage on the rough road caused the stick to bob against the Judge's head sometimes, when he quietly laid it down against the opposite seat ; but the Sheriff replaced it as before, saying, he could not part with his old friend so easily. On proceeding towards Carlisle, the Sheriff remarked. " Now, Mr. Judge, if ye like a draft o' good yel, we can have a quart at this public-house, sek as ye'll hardly teast agean out o'

Cummerlan." The Judge declined the offer with thanks, and asked Mr. W—— if he killed his own mutton, as he always enjoyed the Cumberland sweet mutton. The Sheriff replied, "I'll nit say bit what I may have kilt an odd an' or two i' my time."

By this time the Judge would doubtless discover he had a great oddity for a sheriff, if not, a great fool. But the Sheriff was a shrewd droll under the guise of a blunt simpleton, and scorned to use a polished phrase if a homely one would answer; and, being quite aware of his defective education, was unwilling to risk a reputation for learning, lest he should blunder into his native dialect.

He used to call his carriage a "cwotch," and when he wished to halt would call out, "Now, stop t' cwotch, lads." On one occasion, as he was conveying a friend to Carlisle, and, according to the fashion of the time, had been indulging overnight with new ale, he bawled out "Stop t' cwotch, lads ; I mun be out at o' resks, and it's o' lang o' that blesh yel."

It was Justice W——'s custom to drop in at the Bowling Green Inn, at Penrith, for his forenoon's draught of ale, and one day he detected the smell of bacon frying in the kitchen. Thinking to bother the landlady, he called her, and told her very seriously she was doing an illegal act in frying bacon, for he had read it in his law books. " Bless me, Justice, it cannot be wrang to mak' t' dinner riddy." " Yes it is, and I'll bring thee t' beuk." Away he went, and brought "Burns' Justice," and laid the book open before her—" Now, Betty, read for thysel." Betty could read better than he suspected, and called out, " Wey, Justice, this is firin' a beacon, nit fryin' bacon. What ! I knew it wad be wrang to set fire to Peerith Beacon."

When Justice W—— lived in Penrith, he kept a

cow for dairy purposes.   As the time drew on for the cow to calve, there was no milk or butter for the family, and Mrs. W—— regarded this as a great privation.   However, the cow did calve, and about this time the Justice was called upon to decide between two neighbours on the liability to repair a piece of road.   During the hearing, one of the litigants withdrew his case, and having been no favourite with Mr. and Mrs. W——, the Justice hurried into the parlour to report to his wife, saying, " He's teann t' cowe."   The lady, mistaking the expression, asks, " Then, I do hope he takes the calf too ? "   " It's nit our coo.   He's teann t' cowe, and 's knockt under." This was understood as it was intended, and the lady consoled.

AWARDING PRAISE WHERE PRAISE IS DUE.

H—— S——, of H—— Windmill, when dining at Whitehaven Castle on a rent day, was so enchanted with a second plate of rice pudding, that he exclaimed aloud, " Wuns! t' woman 'at meadd this sud niver dee owt else."

A WISE RESOLVE.

An industrious Irishman rented a small walkmill at Bassenthwaite, and, with much care, prospered on it till his horse was hard put to it to do the work required.   One of his neighbours recommended him to purchase another horse to ease the one he had.

"Och," says Pat, "an' if ever I'm able to kape two horses, one of them shall be a cow."

ORNAMENT AT A DISCOUNT.

A steady going farmer, who knew little of the process of building or of its requirements, was inspecting a workman employed in plastering the farmer's parlour, and observing the man to score the stiffening-plaster in diamond fashion, previous to putting on the last coat, said, ' Nay, nay, now ; we'll hev nin o' that. I want nea ornament in my parlour, and I'll hev nowt bit good flat plaister."

THEORY *v.* PRACTICE.

WHEN the late Mr. Ewan Troutbeck was young, he often took the field with his elder brother in the shooting season, to practise partridge shooting ; but practice with him did not lead to perfection. During his after college life he got hold of a sporting book, which taught him to fix his eye on the flying object before raising his gun.

On going out again, he surprised his brother by bringing down his birds right and left. This caused George to exclaim, " Hollo, Ewan ! what's the matter now?" Ewan was very much of a droll, and had an answer ready. " Oh, aa's beuk-larnt now, man."

A GOOD SELL.

DURING his college days, Mr. Troutbeck was spending a vacation in Newcastle with some young men of his kidney. One of them remarked to him that their landlord appeared to be a very smart fellow, and any one wishing to get to the blind side of him must rise early in the morning. Ewan did not assent to this, but proposed to put it to the proof. Approaching the landlord, he addressed him with, " One of my companions and I have laid a friendly wager of a dinner and trimmings. Can you let us have it to-day?" " Oh, certainly. What would you like to have ? " " The best you can provide." When the capital dinner was over, the landlord inquired to whom he might book the account. Ewan told him the bet was not yet decided. Might he ask what the bet was? " Certainly," says Ewan, rising and pointing out of the window. " You see that beautiful spire yonder, which seems recently erected?" " Yes, sir." " The wager is, when that spire falls, will it fall to the right or the left?" The wager may still be undecided, but the bill was honourably settled, amid much amusement ; and the landlord gained wisdom from his experience.

HARD TIMES.

A gravedigger in Wigton complained to a tradesman of times being bad in his business, when the latter replied that times must be nearly alike to a gravedigger. " Nay, but they warn't. It was nobbet last week, I hed a grave thrown o' my hands." It appeared that he had dug a grave unordered for a dissenter, whose friends refused to have him buried in consecrated ground.

⁓⁓⁓⁓

IDIOT OR INVALID?

THE landlord of a good hotel, not many stations south of St. Bees, finds it advantageous to dispense with his "boots" in the winter season, and occasionally to act in that capacity himself. Being in attendance on the platform when the train arrived, he was asked by a gentleman if an invalid could be accommodated at the hotel. "Aa'll tell you in a minute." Away he scuds into the house, asking of a facetious neighbour who happened to be there —"What is invalids, Mr. A.?" "Why, they're idiots, to be sure," says Mr. A. Away he ran to the gentleman, saying, "Nay, we can deah nowt wi' na mad fwoks here."

⁓⁓⁓⁓

PETER AND PAUL.

MRS. I——, of Broomhills, not having attended service one Sunday, questioned her son, a lad in his teens, about the sermon, and where the text was from. The lad said, "Aa divent know, mudder, but t' priest talkt a deal about Peter and Paul, and they would likely be some girt men about Lunnon 'at my fadder hed selt horses tee." Mr. I—— was an extensive farmer, and dealt in horses.

H

"DEVIL'S DICK" GRAHAM AND HIS SON OF THE SAME OPINION.

How a member of the Society of Friends acquired this *soubriquet*, or whether he had fairly earned it, is not on record; but Dick wore it. James, the son, was a hectoring sort of fellow, but professed, as a Friend, to be very sober, although his acquaintances knew he liked a glass when it could be had snugly.

At a nomination in East Cumberland, James was over-persuaded by some young men to take more election drink than he could carry, and he and his load were conveyed to a quiet inn to rest till he came round. Another Graham (of Riggfoot), who had a spice of mischief and a great deal of fun in his temperament, was elated at the idea of " Devil's Dick " Jemmy being caught outraging the Society's principles by transgressing so far, and hurried to Jemmy's father at his home, saying, he believed the son had come to the misfortune of having a leg broke at the election. Dick posted off with a cart and a bed upon it, to have the injured man conveyed quietly home. On arriving at the inn, he was shown into the room where his son lay asleep on the floor, and tried to raise his head and body, in doing which he awakened Jemmy. Dick smelt the whisky, and soon knew he had been hoaxed. Starting back, he exclaimed, " James, I perceive thou art drunk." James (loudly), " And I am of the same opinion."

PUTTING ON MOURNING.

At the time of the death of King William the Fourth, the rector of Egremont directed one of his churchwardens to provide black cloth, to put the king's arms into mourning. The churchwarden, mistaking the king's arms in the church for the hotel of that name, innocently asked, "Sud we wap t' post or t' sign, Mr. Leech?"

⁂

WELL-AIMED THRIFT.

DURING the war with France, tallow rose to a high price, and candles were so dear that as few as possible were used in farm-houses, and stick fires were substituted for giving light in the evenings, where that kind of "elding" was attainable. Rushlights had also gone nearly out of use, because tallow was required in their manufacture. When light was desirable, the grate was replenished with a handful of small sticks or chips, or a turf at intervals to keep up the light, and this was called " beating the fire."

In a farm-house where oatmeal porridge was the staple of both morning and evening meals, as it was sometimes for dinner also, the custom was to serve the viand in a bowl of size corresponding with the number of the family present. The well-laden bowl was placed on the centre of the table, and the family sat round it, dipping their spoons into the fragrant mess, bringing out each a portion, and again bringing the charged spoon into a basin or tin of skim-milk, conveyed the relished contents to the mouth, and often with considerable despatch.

In a certain house, where the mistress was a clever contriver, and the saving of an inch of candle an act of merit, the supper was served in this manner, hot from the fire as usual, and a dip candle placed on the table, so that all might see what was before them, as well as see each other—the servant-man socially sitting next his master.   It had been the custom there for the mistress to take away the candle as soon as the members were set around the board, and the servant felt much annoyed with this.   He endured it for some time with respectful but ineffectual remonstrance, and set his wits to work to remedy the evil.   One evening the good dame came and took away the candle, saying, "Now, fwok, you can see wi' fire-leet to hit ivery yan yer own mouths, and aa want this cannel.   If ye can't see, ye may beat up t' fire."   The light was gloomy, and when the master opened his mouth to admit his spoon, cooled in milk, the man adroitly contrived to slip in a large spoonful of hot porridge without milk.   The master was not slow to sputter it out ; and commenced, as well as his blistered mouth would permit, to scold in no gentle terms both man and mistress, the children screaming, and the man calling out, "O mistress, pray ye, bring a leet. Aa mis't my oan mooth and hit' t' maister's wid a speunful o' het poddish, an' aa doubt aa've scoadit him."   The supper table was never without a candle, when needful, after that night.

⸺⸙⸺

ARCHY GOODFELLOW.

ARCHY was a farmer in the far east of Cumberland, and occasionally bought two or three fat sheep to slaughter and retail among his neighbours.   He was eccentric in his language, and most original in his oaths ; and, on account of being unable to pronounce the letter R, was peculiar in his delivery, often substituting the letter Y.   One day he went to a neighbour's to buy some sheep, when a few were brought into fold as fat, and were offered for sale to him. He took up and handled one he thought to be the best, and asked the price. "Thirty shillings." Being a very powerful man, he pitched the sheep to the opposite side of the fold, as if it had been a hand-ball, saying, "Thetty sheelin, man? By the mud an' the holy poka (poker) o' Dublin, I could yattle the hundyad psalm on his yibs;" and off he walked.

Archy once put a sudden and effectual stop to a windy political opponent, who was about to address the electors of East Cumberland, and had commenced with, "Gentlemen and ladies," when Archy broke in with, "Wully, thou's yang the vayya fust wud." Wully was so abashed by the laughter and derision of the crowd, that he shut up at once, and spared the infliction of an hour's listening to what Archy evidently did not wish to hear. On being bantered and complimented on his success, he said, "Wully hed putten the caat afooa the hoss."

GHOSTLY OR BODILY.

A MARYPORT man, who was thought by some of the clever ones of that town to be not quite so clever as themselves, went to Flimby one evening; and on his return at a rather late hour, saw a white object on the parapet of the bridge. Quite undaunted, the man called out, "Ghostly or bodily?" "Ghostly," replied the object. "Ghostly or bodily, thou sall hev't;" and, suiting the action to the word, he thrashed the ghost well, and tumbled him into the Ellen, out of which he was drawn by his friends, who had been in hiding to witness sport of another kind, as they thought.

ALWAYS GRUMBLING.

"I wish I was in heaven!" said a peevish old wife at St. Bees to her patient husband, as they sat by the fire one winter's night. "Thou's far better by thy own fireside. What wad ta de theer? Thou's niver satisfied."

ONLY ENOUGH.

A commercial man, accustomed to the route, called on a Quaker friend not far from Keswick, and was hospitably invited to partake of bread and cheese and ale. After doing justice to the bread and cheese, he drank the glass of ale with some relish, and was asked, "Friend, wilt thou take another glass of our home-brewed ale? I believe it is very good, if thou only take enough." He took a second glass and went his way, and found the ale affected him more than he expected or wished. On his next visit, some months after, he accepted another invitation, and was slily asked to take a second glass of home-brewed, with a recommendation similar to the preceding one. "No, I thank you; I remember your words on my last visit." "Yes, friend; I told thee my ale was very good, if thou only took enough; but thee took a glass more than enough."

CLEVER CABMAN.

A few years ago a Cumberland man had occasion to go to London, and took up his abode at the Gerard's

Hall Hotel, then kept by Mr. Younghusband, who was from Caldbeck originally. At night he sallied forth to "spy farlies," and having met with one or two acquaintances, and enjoyed himself too long in their company, he forgot the name and locality of his lodgings ; so he wisely called a cab. Being seated, Cabby politely touched his hat, and asked where he must drive to. "Heamm, thou feull, thou ; whoar else sud aa gang to at this time o' mwornin'?" Not without difficulty the man understood his meaning, and said, " Please, sir, I don't know where you live." " Thou's a bonny beggar to be a cabman, when thou dizzent know whar fwok leevs. Thou mun just guess till thou fins 't out." Cabby ran over the names of several hotels which he thought most likely. " Shelleywelly ! Dista think I wad put up at common pleaces like them ? It's some castle, or tower, or ho'." " Elephant and Castle ?" " No." " Tower Hill ?" " No." " Gerard's Hall ?" " That's it ! Thou's t' cleverest fellow in o' Lunnon. Thou can tell a body whoar he leevs when he dizzent know his-sel."

OBEYING ORDERS.

Mr. T. E. F——, the eminent colliery viewer, was appointed to value the engines and machinery at a colliery, and took a rough but skilled mechanic with him to inspect the parts Mr. F. could not easily reach, and which might soil his dress. The work finished, Mr. F. was invited to dine with a neighbouring gentleman, and directed the man to go to the hotel for his refreshment. Being unused to that class of inns, he asked his master what he might order. " Just go and order whatever thou sees others are getting." He went into the nearest room, and sat down behind the door; soon after two gentlemen came in, one of whom ordered a glass of brandy. When the waiter came with it, he said he thought Jack had made a mistake, and had gone into a wrong room. "Nay, I hevn't. Bring me yan, tee." Shortly after, the other gentleman ordered a Welsh rabbit. Jack, thinking of a cooked rabbit, said, "Bring me yan, tee." Soon the gentleman wanted a glass of beer. To fulfil his instructions, Jack quickly said, "Bring me yan, tee." The first gentleman ordered a bit of dinner. "Bring me yan, tee." He kept strictly to his master's orders till Mr. F. came to pay, when he said, "Ay, maister, it's weel ye've come. I cuddent ha' held out muckle langer, they ordered theirs in sa fast."

HARD BARGAINING.

THE late Mr. R—— W—— would sometimes worship at the shrine of Bacchus for several days in succession, and during those times the inn at Bolton Gate was the chief seat of his devotions. When others tired of his company, he would send for George Irving, best known as Gwordy Urran, the noted wrestler, to join him. However sweet "gi'en drink" may be, and doubtless was, George at length tired, or professed to be tired, of his job, and struck for higher wages. This was rather a risky experiment, but R—— agreed to advance him to three shillings and sixpence per day for the work. When the end of the week came, and payment was duly made, R—— said, "Now, Gwordy, thou must be douce again"—meaning that he should be generous, and treat his employer.

"Nay, Mr. W——," says he, "I cannot afford any luckpenny, but I divent mind givin' ye a day ower."

A GUIDE AMONG THE LAKES.

WHEN Mrs. Arrowsmith was staying at Keswick and doing the Lakes, she wished to explore the neighbourhood by short rambles on foot. Asking for a female guide, a girl was recommended who knew all the country round. On going out, the lady told her guide she wished to know everything about that part—"And you must tell me all you know about it." "Yes, mam. Yon's Mr. Marshall's bull." This information so astonished the lady, that she paid and dismissed her guide at once.

NEW MUSICAL INSTRUMENT.

A WOMAN at Flimby asked the rector's lady what kind of a musical instrument they were advertising for sale at Orton, saying, "It was not an organ, nor a harmonium, but it was summat they co't a advowson."

ECCENTRIC PREACHING.

HODGSON CASSON, of Workington, an enthusiastic preacher in the ranks of Methodism, was very much of an outspoken oddity, and very careless in his choice of words and expressions. In one of his exciting out-door preachings, he said to his audience,

"It's as easy for a swine to climb t' wrang end up a tree as for a rich man to git to heaven."

It is probable the above and the following have had the same origin :—

A ranting preacher was holding forth on the horsing-stone of a village green, when some pigs came wandering through among the straggling audience and were immediately utilised in the discourse. After sundry cautions and warnings, the listeners were told that, unless they mended their ways of living, they had no more chance of getting to heaven than *that* swine had of going hinder-quarters up yon ash tree and whistling like a throstle.

SOGLAN TOM.

Tom was a butcher, and lived at Soglan, between Brampton and Bewcastle, and was noted for selling his meat below the market price. Through the officious faithfulness of his dog, which he had trained to drive sheep home without its master, he was apprehended, tried, and condemned for sheep stealing. On the way from Carlisle gaol to the Sands, where criminals were executed, he said to the people who were hurrying to Rickergate, " Ye needn't be in sek a hurry, for there'll be nea spwort till I git thecar." On looking around him, he discovered some acquaintances by whom he did not wish to be recognised, and told the hangman who drove the cart to " drive on, for them beggars o' Branton butchers hes come o' purpose to hiss me for ondersellin' them, if they can git near."

STICKING TO IT.

AT a Cumberland quarter sessions, a young man from St. Bees was examined on an assault case, and gave his evidence in a pert manner, as if he had been schooled beforehand, adding after each answer, "And I'll stick to that." The Chairman, (E. W. Hasell, Esq.,) said in his quiet way to the witness, " If you do not give your evidence in a more respectful manner, I'll commit you to prison ; and I'll stick to that." The court enjoyed the joke, and the rebuke had the desired effect.

THRELKELD HALL.

WHEN Mr. Barker, the land steward of Henry Howard, Esq., of Greystoke Castle, was superintending some repairs going on at Threlkeld Hall (once the seat of Sir Lancelot Threlkeld, where he sheltered his stepson, the Shepherd Lord Clifford, when sought for by his enemies), he observed the stone floor of the principal sitting-room, (provincially, the house), was much broken up, and offered to floor it anew with stone flags. All the family, except old William Taylor, the tenant, gladly accepted the offer, and volunteered to cart the materials. The old man said, " I"fleur hed deun a gay while for him, an' it med dea on." However, decency prevailed. The flags were brought, and the men set to work.

The old man held to his principle to let well alone ; placed himself in his heavy arm-chair, at his usual corner of the fire-place, and there he doggedly sat and would not move an inch, till all was completed around him to the very square his chair covered. When other necessities compelled, he was obliged to give way; and, to the great annoyance of his feelings, the whole was completed during his short absence, but he could never bestow an approving word on the smooth new floor, though the old one had been almost as uneven as a newly-ploughed field. William was an honest and upright man, and was much esteemed by both landlord and steward, as well as by his neighbours.

HOGG'S IDEA OF MERCY.

ONE of the Hogg family of Bewcastle, was tried at Annan for poaching, and was ably defended by Mr. Armstrong, a solicitor of Carlisle. In the Scotch courts at that time the prisoner was allowed to give evidence on oath, and Hogg swore he did not commit the offence he was charged with. The gamekeeper swore he saw Hogg shoot game. But, as his evidence was unsupported, the prisoner was allowed the benefit, and acquitted. After the trial, Mr. Armstrong asked Hogg why he perjured himself by giving false evidence after confessing to him that he was guilty. "Hoot man," said Hogg, "I wad far rayder trust the marcy o' the Lord, ner I wad trust to that oald deeval on the bench."

A NIGHT WALKER.

A SCOTCH labourer, at Branthwaite, whose love of good eating was stronger than his prudential resolves, unintentionally disturbed his English wife's sleep by getting out of bed at an unusual hour of the night.

She called out, "Whoar are ye gaan, Jimmy, at this time o' neet?" "Ma woman! wha could lig i' the bed an' a guid veal peye i' the house?"

CHURCH AND COMMERCE.

WHETHER the following was a remnant of a very ancient custom or merely the outcoming of a thought the clerk had just indulged in, is not known. But it is recorded that at many churches it was not unusual in former times for a parishioner to bring the carcase of a fat sheep into the church porch, to cut up and sell to the congregation at the close of service. And lest the market should be overstocked it was arranged to take it in turns.

At the close of divine service at Whicham Church, the parish clerk was descending the steps from his desk, when he whispered to a Whitehaven tea dealer who was passing with the rest of the congregation—"Wad ye pleaz, Mester Lammin, to let me hev three pawnd o' teah, seamm as ye sent to Tibby Sheels?"

JUDY CRONE.

BEFORE the introduction of railways, there was a considerable traffic by carriers' carts, and of passengers by coaches and other vehicles, between Cockermouth and Carlisle. Some years before that, business began to diminish, George and Judith (Gwordy and Judy) McCrone had long kept a lonely, roadside public-house, at Moota Gate, about four miles north of Cockermouth, where few people passed without calling on the honest and respected, but rough-mouthed old couple. They were reported to have saved money, and were likely to have some with them at all times; it was also known that their only protection was a mastiff, with occasionally a little girl to assist in the house.

One night a mason of the name of Toole broke into the house, shot the dog, and ransacked the premises. The old pair were too frightened to make any resist ance; but Judy saw sufficient of the burglar to enable her to recognise him, and had him apprehended. He was tried at Carlisle and found guilty; and, on the judge asking if he had anything to say before sentence was pronounced, Judy stood up, and her kindly feelings overcoming the sense of her loss, said, " Now, Judge, thou munnot be ower hard o' t' peer lad. He's somebody's bairn." Then, turning to the prisoner, she said, " I dunnot mind about t' bit o' brass thou gat frae me, good lad; and I dunnot want to hurt thee, good lad; but thou shot my dog, and thou steall our Gwordy's brutches, thou dud."

⁓⁓⁓

BOTH DEFEATED.

At a period when the adulteration of intoxicating drinks was less understood than it has since been, or when it was less harmfully practised, a strong-headed toper, who had been drinking in a public-house all day, rose to go away about nine o'clock in the evening, when the landlord asked him where he was going. The reply was—" I's gaan to t' Cross"—a rival public-house. " What's ta gaan to dea there?" asked Boniface. " I's gaan to git drunk." " Git drunk! what for can ta nut git drunk here?" " I've been tryan iver

sen nine o'clock this mwornin', and I can't; sooa now
I's gaan to t' Cross."

A SURPRISE.

An eccentric attorney met a country client in Main
Street, Cockermouth, who stopped him and said, " O,
Mister Nicholson, can ye tell me if this sebben shillin'
piece is a good un ? "   " Yes," replied the lawyer, putting it into his pocket and giving him fourpence
change—"it is perfectly good, and I'm obliged to
you."

RATHER ILL-TEMPERED.

A man going to pay his lawyer's bill, and feeling
aggrieved at the amount remarked, " I doubt you've
meàdd a mistak.   I see you've charged six and eight-
pence for coman to see me, but you've forgitten to
charge ought for gangan heàmm ageàn."

A PLEA FOR POVERTY.

Before the days of Union Workhouses, when each
parish separately maintained its own poor, a blind
pauper married a woman who was also a pauper,
belonging to an adjoining parish, whereby both became
chargeable to his own.   Such contumacy could not be
allowed to pass unnoticed, and the poor fellow had to
appear before the vestry.
    When he had patiently listened to a severe but un-

availing lecture from the chairman, he meekly observed,
" Nea doubt it's a varra bad job for us o', but howiver
its o' done now, and can't be helped."

<hr>

CONCEIT OR SPIRIT?

IT is a happy circumstance that many of those whom
Nature has deformed are seldom fully alive to the fact.
Indeed, some appear altogether ignorant of it, as was
the case with a spirited hunchbacked village tailor,
who lived in the delusion that he was a well-made
fellow, and possessed of what he especially lacked—
great muscular strength. He used to say, " Ther niver
was nobbet ya man about G——fit to wear his (the
tailor's) coat, and that was "—naming an individual
with the powers of a Hercules.

On one occasion he accepted a " lift " in a farmer's
cart, when the horse chose to run away, and the driver,
who was a very powerful man, failed for some time to
check it.   " Let me see hod o' t' rynes," said the
plucky tailor, " I'll owder stop't, or I'll rive t' chafts
off 't."

A neighbouring gentleman got a new dress coat,
made by Stultz, or some such fashionable west-end
maker, which proving to be a little tight under the
arms, he sent for the local artist to make the needful
alterations.   When that functionary, holding the gar-
ment up to the light and examining it most minutely,
with a countenance expressive of the most withering
contempt, asked, " Who meàdd this thing ? "   The
reply was, that it was made in London.   " I thought
seah.   Thur Lunnon taileors ! they dooant know what
a cwoat is."

HOPE IT IS NOT A RULE.

In cautioning his nephew not to marry for money, an old uncle said, " Niver thee wed a woman wid a fortun. My wife had five pund, and I niver hard t' last on 't."

COSTLY WORK.

After listening to a description of the great cost of opening out a valuable and extensive mine in his neighbourhood, a yeoman remarked with a sigh, " Ey, thur publik warks is varra expensive. Ey, they cost a deal o' brass. Now I's buildan' a lime kiln, an' aa 'll be bund afoor it's done, it 'll cost varra nar ten pund."

A LIVING GUIDE-POST.

A stranger called at a farm-house in the village of Arlecdon and asked to be shown the way to Brown-rigg. He was very particularly answered by a female, who was busy at the butter tub and who scarcely looked up : " Wey, aa 's thrang ; but you mun gang down t' foald, an' through t' yat, and on by Sunton's, an' on through Helsigill yat, an' than turn down be-fwore you git to t' Lime-kill neuk, an' through t' Wood lonnin yat, an' down t' Wood lonnin by t' Wood lon-nin shades, an' ower t' Dub beck brig, an' up Brown-rigg brow, an' you 'll be theer directly."

I

WHITEHAVEN TRADESMEN LONG AGO.

MANY years ago there flourished at Whitehaven two bachelor brothers of remarkable quaintness, both as to sayings and doings, who, although in a small way of business, amassed considerable fortunes by dint of industry and extraordinary thrift. They were by no means young men when Paul Jones made his famous raid on the port in 1778, and the elder one calmly watched the attack and retreat from the heights where the Wellington coalpit now is. Although none of their relatives are believed to be in existence, and probably not half a dozen of their personal acquaintance are now living, it may be well to so far attempt disguise as to call them Jacob and Joseph. Their book-keeping must have been of the most primitive description, for they struck a balance and divided their profits in true brotherly way every Saturday night.

During the war time, Joseph was tempted to invest a portion of his savings in shipping—at that time, and in general, very lucrative, but exceedingly hazardous from the numerous French privateers which infested the routes of home-ward bound vessels; while the more cautious Jacob confided *his* treasure to the security of an old stocking-foot and the corner-cupboard.

Joseph's ship made one or two most successful voyages, and after each "ship's settlement" he exultingly chinked his golden dividend before his brother's face, taunting him with the fact that *his* money was "liggin' in t' corner-cubbert" idle and unproductive. In time a change came, and one evening the younger brother came home dejected and morose, when the following conversation occurred :—

"What's t' matter wid tha, Joe?"

"Nay, nowt."

"What theer mun be summat wrang wid tha."

" If there is, what odds is 't to thee ? "

" Wey, wey ; thou need n't be seah cranky ; but theer mun be summat wrang when thou comes heàm hingan thy lugs that way."

" Wey, Jacop, if thou mun know, t' ' West India ' 's teànn, an' me nut insur't."

" My brass is in t' corner-cubbert, Joe."

When these brothers retired from business, they divided everything equally, even to the shelves and fixtures of their little shop ; but the apparent indivisibility of the counter puzzled them not a little, and seemed likely to lead to some disagreement, until one of the pair exclaimed, " Aa tell thee what, I'll git t' hand saw, and saw her i' two : I'll tak my hofe, and thou may tak thine ; " and the dispute was amicably settled.

At the death of a relative, Jacob was very anxious that the remains should be interred in the burial-ground attached to the dissenting place of worship which he himself was in the habit of attending ; but, owing to the very limited space, his request was refused, greatly to his annoyance, if not to the injury of his feelings. Shortly after, he called upon one of the leading members of the congregation, and, throwing a bundle of bank-notes upon the table, benevolently exclaimed, " Theer, William, theer two hundred pound. Gang an' buy mair grund wid it, and niver set up sec a teàll ageànn 'at ye hevvent a bit o' grund to bury a poor fellow in."

Jacob had a virago for a housekeeper, of whom he lived in almost abject terror. He was once seen wiping up his own dirty footmarks with a dishclout, rather than brave a scolding for neglecting to use the door-mat. On one occasion he so far ventured to attempt to assert his independence by buying a couple of ducks in the market and taking them home without consulting the home authority, who muttered that he might pluck and dress them himself, and angrily enquired, "Who's to poo t' pens out, I would like to know?" "Wey, thee, to be sure." "Me?" "Ey, thee; it's nea use keepin' a dog and barkin' yan's sell."

This servant afterwards married, and on the wedding-day the old gentleman was seen pacing to and fro, with his eyes on the ground lost in meditation—slowly wagging his head from side to side, and muttering, "He *will* git it! he *will* git it!" To a friend who was ready to sympathise with him in his apparent distress, and who inquired to whom the allusion applied, he explained that he was thinking of the poor unfortunate bridegroom.

In their younger days the brothers were addicted to poaching, and netted both fish and game. On one occasion they were casting in the river Liza, in Ennerdale, a new net, which was of their own handicraft and of unusually choice material, when they were suddenly come down upon, and had to run and leave the net behind. A year or two afterwards, being benighted in the same locality, they begged a night's lodgings at a farm-house, which the hospitable owner readily granted to such respectable-looking men. After due refreshment and evening chat, they were shown to their sleeping apartments, little thinking their kind host was the custodian of the trout stream of their previous adventure. In the early morning the younger was awaked by the elder exclaiming, "Dy-pend, Joe, that's our net:" and, sure enough, there it was hanging on the rafters overhead. Prudence prevailing over gratitude, they took a precipitate departure without waiting to thank their entertainer for his kindness.

In presenting a hare to a friend, Joseph apologised for its mauled condition by saying, "That feull of a Jacop thought she was gittan' out o' t' net, and flang his-sel on t' top on her and brast her bags."

SAVING A CANDLE AND LOSING A WEB.

The two brothers before mentioned were of so saving a turn that the cost of a light in their shop, whilst they retired for tea on a winter's evening, was a subject of consideration. One day, before the use of gas was known, they, as usual, closed the shop door without fastening it, and went to the inner room for tea, leaving the shop in darkness. In a little time they heard the outer door opened, and some one knocking on the counter and saying, " Old friends, I suppose you are well employed ; I will look in after you have had your tea." Dreading no evil the brothers quietly finished their tea, and took the light from the table to the shop to discover that, by saving a candle, some clever thief, who knew their habits, had walked off with a web of cloth, the value of which would have covered the cost of shop candles for some years.

CONSCIENCE-SMITTEN.

This and the next following may be best understood by persons engaged about mining : --
The overlooker of a colliery, through some real or supposed neglect, lost a valuable mine for a time by a collapse of the shaft. This was a source of great trouble to the honest man, and, after unburthening his mind to a fellow-craftsman who belonged to an opposing firm, he expressed a wish that he was dead, adding, " Dusta think, Jwohn, if I was deed I wad gang to heaven ? " He received the consolatory reply, " I doon't kno' whether thou wad or nut, Jemmy ; but thou wad ha' studden a vast better chance if thou hed n't setten t' creep on t' pit."

DEEP PIT.

A poor workman said of a large colliery proprietor, against whom he had a grudge, "Ey, he's boddomed many a pit, but he'll be gittan into yan efter a bit, 'at he'll be pinch't to find boddom on."

―――――

SELF-HELP.

An illustration of the proverb that heaven helps those who help themselves occurred to a man of the name of Woodville (pronounced Woodall).

He had imbibed too freely, and was crossing the low Cloffock at Workington, over which a recent high tide had flowed and left the muddy surface in so sticky a state that his feet stuck fast in it. Fearing the rise of the tide again, he shouted, "God help Woodall," but without result. After patiently waiting a few minutes for a miracle, he cried out, "The divel help Woodall." Still no assistance came. A little longer, when he became more sober and began to reflect on his situation, he said, "Help thy-sel, Woodall," and with a strenuous effort escaped from his difficulty.

―――――

VERY SHARP.

A gentleman of an irritable turn was met by an acquaintance who saluted him with, "A fine morning, sir." The immediate reply was, "Ey, who said it was n't? D'ye want a fratch?"

HARD PRESSED AND CONQUERED.

THE late John Steel, of The Gill, in Kinniside, was a shepherd yeoman of the John Bull type—of few words and slow of speech. On a general election for M.P.s, he had, for some manorial reasons, promised to give his vote under the direction of the late Mr. Robert Benson, of Cockermouth, on the liberal side, while his predilections tended another way. But he was a sturdy man of his word, and having pledged it, he would not swerve.

On appearing at the polling-booth at Egremont, he was asked for whom he would vote.

John—" I vwote for Mr. Benson."

Officer—" Mr. Benson is not a candidate, and you cannot vote for him. The candidates are so and so. Which will you vote for? "

John—" I vwote for Mr. Benson."

Officer—" But he's not a candidate, Mr. Steel, and you must really say which of the others you vote for."

John—" I say I vwote for Mr. Benson, and neabody else "—and he was turning away, when some one whispered the name he was wished to vote for ; being so reminded he could carry it no further, and turned and gave his vote for Major Aglionby.

SAVING TO THE LAST.

A WEALTHY old yeoman in the west of the county was of exceeding miserly habits. It is said that once, when he was out of health, he sat by the roadside for three weeks, in the hope that he would be able to extract some gratuitous advice from any passing doctor of his acquaintance whom chance might lead that way. On another occasion, in order to save medical fees, he consulted a respectable druggist who thought he could give him a box of pills at the cost of a shilling which would afford relief; on telling him that two of the pills constituted a proper dose, he received the characteristic and saving suggestion, "Does n't thou think, if thou'd meàdd them rayder strangger, that *yan* med ha' done?"

VERY CROOKED.

Two neighbouring shepherds having quarrelled, one accused the other of having a "creùkt temper," when he received this reply; "Thou need say nought about creùkt tempers awivver, for thy temper's meàdd o' nought bit tip horns and grunstan hannels."

OF A SAVING TURN.

A CARRIER, speaking of a lady who was of a saving turn, said, "Gittan tuppence of her for a parshel's like rivin' a teùth out of her head."

OUTLANDISH WORKINGTON.

A VERY stout, homely couple were seen at the Workington railway station, a short while ago, and the good wife was heard to say to her husband, " Maister, this *is* an outlandish kind of a spot, awivver, and I wish we war beàtth scàff heàmm ageànn at t' feút o' Cross-fell."

ISAAC TINNION.

As an instance of ready reply Isaac may be quoted.
He was a strong and powerful man, and took a delight
in being employed as flag-bearer in the processions of
the school and other festivals in Workington, "because," he said, "he could carry 't flag straight upreet
in a windy day."   He did not confess to a liking for
ale; and one day Miss Howe, the rector's daughter,
who organised a procession, anxiously inquired what
had happened to Isaac, for the flag was dangerously
near the windows in passing, and Isaac was leaning
forward.   He heard the inquiry, and turned to the
lady, saying, "O Miss Howe, I's very bad.   I've gum
biles in my back."

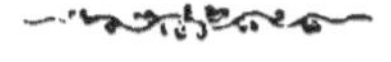

OLD ELECTION TIMES.

A FORMER Countess of Lonsdale, who took great interest and amusement in elections, went to Sandwith to
try her skill in winning over a yeoman farmer through
the influence of his wife to vote for the earl's friend.
The nearest way to the voter's house was through a
small inclosure called the garth.

The dress of her ladyship was rather long, and the
path not over clean.   The inmates saw through the
window a lady approaching, and the goodwife exclaimed, "What gars t' gowky gang through t' garth
to jarble o' her cleàzz!"

THE WINKER.

WHEN the tithe commutation was going on in a parish
not far from Cleator, the commissioner was examining

the lessee of the tithes and did not approve of the prevaricating answers he received as to their annual value distinct from the farm held along with the tithes. Whilst endeavouring to elicit more straightforward replies, he overheard one of the company say, " Now, Jemmy's winkan', and when he winks he lees."

VERY WRONG INDEED.

A SANDWITH farmer walked down to Whitehaven with his wife, and arranged to call for her after his business was finished.   A neighbour returning from town met the farmer hurrying to Whitehaven, and inquired if anything was wrong with him.   " Ey, wrang far eneugh ! I left t' wife at Peter Leech's and clean forgat to co' for her."

SUPERSTITIONS.

Of all the absurd beliefs entertained by the credulous, none seem more weak than the idea that toothache can be cured by a charm; or that warts can be dispersed, or a bleeding stayed, by a few unconnected words, or by two or three short sentences written, or a few hieroglyphic scratches made by some quack, and given to the sufferer to be worn near the heart; not to be read or examined by the patient or any other person.

Certainly, if read, the absurdity would be apparent, and the belief annulled; and so the charm could have no effect, except on the imagination. As one instance may be given—

THE CHARM TO STOP BLEEDING.

"In Bethlehem a child was born,
In Jordan was a flood;
Sweet Jesus, stop this blood,
In the name of the Father, Son, and Holy Ghost.—Amen."

It was not until near the end of the 18th century that the belief, hitherto so prevalent, in seers and witchcraft began to give way. It lingered through the first quarter of the 19th century, gradually tapering into small and smaller dimensions as education advanced, and the rural classes, among whom had been its stronghold, became more enlightened.

The fear of ridicule had in a great measure suppressed the outward belief; and when that was stayed, the rising generation had fewer opportunities of hearing the exciting but exaggerated stories of times gone by. Many are the stirring narrations I have listened to in early youth ; and doubtless at that time many of them were believed, because not contradicted; and because the young mind is so prone to accept the marvellous as truth in preference to that which is reasonable.

In more mature life, the absurdity is more easily seen through, and reason generally asserts her supremacy, and discards the high-drawn miracles.

THE SEER.

About the years 1817 and 1818, several farmers in the neighbourhood of Lamplugh and Arlecdon had geese stolen from their stubble fields in the autumn, and from their outhouses in the early winter season, without detecting the thieves.

Among others, Thomas Fisher, the then tenant of North Mosses, lost a few from his field. He had heard of George Lawson, of the Gill, near Egremont, who could find out stolen goods and reveal many mysteries relating to matters stolen or lost, and who sometimes could denote the depredators. Fisher's belief in seers was not strong, but he thought and said if Lawson had been successful in some cases, he might be again, and he should have a trial. I was invited to ride over with him to see the man, and, my curiosity being greatly excited with the novelty, I readily consented to accompany him. To avoid being observed and chaffed, as we assuredly should have been

in daylight, on a chosen dark night we quietly reached
the place a little before the family bed-time, when
Fisher explained his errand and requested such aid
as the seer could give.

Lawson was a handloom weaver, and a well-esteemed
man in very moderate circumstances. Having a numerous young family, his small cottage did not afford
much accommodation for strangers, and we were
shown into a small upstairs bedroom, the candle placed
on a round table, and soon blown out. A globular
ball of dark glass, the size of a large orange, had
been produced whilst the light burned, and it was now
explained to us that the ball was to be held between
the two hands of a young person of pure morals and
of upright conduct, and closely looked down upon in
the dark, and the person holding it would answer
questions as to what he saw in the glass, if any discovery was to be made. As the youngest person present, the ball was offered to me, but not having seen
or heard of anything of the kind, I declined, and Lawson's eldest son was called up, a lad of twelve or thirteen, who had acted in similar performances previously.
Virtually, the lad had been the seer under his father's
surveillance; and now, after two or three minutes of
silence, the father began to question him, and the reply
was, "The light is only just coming on, and it is very
dim." After another interval of silence, the lad said
hesitatingly, "It is better now." "And what do you
see?" "Two men catching geese in the corner of a
field." Still with hesitation : "They've got one—they
are putting it into a sack—the rest have broke away—
they have driven them into the corner again—they
have caught two or three more." "Do you know the
men?" "No." "What is the field like?" "A
sloping field, and they are in the upper corner."

All this was slowly given out, and the description

of the field agreed well with the one from which the
geese were lost, and where marks of the taking had
been seen.　He then said the light was going off;
but on Fisher's wishing to know something of the
thieves, we were told to wait awhile in silence, and he
would try further.　After about a quarter of an hour,
the father asked again if he saw anything.　"The
light is coming on."　A short wait, and—"I see a
farm-house with a tree before it."　"Only one?"
"One."　"Do you see the men?"　"No."　"Do
you know the house?"　"No—the light is going—
all is dark."　This again was all slowly said, as if there
was difficulty in making out the objects; and we were
told it was in vain to try any more on that occasion.
Lawson promised to try it on some future night, and
would inform Fisher if he could give more information; but no more was heard of it.　The farm-house
and the tree before it brought strongly to mind the
residence of a family who had been selling cart-loads
of geese in the different market towns for some weeks;
and from the great number passing through their
hands, suspicion bore strongly upon them.

Whether or not Lawson had some private intima-
tion of the transaction, or he had sifted others who
had been to him on like occasions, we could not learn;
and the answers, though pointed, were too vague to
found action upon.　One thing rather suspicious was,
that our neighbour, Mr. Jonathan Boadle, who was
acquainted with Lawson, and was well up to and
delighted in a lark, knew the way to the Gill and we
did not, and was invited to be our guide, being present all the time.　On taxing him, he denied giving
any hint; and, after many months, he declared he
had done nothing of the kind, and never had any
thought of it.　He was of too candid a nature for me
to entertain any further suspicion, especially as he had

joined us in rewarding the seer with an unasked con-
tribution. This was the first and last circumstance of
the kind I had anything to do with, and I see no reason to suspect collusion in the matter.

The late Dr. Jonathan Langrigg Lawson, of Egremont, a most worthy and talented man, and my intimate friend of many years' standing, was own brother
to the seer, and he told me he had not believed in
the special gift of his brother, until one morning a litter
fork was missing from his stable. To test the reputed
skill of his brother he went one evening to ask if he
could throw any light on the matter; when, after going
through a ceremony similar to the one described,
George told the Doctor the fork was then under a bed
in an upstairs room of a house in Egremont, which he
described so plainly that the Doctor was led to carry
out his investigation at once, and to learn the truth or
fallacy of the indication and of his brother's repute.
No name or place was given; but he went direct to a
house agreeing with the description, and upstairs into
a room which, as a professional man, he had before
known, found the fork, and brought it away without
speaking to the astonished family, but not without
showing them what he took away.

FORTUNE TELLING.

An old servant of Cunningarth, near Wigton, when in
the act of making black puddings, always "likkent"
them to some newly-married couple. If the puddings
came sound and whole out of the pot, the said couple
would lead a happy life; but if under too rapid a boil
they came out burst or damaged, it was a bad omen
for the conjugal happiness of the couple.

CARD-PLAYERS.

In November, 1829, Mr. John Swinburn, of Bewald-eth (then about 84 years of age), related to me the following :—

The parish of Bassenthwaite was noted in former times, as now, for the indulgence of its inhabitants in card-playing. One Saturday evening a number of both sexes had assembled in the inn, at the Haws, to amuse themselves with card-playing. They played at loo—and played deep and late—into Sunday morning, At an early hour in the morning, a woman of the company, noted as a keen hand, began to boast of her cleverness and success. By-and-by she held three aces in one hand, and was so overjoyed that she exclaimed she was now a match for the devil! The next moment a horse was heard to gallop fiercely up to the door, and, on its being opened, a gentlemanly-looking man alighted and requested that his horse might be taken to the stable, the request being at once complied with. The horse was remarked to be an exceedingly fine animal, coal black, and with a peculiar fierceness in its look. It seemed to have been hard-ridden, and suffered itself to be quietly tied up, but not without the servant exhibiting signs of fear on being near him, and of joy on closing the stable door after leaving the horse. The gentleman was dressed in black, and, on seeing the occupation of the company, requested permission to join their sport. His request was acceded to, and he made himself agreeable to all by his hearty good humour. He was invited to sit at the table next to the woman who had been so successful, and he took a hand with them. His luck or cleverness enabled him soon to draw all her winnings, as well as most of the cash from nearly

all present. Amid the surprise and confusion attendant on seeing their money disappear so quickly, and
in their eagerness to have a return of luck, time was
forgotten, Sunday morning advanced, and every one
was more than usually intent on his or her hand of
cards. By some accident a card fell on the floor, and
on one of the company taking a candle to look for the
card, his eye accidentally glanced on the gentleman's
feet, and observed (what none had seen before) that
one of them was a club-foot. He looked up for the
gentleman's face, but he was gone !—gone in an instant ! and no one knew how or where, although he
was present the moment before.

Some sly trick was suspected, and one of the company began to condole with the rest, saying that if the
gentleman was gone, they should still be a good horse
into pocket, as *that* was safe under lock and key ; but
on going to look for the horse, the stall was found
empty ! Man and horse had both vanished ! Fear
struck at the hearts of all. They now discovered they
had been playing at cards a few hours into the Sab-
bath, and, for anything they knew, with the evil one
himself. A consciousness of evil affected some of
them so much, that they were never known to play
cards again.

On mentioning the above soon after to the late
Mr. Norman, of High Dyke, my father-in-law, he said
he had often heard the same story, and in his younger
days it was generally believed. He also related an
instance of superstitious fear which occurred in his
presence.

A party had met at Mr. John Sibson's, at The Brow,
near Lorton, and were amusing themselves at three-
card loo. Mr. Scott,* of the Sun Inn, Cockermouth,
was one of the party, and for a few deals in succession

* Whom I well knew.

he happened to have the club knave dealt to him. He laughed with the rest at the occurrence for some time; but on its continuing to be repeated he grew angry; and supposing some one at the table had put the trick upon him, he threatened the sleight-of-hand performer with instant vengeance if he should be found out. The play continued, and, more frequently than welcome, the hated club knave stared among his cards, till fear began to predominate, and to such a degree that his knees and even his jaws and teeth shook. This went on until he declared that if his hand should again open with that "devil card" in, he could play no longer. He had hardly spoken till there it was again, as black as ever! Down went his cards, not in anger now, but in actual fear. He turned pale, and staggered from the table almost fainting, begging Mr. Sibson to send a person to Cockermouth for one of his chaises to take him home. He was so much affected by the incident that he could scarcely walk to the carriage, and his wife has said he could not compose himself to sleep that night. The fear gradually subsided, but never entirely left him, and it was never declared if the cards were tampered with.

THE LAST FAIRY.

THE tradition runs that the last fairy seen near Whitehaven was by a man standing on what is called the "fairy rock,"* near Saltom Pit. The man was looking towards the Isle of Man, when he saw a calf coming, at some height in the air, over the sea, and alight on the rock beside him, In astonishment he exclaimed, "G—d! weel loppen, cofe!" At the sound

---

* The Fairy Rock fell in one of the violent January storms of 1872.

of the sacred name the calf disappeared, and no fairy has since been seen.

BEWILDERING.

THOMAS BELL, of Thornthwaite, was born and lived at Peelwyke till grown up to a man, and gives the following proof of the superstition prevailing in his young days :—

A family named Watson lived near, and three or four of the young sons were accustomed to play on the Castle Hill, which is believed to have been a British fort guarding the pass or wyke. These boys made an excavation in the side of the hill and uncovered a neat hut roofed with slate. Dinner-time came before their exploration was completed, and they were called home. In hopes of having made a great discovery, they hurried back to the hill, but could not even find the place, for all was covered with soil and green sward as when they first found it, and no one has found the place since.

Watson, the father of these boys, kept an ill-tempered cur. One evening, about sunset, he saw two tiny people dressed in green in a meadow near Peelwyke, and set his dog on them. The dog went fiercely to them, but immediately began to yell, and rolled over. It continued to cry out, and occasionally to tumble, till it reached Watson, and the little people were never seen after.

JOHN STORROW.

THE belief that God made everything so completely adapted to man's use that no need existed to try to improve the land is exemplified in the following instance, wherein the speaker seems unaware that our first father was placed in the garden of Eden "to dress it and to keep it," and that his successors were commanded to "till the ground." John's idea, doubtless, arose from a reverential motive, but its application was inappropriate.

John Storrow, of Plumpton Head, went to his neighbour, William Birkett, who was cutting a drain in a piece of wet land, and said, "What is ta aboot, Willy? Does not ta think the Almighty knew best how to mak land? It's t' height of wickedness, thee tryin' ta mend his wark!"

NEEDFIRE.

ALTHOUGH superstitious practices are slowly and gradually becoming fewer, the last generation was not wanting in instances, amongst which the "Needfire" held a conspicuous place as a means of prevention, at the time when the foot and mouth disease (then called the murrain) prevailed among cattle and all cloven-footed animals.

The disease had not been known in Cumberland in the present century till about 1840, when it broke out or was imported, and by its disastrous effect and active progress spread dismay among all classes. Dairy cattle suffered most by it, for it not only dried up the supply of milk, but incapacitated them for further utility by destroying one or more, and in some cases, all the teats. Thus all classes in town or country suffered by being deprived or restricted in the use of milk, so needful and acceptable in all families. No cure was known, for no one knew anything about it;

and the cow doctors of the day, after various unsuccessful experiments, one and all gave it up as beyond their skill. It astonished people by being so easily communicated. Even the smallest touch by a sound hoof on the footstep of a diseased one sent the mischief flying from one animal to another through whole herds in a few days ; and people were afraid to walk along the roads for fear of stepping where a murrained cow had trod, and being the means of conveying the virus to their own or other stocks. They even began to be under some alarm lest the human subject should become liable to contract the disease.

Old men were consulted, and old books were ransacked for remedies, without effect. No doubt wise women were consulted ; but nothing availed, and the disease spread quickly. Preventives were next looked for, and a rumour got afloat that the Needfire was coming from the eastern parts of the county. At first none knew what the Needfire was to be or to do, only it was said to be a charm to check the ravages of the murrain ; and in the panic some were afraid we should be in danger of suffocation by the smoke, or of being burnt up by the fire—so outrageous were the exaggerated stories about it. After a few days of mystery and much talk, columns of smoke were seen to arise to eastward, to become more numerous, and to approach day by day. Information came in advance that it was to stay the plague. Where it was first kindled no one could tell, but it was said to have been originated in Yorkshire by some one rubbing two pieces of dry, half-rotten wood together till they took fire, and that there it had worked wonders. The fire was not to be suffered to go out, nor to be taken into any house, or the charm would be lost, till got up again in the same way ; and the greater the smoke the stronger the charm. Having been from home one day, I was not a little surprised, on returning in the evening, to observe a grass field near my house so trampled with cattle, that herbage was scarcely visible on it ; and, without much inquiry, was quickly informed that Need-fire had been in use. I had previously scouted the idea, and directed that it should not be admitted, and was inclined to feel annoyed that my orders should have been disobeyed. This feeling was soon dispersed when I was told that John Steel, of Whitekeld Farm, who had been an old and valued servant with my father, had brought the fire direct with the haste of the "hot-trod" of ancient border warfare, from the last kindling ; and, with great pride and bustle, would neither taste "bite nor sup" till the fire was lighted in the field, and the men sent out to draw in the cattle. His proceedings had at first been strongly objected to, but he had seemed so much cast down by the refusal, that consent had been given on the score that if no good came of it, no harm was likely to be done ; and all knew his intentions to be good, and his anxiety for the welfare of his old master's family was beyond doubt. So the business went on. As the fire rose, it was plied with weeds, old thatch, rushes, brushwood, or any kind of fuel that had *never been in a house*, and heaped again and again with whatever of that character was at hand and best adapted for raising a great smoke. The great smoke was partly levelled in one direction by a gentle breeze, and the men crowded the cattle into it, and drove them in a continual ring, sunwise, through it ; while John continued the hot-trod to the next neighbour, and so on with it till relieved by some one willing to take his place. The ring driving was repeated till the poor animals began to sneeze, and then to cough—and so did the men— till cattle and men were nearly suffocated, and then the play ceased. Then it was thought the old man's

directions had been fully carried out, and the charm
was left to do its work, if it was to work at all. The
cattle were driven staggering to their several places
by the men, wondering at the strange incantations—
some impressed with fear, others (unbelievers) scoff-
ing at the ceremony, and railing not a little at the
outrageous smoking they had undergone. However,
the charm was not effectual in this instance, for the
herd was invaded by the disease on more occasions
than one during that summer; but, by a careful system
of isolation, it did not extend to any great numbers.

Since that time no smoking by Needfire has been
practised to my knowledge, although numerous instances of foot-and-mouth disease have occurred in
various years.

CATTLE CHARMS.

THERE are other matters of superstition which have
escaped the notice of both Bourne and Brand, or are
not recorded in their elaborate works on popular
antiquities and superstitions.

Old people of two generations ago have said it was
a practice formerly with owners of cows subject to
abortion, (which malady is often known to continue
nearly three years in a herd,) to watch for the first
abortive calf showing signs of life, and to dig a hole
under the threshold of the byre, and bury the calf in
it—alive, if possible, but there to bury it, alive or
dead.

A still more barbarous practice was to take the first
living abortive calf, and at midnight to burn it alive.
It was allowable to despatch the calf with the aid of a
pitchfork as soon as it was thrown into the fire. If a

cure was to be effected by this, the evil spirit which caused the disease would enter the byre or field where the cattle were, and in parting revenge would set the whole herd bellowing like so many mad creatures. If in the byre, they would break loose, and a general fight would ensue during the burning.   If in the field, they would break through the hedges, galloping furiously, with heads and tails erect, bellowing and surrounding the fire ; and woe be to the man who undertook the sacrifice if he had not time to secure his safety by flight.

If so near as seven months to the natural period, the calf might be able to bawl lustily when the pitchfork was used ; and in a still night this would be heard to a distance, and rouse the herd to fury.

These operations were to be performed by one person alone, and no man would undertake it if he did not believe in it.   And believing that the evil spirit was to be present, and to take part in it, or at least to drive the cows mad for a time, it seems improbable that the mystic charm would be undertaken by any one ; and it certainly would not be adopted in sport.

A later and more rational practice has been to endeavour to rear the seven-months calf ; and this has been followed with success.

As the malady gradually abates, which it usually does towards the end of the third year, the calves are dropped with increasing strength ; the charm is broken, and all goes well again.

THE PHANTOM BELL.

PERHAPS no class of men have been more prone to believe in supernatural sounds and appearances than those who work underground in coal and other mines ; and the belief is perpetuated to this day, in a gradually weakening degree.

A man working in a solitary part of the Graysouthen colliery was annoyed, day after day, by what he took to be a bell ringing in a distant part of the mine, where he knew no bell could be, and where no one was working. This continued ; he could make nothing of it, and his mind brooded upon it till he believed the place was haunted, and he got so afraid that he durst not work there any longer, begging of the overman to put him to work in another part of the mine. The overman consented, but first desired the man to show him the place he dreaded so much. On reaching it, the phantom was soon discovered to be a drop of water falling at considerable intervals into a still pool at a little distance, round the corner of the workings. The poor man was at once convinced ; his fears vanished ; and he continued to work contentedly at his usual place.

JWONY AND THE FAIRY.

An old miner came from Tindal fell to Bolton collieries, and used to relate many stories of witches and warlocks ; among them was one of his own experience, in which he firmly believed. When at Tindal fell, he and some of his fellow-workmen agreed to enjoy themselves with having a *black drink, i.e.,* in their working-clothes.

There was an illicit still some three or four miles away, where they could have whisky cheaper than from an inn, and Jwony was deputed to go there for a gallon and a half. Though attended by a total

abstainer in the shape of his dog Swan, he could not
resist the liberal offers of the distillers, which took
effect accordingly.   On his way home he had a brook
to cross ; and feeling uncertain whether he could safely
cross by the stepping-stones. he took the wiser course
to lay down on the bank, but eventually rolled into
the stream, where fortunately it was shallow ; and
there he lay helpless.   With more than common sagacity, the dog seemed to understand his predicament,
and hurried home ; and by its anxious gestures and
continued whining, induced Betty, the wife, to accompany it to where her husband was left, and in time to
save him.   During the time he was in the water, he
chanced to turn his head round, and saw a little man,
of less than a foot high, dressed in green, and perched
on his shoulder ; he remained there till Betty came,
and then he vanished.   Jwony fancied the little creature had the power, and kept him down, and he used
to say, " If it hedn't been for Swan and Betty, I med
ha' tofert in t' beck ; for it was them 'at freetn't t' laal
thing away."

The old man believed in this till his dying day ;
and doubtless many a fairy story has sprung out of
similar materials ; and he could never rationally account for some missing whisky, but said the wind was
so strong that it blew him down at different times in
coming home.

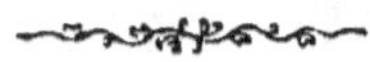

IRISH SOIL.

THERE is a lengthened conical hill at Stockhow Hall,
called " Henkam Hill," where it is said a former lord
(Patrickson) caused a cargo of soil to be brought from
Ireland, and spread it over the surface of this hill to

banish all venomous creatures, that his children might play there in safety.

A similar tradition is given relating to the hill on which Egremont Castle was built; there is, however, no record of any venomous thing being known at either place.

BEES.

CERTAIN people believe that bees sing the Old Hundredth Psalm on Christmas morning. If one of the family die, one of the household goes and taps at the hives, and conveys the intelligence to the bees in a whisper; and on the day of the funeral, before the procession leaves the house, the bees are again informed that the body is about to be lifted.*   This is done to prevent ill-luck to the hives and honey.

THE BOGGLES OF WHITEHAVEN.

WHITEHAVEN has been noted in old times for a Newtown boggle, which occasionally rendered night hideous by its howlings, and especially before fatal accidents occurred in the collieries. It was said sometimes to exhibit itself in the shape of a very large dog; but it has not been seen or heard in warning or otherwise for two or three generations past.

Towards the end of the last century, before street lamps were in use or night watchmen employed in Whitehaven, it was firmly believed that a ghost, in the form of a tall female, haunted and perambulated the

* The last case known was at Asby, in the parish of Arlecdon, in 1855.

streets of the town and quays of the harbour, and was occasionally seen on the roads at the outskirts. This was averred to be the ghost of a Miss G——, whose family resided in a large and well-appointed house situate opposite the west end of the present market-house. A large garden behind was laid out in terraces across the slope of the hill, and a mulberry tree grew in the centre.

The corpse of the lady was found one morning, apparently as having fallen from an upstairs window; and it was conjectured by some foul play.

The apparition was a silent one, and peaceful as well; always disappearing round some corner, or by some dark and narrow entry to avoid being met, and no one mustered courage to speak to or meddle with it.

A room in the house was stated to be haunted by the ghost, noises being heard there during the nights; and none of the servants durst look into the room. This continued for some years, when the Rev. Wilfrid Hudleston, unwilling* as some say, to lay the ghost, not in the Red Sea, but under the mulberry tree in the garden. His tact and efforts were successful, and the appearance was never seen after.

Tradition tells us that a gentleman belonging to the family was missing from the time the body of the lady was found, and none could account for his absence or tell of his whereabouts.

The G—— stood high in mercantile matters, having plantations in the West India Islands; and the rumour went that the missing gentleman might have gone out to superintend them, and so suspicion was quieted. It is stated that by some oversight the door of the haunted room stood ajar one morning, and that a servant in passing espied the figure of a strange man slip

---

* There was then a belief that any one who succeeded in laying a ghost could only do so under the inevitable penalty of being deprived of some faculty; as, one of the five senses, for instance.

hastily into a closet or cupboard and shut himself in. The girl was terror-struck, and could not refrain from reporting to the family what she had seen — that a man was in *hidlins* (hiding) in the mysterious room. It appears that Mr. Hudleston had the confidence of the family, and possibly of the ghost too; and that immediately after the above discovery he had waylaid the figure in one of its rambles, and advised it to give up its unearthly practice; saying it (or rather he) had been a street-walker long enough, and under present circumstances must at once undergo the ceremony of being *laid* under the mulberry tree, and must take his departure from Whitehaven. Night walking exercise had doubtless been beneficial on the score of health, even to a ghost; and as it could now no longer be enjoyed in safety, the advice was promptly followed, and the ghost never more seen, and the noises in the dark room ceased.

PADDY CORE'S WIFE.

A GOOD number of years ago a small farmer at Graysouthen suffered by the deaths of four swine and three cows, within the space of a few weeks, from some mysterious cause which he could attribute to nothing but witchcraft. One morning he went to the byre where the last cow died, and on opening the door out sprang a hare, which escaped him. Believing that witches could transform themselves into hares or other animals, he at once concluded he had discovered the secret he had long suspected; and that his next neighbour, Paddy Core's old and repulsive-looking wife, was the hare, and had been brooding further mischief to him. Acting on this idea, he rushed into Paddy's

house in great fury, and dragged the infirm old
woman into the byre, and swore that if she would not
break the charm she should never bewitch cow or pig
again, for he would be the end of her there and then.
In spite of her screams and protestations of innocence,
he shook her still more roughly, till she begged him
to desist and she would do her best. She muttered a
few words, unintelligible to him, and he then let her
go; and fortunately he lost no more of his stock.
He is yet living, in 1874, and is firmly convinced that
Paddy Core's wife was a witch, and that he put a stop
to her cantrips so far as regarded his cattle.

BRANTHWAITE NOOK BOGGLE.

A young man of Branthwaite had an errand to the
neighbouring village of Ullock on a dark winter night,
during the period when the headless boggle of Branthwaite Nook (so celebrated by Dr. A. C. Gibson) was
much talked about, and by some much dreaded.

He stayed till near midnight; and when he returned
his mother expressed her satisfaction, saying, "Loavin
days, John! I thought thou wad be sa freeten't o' t'
boggle 'at thou durst n't come past t' Neuk." John
had duly considered the matter before and replied,
"Nay, mudder, you ned n't ha' been sa freetn't, for aa
left my clogs at heàmm an' went i' my shun, an' I com
sa deftly it couldn't hear me; an' it was so dark I's
sure it could n't see me."

REMINISCENCES OF CLERICAL LIFE

IN THE

EARLY PART OF THE 19TH CENTURY.

In recounting the following it must not be thought I intend to hold up the sacred calling, or its members, to ridicule; or that I am wanting in respect to the office. My aim is to record a few instances of successful struggles for existence, or of eccentricity of character, as observed at the end of the eighteenth and beginning of the present century; examples of which are now as rare as they were then plentiful. "Wonderful Walker," whom Wordsworth has so justly celebrated, and many others, have been recorded by abler hands. Of these I only intend to relate such as came under my own observation, and chiefly in my own neighbourhood.

The rage for collecting subscriptions had not then started among clergymen, except for purchasing a new bell rope, or renewing a pitch pipe; and then only pennies were looked for. Churches, and some few schools—one serving for each parish—had been built in former times; and in spite of their damp floors and mouldy walls, and other uncomfortable and unhealthy properties, served the purposes of their dedication without complaint or murmur on the part of the parishioners; and the clergy had neither power nor inclination to agitate on behalf of new parochial edifices. The bustling anxiety of the curate of the present day was altogether unknown to

the steady-going minister of that period.　The difficulties and privations of the meritorious class of poor
country parsons of that day should also be recorded as
a contrast to the status of the class at the present time;
and many are even yet *sadly underpaid.*　Many of
the rural clergy were constrained by necessity, as well
as by duty, to become teachers, after the primitive
custom of Whittlegate* was abandoned; and until
schools were built, they taught in the chancels of the
churches, in the cold of winter and the heat of
summer.　No fires or stoves were in use, and the only
way to maintain a comfortable heat of body was in
warm clothing, when it could be afforded, or a smart
walk to and fro for the master and a run for the
children.

When it was parochially decided that a school should
be built, it was erected on the edge of the common, or
on some roadside waste; and great part of the work
was done gratuitously by the inhabitants of the parish.
Some tore out a few cartloads of stones from the
breast of a quarry.　Others collected from the fields
or commons, and conveyed the half-loads to the site,
in clog-wheeled carts—then the cart of the day—for
the unmade roadway would not admit of a reasonable
load.　Seldom was the mason's chisel applied, and
"rough and ready," if substantial, was the order of
architecture.　Some cut a tree or two from the hedge-
rows for timbering.　A general boon-day was organized
for bringing the cheapest slate from the quarry.　Some
contributed a pack-load of lime, and others of sand,
for mortar, to which clay was sometimes added by
way of sparing lime; and this mode of conveyance
was considered safer than risking the overturning of
the cart, as the matter of time was not then important.

* Clergymen and schoolmasters were privileged to use their whittles or
knives at the tables of their parishioners, in a rotation known and sanctioned
by them to aid the scanty stipends.

Some volunteered in turns as masons' labourers, or assisted in anything they could put their hands to. No bricks were required, and the floor was of earth or clay, trodden hard down. The little money required was asked from those who could not contribute in labour, or who had not the opportunity, and a rude but serviceable structure erected, of a more comfortable nature for teaching in than the damp and fireless church. Many of these little edifices may still be found, but are gradually being superseded by more pretentious, and much more costly buildings, and most of the modern clergymen find their time sufficiently occupied with their other duties.

Few old parish schools exhibit dates of erection; but we have a clue to their approximate age in the absence of thatched roofs. Of these I cannot call to mind even one example, though many of farm houses and out-buildings. Towards the end of the eighteenth century slate roofs became more common, and the dangerous and unthrifty thatched roof, with high and stepped gables, began gradually to disappear; and it may be reasonably concluded that the schools of country parishes were mainly built in the eighteenth century, and most of them in the latter half of it.

If a country church was to be built, or required rebuilding or heavy repairs, a royal mandate, called a *brief*, was issued to the bishops, and by them to the clergy, to be read in all the churches, and collections made. Sometimes these resulted in nothing, and often in only a few pence.

REV. OSBORNE LITTLEDALE, who was long curate of Buttermere, was a native of Whillimoor, and was born and brought up at High Toot Hill, in the parish of Arlecdon, of which Whillimoor forms one of four townships. His father was a dry-stone waller, and managed to afford his son a clerical education at St. Bees, on the products of his daily labour, and of his estate of eighteen high-lying acres, tilled by his own hand. The young man was tall and robust, and although fond of and skilled in athletic sports, he did not neglect his education. Of a good figure, he might be thought a little too uncouth for the ministry of a populous parish. His manners were of the homeliest character, and his very dark complexion, rather repulsive features, and a somewhat disagreeable squint with one eye, would in some measure disqualify him for attaining celebrity as a popular clergyman in polished society. But popular he was in his ministry at Buttermere; for he was strong and active, willing and ready to put his hand to work when his neighbours were in need of help; and having been brought up to farm work, nothing of that kind came amiss to him. The place almost appeared as if made for him, or he made for it, and for the people, by whom he was looked up to as a friend and favourite, as he truly was. His ordinary dress was becoming for his week-day work, consisting of a drab fustian coat, corduroy knee-breeches, grey stockings of the coarsest yarn, with clogs, or strong calkered shoes, stuffed with dried brackens, and hat brown, bare, and crumpled. In climbing or descending the steep mountains, calkers are as indispensable to the Cumberland shepherd and others whose business leads them to frequent excursions on the fells, as the alpen-stock and spiked shoes are to the members of the Alpine Club. And the brackens, where straw was scarce, and such ample foot room given in shoes as was the custom of the day, made a shoe or clog of any reasonable size hang well on the foot, when aided by good iron clasps.

Parson Littledale's ability and willingness to help, always without money pay, made him a great favourite with his flock, especially as he would undertake and perform feats of exertion that few others could accomplish.

In that neighbourhood the best peat earth is found on the mountain heights; if any poor family wanted peats cut, and they could not afford to hire, he would volunteer a day, shoulder his spade, with bread and cheese in his pocket for dinner, and labour with or excel the best from early morn to sunset. When sledging time came, and peats were dry, he would shoulder the sledge, take it up to the top, load it and run it down, and rally those who were unable to do as he could. At the sheep-clippings he was always busily employed, and could keep the whole gathering in a roar of laughter with his stories and anecdotes; and when the work was done, could enjoy his glass without excess. In haytime, if any had more work set out than his available force could accomplish, he'd "gang an' ax t' priest to help a bit." And " t' priest," ever ready, would exert his strength and fork to the cart or the hay-mow in a way that few could follow. He could handle an axe, and cut down a tree, and strip the bark as well as any woodman ; and whatever he took in hand, he did it with a will, and could show his parishioners how they ought to work. His stipend was very small when he commenced—only about £28, and eventually it was augmented to about £40 per annum ; and to eke out a subsistence for himself and family, he farmed the fishery of Buttermere lake, which would make a small addition to his income. Net and rod together (and with the latter he was an expert), he could have a dish of excellent trout in the season, when probably his means would not always afford a joint of meat, and none could be had nearer than Keswick—a journey of ten miles each way, and no carrier on the road. When char were netted, (none took bait,) they were sent to Keswick as the bread-winners. When a fox hunt was organized, he was out with the first and foremost, could scale the crags with the best, and tire most of the hunt in a long day's run. Otter hunting was a favourite sport, too ; and, if necessary, he could swim and dive almost as well as that animal itself. This kind of chase seldom occurred, from the scarcity of the game ; but when it did happen, he enjoyed both the hunt and the fun of slyly hustling some known bully or stuck-up effeminate into the river or lake to cool, without fear of retaliation ; for few durst take liberties with one of his burly frame and spirit. In his early manhood, while attending to his scholastic duties at St. Bees, he became a good wrestler, and won some prizes, and used to say there was more to learn at a public school than Greek and Latin. During a holiday, he and John Sumpton, the then young parish clerk of Arlecdon, agreed to go to Egremont Crab-fair sports ; when Sumpton brought away the prize for running, and the young parson the belt as the winning wrestler. Rather late in life he obtained a Lancashire curacy, with an improved stipend ; but the turmoil of a busy manufacturing community, with its accessories of steam and smoke, was in no way congenial to his feelings. The population and dialect were so different from his former associations that he became dispirited ; and unable to rally against a severe attack of illness, he finally succumbed to it, leaving somewhat comfortable circumstances to his family, by an undeviating course of care and economy, without parsimony, during many years.

THE REV. JOHN GREGSON, Senior, was curate at
Lamplugh, on a small stipend, and helped it by teaching the parish school boys and girls for several years,
till age and infirmity incapacitated him for active
duties.   He was of a mild and gentle spirit, with
scarce energy enough to preserve due order among
his forty or fifty restless pupils. of whom the writer
was one of the juniors ; and liberties were occasionally
taken, which he did not often resent.   He was brought
up a hand-loom weaver in Wigton, and, by a course
of hard saving, had managed to fit himself for the
clerical life of that day, and finally to accumulate a
little property.   His school-day dress was of the
plainest, and generally consisted of a checked linen
shirt, blue duffle coat with large metal buttons, waistcoat of like cloth, drab corduroy knee-breeches without braces, grey yarn stockings, and often clogs.
These homely habiliments were supplemented by a
blue linen apron, such as weavers used to wear, wound
about his waist, helping to conceal the space between
the waistcoat and breeches, where otherwise his linen
would have been visible.   This dress was seldom laid
aside, except on Sundays or at funerals.   At weddings
or christenings, his chief change in dress was to don a
black coat and waistcoat, and sometimes a white
neckerchief; the surplice, having been for a taller
man, doing useful service on such occasions.

Tourists had not then begun to scour the country
and criticise its population ; and a worthy man might
wear whatever was most useful to him, and his finan-
ces could best afford, without being subject to remark.

The reverse of teetotalism was the fashion of that
period ; but he was a consistently temperate man,
neither refusing to join the social circle nor indulging
beyond the bounds of reason.   He lived in frugal

lodgings, and obtained and kept the respect of his parishioners by his uprightness and meek demeanour. In person he was rather below the middle size, and broad-set; and his long blue coat and other outfit bespoke the handicraftsman, in a clean-looking, ordinary working dress.

He was succeeded in the curacy of Lamplugh by his son, the Rev. John Gregson.

THE REV. JOHN GREGSON, Junior, was chiefly educated by his father till fit to go to the Grammar School at St. Bees. He would be a man of more than thirty years of age when ordained, and I believe his first curacy was Lamplugh. He had been pretty well grounded in the classics; and in following his father as teacher of the parish school, gave most of his attention to the advanced pupils. When I went to his school for about two years, he had a few young men of over twenty years old, educating for the Church, who made good progress under him—not greatly to the advancement of the younger classes. He dressed in a rather more refined style than his father, and always wore a black coat and waistcoat, with the serviceable dark drab or olive corduroy breeches and dark grey stockings, without gaiters or leggings. He commonly wore strong calkered shoes, and was rather fond of trying their speed against those of any young men of his parish who felt disposed to give him a trial, and was not easily beaten on fair ground.

He also lived in frugal lodgings, and saved up what he could. He was a man of few words, and mixed little in society, his chief amusement being an occasional game of whist, when invited to spend a winter's evening with a neighbour. In summer he

took long, solitary walks on the holiday Saturdays.
He was of good stature, and well built, with little of
the clerical in his appearance or demeanour, and
might have been taken by a stranger for a farmer in
market-day dress. He had not learned to dispense
with his native dialect of Wigton, and occasionally
introduced its peculiarities into his reading and
preaching, and more often in his sparse conversation.
Now and then he had to undergo a sarcastic remark
upon it, which had the effect of increasing his reti-
cence; and, being of modest and retiring habits, he
would often have to pay the penalty for neglecting to
acquire the orthodox pronunciation in his younger
days. He had a strong ambition to become son-in-
law to a neighbouring " statesman," of good substance
and some drollery, and was a frequent visitor at the
house. The old man was somewhat loquacious, and
fond of repeating his anecdotes and reciting his
home-spun rhymes, but could never extract a rejoinder
from the parson, and not often a remark or a question.
One evening, after a vain endeavour to draw out his
visitor, the old yeoman sat silent for a time, whilst
concocting an appropriate couplet; and getting impatient, and still without a word from the young man,
he said :

> " Will ye nowder sing nor say,
> Tell a teall, nor gang away?"

This sally only had the short-lived effect of driving
him away on that occasion, for his visits were soon
renewed with the same silent admiration. In time
they became tiresome to the old man, who, though
eminently talkative, felt the annoyance of constantly
sustaining a one-sided conversation, in which his two
daughters could not assist him, and vented his disap-
probation to them with a groan, and :

> " Thur bishops and priests are not o' my plan :
> I'd rayder our Nancy hed a good husbandman."

After allowing the parson ample time to open negotiations, the young lady discarded him for a rival, who was a "good husbandman," and a thriving one too, and who made a good husband to her.

Not long afterwards the parson retired to his home in Wigton, and married there. He gave way to less temperate habits, and died in middle life.

THE REV. JAMES PONSONBY, of Ennerdale, was a remarkably fine-looking man, and of gentlemanly demeanour. He was said to be of the family of the Ponsonbys of Walton; and being a younger brother, without fortune, availed himself of his superior education to enter the Church as a means of support. Having been reared amid great plenty, it was no small trial to him to learn to exist on eighty pounds a year. But he resolutely set himself to the task, and, imitating the dialect of his parishioners, used to say he had learned to eat "taties and bacon off a bare fir board." He was a bachelor, lodged in a farm-house, and lived as the family did. He mixed sociably with his parishioners and other neighbours who mostly made him welcome, and rendered himself tolerably comfortable on a stipend very much below the amount his early years had enjoyed, settling on his curacy for a long period, and possessing the respect and good-will of all.

When the Wild Dog of Ennerdale was committing so much destruction among the mountain flocks in that and the neighbouring fell districts, it was customary to assemble the hounds to try to kill or chase the destroyer away, whenever the opportunity offered of his locality being known, irrespective of days or times. One Sunday morning, during divine service,

the hounds were passing the church in full cry after
the great dog. The excitement was too much for the
congregation to resist, for male and female, young and
old, felt so much interested in the probable destruction of their enemy, that all arose and ran who could.
And when Mr. Ponsonby found his church and ministry deserted, it was said he stripped his surplice and
followed, as far as his advanced years and impaired
locomotive powers allowed.

Like the great King Alfred, he was once left alone
in the house to mind the pot-boiling, while the mistress was absent. When the good woman returned,
she found the broth swimming with fat. This being
something unusual at Brackenwrea in those days, the
parson was asked, in a not very agreeable tone, to
account for it. He at once said he had found a
pound of butter in the dairy, put it into the broth, and
had enjoyed a good fat crowdy very much. He was
not appointed to the same office again.

Aware of his propensity to indulgence, as he grew
in years, he sometimes warned his parishioners to do
as he said, and not as he did.

THE REV. SAMUEL SHERWEN, rector of Dean,
began life with very moderate means, but apparently
settled in his mind that he would improve those means
by great industry and strict economy. Twice he
walked to Chester to pass his examination and obtain
his ordination from the Bishop ; his walks being from
early morn till dewy eve, and being a strong and willing pedestrian, no idle time was spent on the way.

In early life he was for some time an usher in the
Grammar School at Bolton-le-Moors. He afterwards
held the curacy of Embleton, and taught in the Gram-

mar School at Cockermouth, living in frugal lodgings and saving a little money. In consequence of the pecuniary embarrassments of the then rector of Dean, (the Rev. Henry Sill,) who had, among many other obligations, neglected to pay his curate, Mr. Sherwen, his salary, for some years, and, it is said, had also borrowed money from him, the living was sequestrated, and Mr. Sherwen was licensed as curate by the Bishop, and finally purchased the living—it was said at a very advantageous rate—and became rector of Dean.

He continued to labour at his school in Cockermouth and his church at Dean for some years, having comfortable lodgings in his parish, and letting the rectory farm and a large parcel of land, allotted to the rectory in lieu of tithes, to tenants. The tenant of the parsonage farm having a strong family, and having made money, took the noted Schoose Farm, belonging to J. C. Curwen, Esq., M.P. ; and Mr. Sherwen, being prejudiced in favour of a farmer's life, took the farm into his own hands, and commenced farmer. Till now the energy of his character was hardly suspected, for it was hidden under his peaceful demeanour. His industry was undisputed ; but it was never imagined that such a homely and quiet-going man as he, was capable of the active and untiring perseverance that from this time he exhibited, both in his clerical character and in the management of his glebe. Like most others, he was not without his eccentricities, but they were always intended to do good, and none seemed to point in any other direction.

It has been remarked that a good farmer was spoiled when Mr. Sherwen was made a parson ; but his constant endeavour was to shew that in neither character was he either spoiled or injured. Constant in his duties as a clergyman—in visiting the sick, and in administering the consolations of religion to his parishioners; in secretly aiding the necessitous, and in giving advice, he was unwearied, and always ready when called on, day or night. Being of a social turn, he mixed much in the society of the heads of his own and the neighbouring parishes, when he relished a rubber at whist or a dance, and the temperate enjoyment of the evening.

Once, on the breaking up of a party. the writer of this saw him in a position he did not seem to enjoy. For some time he had been paying attention to Miss Wood, of Pardshaw Hall, and had a rival in Mr. John Fisher, of Coldkeld, a tall and very powerful man. Mr. Sherwen was already on horseback at the door, waiting to escort Miss Wood home, when Mr. Fisher went up, and lifting the quiet pony's hind leg backwards, held it there for some time, in spite of the vigorous application of a slender switch and the strong remonstrance of the parson, amid the laughter of the party. The pony's struggles to get away were quite fruitless under the powerful grasp of the giant, and it gave up the attempt and stood as if held in a vice till Mr. Fisher was satisfied with the effect of his lark, and set it and its rider at liberty. Neither of the rivals were successful in that pursuit, for death—that more powerful competitor—stepped in a few months after, and carried off the fair prize.

Mr. Sherwen afterwards married Miss Robinson, of Cockermouth. who died in a few years without leaving any family. To divert his mind from his bereavement, he took up farming keenly, and particularly the grazing of sheep and cattle, for which his farm was very suitable. In accordance with this, he became a regular attendant at the Monday markets at Cockermouth, where, exercising his judgment, he frequently made purchases of Irish cattle at a reasonable rate, and of Cheviot and mountain sheep, and was not shy at driving his bargains home. So laborious was he in his pursuit, that he went to nearly all the fairs within many miles, most commonly on foot, returning the same day. He has gone in the morning, on foot, from Dean to Grasmere fair, in Westmoreland, purchased sheep, and driven them home in the evening, but stretching a long way into next morning—the distance about sixty miles. Speaking of this and similar excursions, he has often said he never knew what fatigue in walking was, and especially if he thought he had made fortunate bargains, as he frequently did. In his attendance at the sheep fairs, he was not one to judge of the quality or condition of the sheep by a poke with his stick over the side of the pen, nor to purchase without careful examination. With due respect to his clerical habiliments, and care of his own belongings, he mostly took pains to retire and put on his trousers the wrong way, or inside outwards, and then could press in and wade among the highly-coloured flock, to handle and turn them to his heart's content, with the smallest injury to his dress. When his examinations were over, his trousers were as easily turned again in some stable or outhouse, and he was once more a parson in dress.

The labour attending his ministry and farm, extensive as it was, could not satisfy his energy. He was appointed guardian of the poor of the parish ; and his attendance was so constant, and his qualifications for the office so high, that he was elected chairman of the Board ; the duties of which office he discharged satisfactorily until nearly fourscore, when he declined the chairmanship, but continued to act as guardian.

He had a strong and clear voice, with a distinct and deliberate pronunciation, and was most explicit in aiding his hearers to have a due understanding of the subject of his sermons ; but he probably had never heard of the late Baron Alderson's opinion of the proper length of a sermon, which was "twenty minutes, with a leaning to the side of mercy." But his church was well attended.

The difficulty of concentrating the mind upon the matter in hand, was in some measure exemplified in Mr. Sherwen. It is told of him, that in leaving church after service one Sunday, he called his servant, and said it occurred to him, during the delivery of his sermon, that a sheep they had missed some weeks before, and searched for far and near, had been sold in such a lot to the butcher, Johnny Go-faster.* On another occasion, he performed a very useful bit of service, by sending his man out of church to drive some cows out of a corn-field, which he caught sight of through a window when in the pulpit. At another time he spoke to his servant Peter, when in church on a Sunday, and told him there were some pigs in the churchyard which were not his, and said he might go and drive them out.

From long experience and close observation of the ways of mankind, Mr. Sherwen had formed an opinion, and was not shy in declaring it, that we should only believe half of what we see, and nothing of what we hear; forgetting, at the same time, that himself was engaged in promulgating the doctrines of Christianity with an earnestness, he hoped, that none who heard him would disbelieve.

On one of his many essays to preach extempore, having exhausted his stock in hand, he asked, "And what shall I say next?" "Amen," said an audible voice.

He married a second time, and was again left a widower without issue. He died in September, 1870, having completed his eightieth year.

*John Denwood.

Since the above was written, a clerical friend who knew him well, has contributed the following :—

"To a strong, natural sagacity and quickness in 'discerning of spirits,' there was added a considerable power of argument, the result of previous thought and reading. The following anecdotes will illustrate these several qualities of this complex order of mind :—

"A drainer whom he employed, from Pardshaw, and who on Sundays was in the habit of attending the Friends' Meeting House at that place, said to Mr. Sherwen on Monday morning, 'I was thinking yesterday in t' meeting that thou should hae the main drain quite another way.' 'Oh, Jemmy,' was the quick re·proof, 'is that what thou thinks about in t' meeting? There is another *main thing* for Sundays, and main drains for Mondays.

"When Denwood, the butcher, came to Dean, it was well understood that in driving a bargain with the rector, it was a case of Greek meeting Greek. On one occasion, after a hard contest, Johnny, on leaving the house, made a parting shot at his clerical rival in these words—'Weel, I find this, self niver sleeps but wi' ya ee oppen.' 'Eh, Johnny,' was the rejoinder, 'thou has nobbet learnt hofe thy lesson. Self never goes to bed.'

"A friend, one Saturday evening, remarked to him that the article in the Creed, 'The Holy Catholic Church,' was much misunderstood, most people in the country thinking it was a pure bit of Popery. Mr. Sherwen made no reply, but next day, from the pulpit, delivered a most admirable extempore sermon, dividing it thus —'The Church, its Constitution. Its distinction, Catholic. Its character, Holy.'"

It would be unjust to dismiss this sketch without remarking that he was careful in small matters that he might be liberal in large; and his character in the parish and neighbourhood was this, that he would go any distance to visit the sick, to set out a drain, or to knock out a bullock's wolf-tooth !

Towards the end of his ministry, a nephew, the Rev. William Sherwen, took most of the duty, whilst himself formed part of the congregation ; and occasionally, during the delivery of an approved sermon by his nephew, he has been heard to audibly call out, " Hear, hear ! "

Tʜᴇ Rᴇᴠ. JAMES MARSHALL was curate of Ireby sixty-five years, commencing with a stipend of twenty-five pounds per annum, which was at different times augmented by small additions to fifty pounds, but late in life for him. He had acquired some learning, and was well respected.

The pressure of difficult times and an increasing young family put him to sore straits for a decent maintenance, although industrious and very careful. In middle life he kept a couple of work-horses ; and, occupying some of his glebe, performed most of the farm labour with his own hands, assisted occasionally by two daughters, whose skill and energy in cutting corn with the toothed sickle, then the only reaping machine, enabled him to contract for cutting the crops on other farms.

For many years he practised carting coals from Bolton Collieries to Keswick, filling the carts and conducting them to market himself—resting the horses when occasional duties required his presence. As his daughters grew up, one of them sometimes went with the horses when he was engaged.

This carting of so dirty a commodity must have been very irksome to an educated man, whose profession would naturally lead him to anticipate a life of a very different character. Whether he thought it degrading or not, he manfully and unrepiningly struggled with his lot; and though obliged to wear the plainest and coarsest habiliments, clogs, &c., when at his labour, he maintained the respect of his parishioners by his upright conduct and steady industry, and by extraordinary perseverance in early rising, working late, and strict economy, managed to educate a son for the Church; and the education he privately gave his daughters on spare evenings, was beyond what many young people received at that day.

Though a man of peaceful disposition, he could rebuke an offender with stern dignity, and has been known to take the law into his own hands when rudely assailed by a disorderly parishioner, and to do it with more effect than by a lecture from the pulpit. He was once attacked by two cowardly fellows, and soon felled both! The first got up and ran away, calling to his companion to "lig whyet, or he'll seun hev thee down ageann." The advice was taken to the great amusement of the parson. He did not excel as a preacher; and it was said, that through defective sight, in a gloomy church and dark weather, he was sometimes so puzzled with a word that he was observed to quietly spell before he found it safe to utter it.

One Sunday his clerk fell asleep during the sermon, and happening to awake during one of these pauses, called out, "Amen." Mr. Marshall was so disconcerted that he stopped amid the titters of the congregation; and, on leaving church, said to his clerk, "Richard, you cut me rather short this morning." "Ey," was the reply, "I thought you war deun."

He died in January, 1842, at the patriarchal age of ninety-one.

THE REV. ABRAHAM BROWN.—Very common among clergymen, as among most other classes of that day, was the habit of living too freely ; and no exception was the Rev. Abraham Brown, of Egremont. This might in some measure be induced by the broad hospitality of the time, when every one thought the parson's visit an honour, and it was a duty to treat him with the best. At the same time, if he happened to be tithe owner, some would not scruple to mislead him in rendering their dues. Few durst take such liberties with Mr. Brown. or woe betide them ! I remember, when a boy, seeing him in his advanced years ; his broad shoulders and stalwart frame indicating great strength of body.

Of his ability as a preacher I had no opportunity of judging, but have heard many speak of his power and indomitable spirit as an athlete, and of his boast that none could throw him in the wrestling ring, and only a *Mr. Rum* could throw him outside of it ; but he did not like to admit having been once thrown by Thomas Johnstone, of Workington.

He died early in 1822, at a ripe age.

THE REV. WILLIAM SEWELL, of Troutbeck.—In evidence of the home-spun materials of which the clerical character was formerly attempted to be made and placed in country parishes, a few anecdotes of that worthy and eccentric old man, the Rev. William Sewell, may be quoted. He was a tall and bony man, of great strength, and willing to put his strength to a good purpose when opportunity offered ; and it is said he did not decline to use it occasionally in effectually settling disputes among his parishioners.

He was owner of the highest situated house in England, the inn at Kirkstone Pass, and of other landed property in the romantic valley of Troutbeck. He held one farm in hand, and kept a flock of mountain sheep, and was no mean judge of that class of stock.

One Sunday he had mounted the pulpit to preach at Wythburn Chapel. The pulpit was in a dilapidated state, and leaned a little from the wall, leaving an opening behind it. He had laid his sermon on the ledge, and displaced it with his surplice, when it fell down the chink to where he could not reach it. The pulpit was small and low, scarcely reaching to his middle, and was neither convenient nor safe for a tall man to turn in. After vainly trying to recover the sermon, he resorted to an expedient recorded elsewhere, and said to his congregation, "T' sarmont's slipt down i' t' neuk, and I can't git it out; but I'll tell ye what—I'se read ye a chapter i' t' Bible 'at's worth three on't."

On another occasion he was about to commence divine service, when, leaning over the side of the reading-desk, he whispered to his clerk, "Jwon, dud ta see ought o' two black tips 'et I lost?" "I dudn't," says John. "Wilta enquire?" "Ey." And then to work—"When the wicked man," &c.

Dining once at Dalehead Hall, as he often did after morning service, he said to his hostess, Mrs. Leathes, who used to encourage his plain speaking, "How did ye like my sarmont to-day?" "Very well indeed, Mr. Sewell." "It hes a reet to be a good 'un, for it was yan o' Bishop ——'s, o' bit t' tail end;" and unmistakably the tail had not belonged to the carcase.

The late Bishop Villiers used to relate that when visiting the clergy of his diocese he went to Trout-

beck. It being about the end of October, the shepherds were busy salving their sheep. He approached
a solitary salver at work, and enquired where he would
be likely to find the incumbent, the Rev. William
Sewell. The salver, recognizing the Bishop, and
knowing that any attempt to mislead him would be
dangerous, at once frankly said, "He is before you,
my lord ; I am he." The astonished prelate said he
might employ his time better among his parishioners.
The parson readily and honestly replied, "My lord,
when you find me better remuneration, I can probably
afford to lay aside assisting my neighbours ; and I
shall be very glad to give up salving sheep."

Mr. Sewell remained, greatly respected, in his in-
cumbency till near the end of his long sojourn here,
and died, July 31, 1869, aged ninety-eight years.

CLERICAL ANECDOTES.

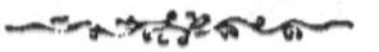

COMPLIMENTARY.

ONCE when a neighbouring clergyman took a Sunday service at Matterdale Church, an aged parishioner drew up to pay him a compliment on leaving the church, and said, " Wey, Mr. ———, they said ye war yan o' t' warst priests et iver waww't, bit what ye'r a fine deeal better ner nin."

A POINTED QUESTION.

IN December. 1863. a young clergyman on the eve of marriage, wishing to be economical, wrote to the Bishop of Carlisle to say he had published his own banns, and to inquire if he could marry himself. Without referring to ecclesiastical law, his Lordship at once replied, " Could you bury yourself?"

WILL RITSON.

WHEN the Rev. Dr. Ainger and two other clergymen were on the top of Scawfell, with the eccentric Will Ritson as their guide, and were indulging in hearty merriment, the Dr. asked Will what he thought of their doings. Will quickly replied he thought they were nearer to heaven than they ever had been, and may be nearer than they ever would be again.

ON FOOT OR ON HORSEBACK?

In a whisper loud enough to rebuke the offender, the clergyman of Eskdale, who was near-sighted, hearing some one walking noisily up the aisle during divine service, stooping toward his clerk, said,

"Whaa's tat?"

Clerk—"It's aad Sharp o' Laa Birker."

Priest—"Afooat or o' horseback?"

Clerk—"Nay, nobbet afooat, wi' cokert shun."

CUT AND COME AGAIN.

When Thomas Newby removed from Bracelet, near Broughton-in-Furness, to Muncaster Head Farm, the curate of Eskdale, the Rev. Robert Powley (not the near-sighted curate), met him on his way; and, after a little chat, Mr. Powley, in his homely way, said, "Tom, I'se caa to see thee some day." Tom, knowing the convivial habits of the parson, answered in *his* rough way—"Thaww need du nawwt o' t' sooart, I want nawwt wi' tha." The parson was as ready with a caustic reply as Tom, and immediately said, "Wey awivver I'se come to t' seall," implying that Tom would be sold up ere long. But Tom and his son have thriven on the farm for thirty years or more, and are likely to continue thriving and well respected.

NOT BAD—FOR A FARMER.

St. Bees Grammar School has frequently sent forth bright scholars ; and a few farmers have, from time to time, received a fair classical education there, one of whom is Mr. C——, of that village.

One day Dr. Ainger, Principal of the College, the Rev. Mr. Heslop, head master of the Grammar School, and Mr. C——, happened to meet, when Mr. Heslop said in a jest, " I wish you would take my class to-day, Mr. C——, for I have a bad headache." The immediate reply was, " I doubt my classics will be getting rusty for your class, Mr. Heslop, but if the Doctor will take your class, I think I can manage his." Mem.—No bargain made.

WELL PUT.

The clergy of St. Bees have usually a good amount of Charity Money, arising from different sources, to distribute every Christmas, and they sometimes have a difficulty in finding a needy recipient, for the village is and has been long remarkable for the absence of poor people. On the Principal of the College asking his churchwarden if he knew any deserving poor, he was naïvely told that the most destitute family in the village was that of a student at the College !

CHARITABLE ON BOTH SIDES.

Dr. Ainger offered an old woman, whom he thought poor, five shillings from Miss Shepherd's alms fund.

The charitable woman turned seriously towards him and said, " Nay, nay, Doctor, keep 't yer sel. You've a girt family. and you doant know what you may stand need on befwore you dee."

TRUE, NO DOUBT.

THE late Provost Fox used to tell a story of a man asking a clergyman what he would charge for preaching a funeral sermon. The reply was, " My regular charge is thirty shillings. I *could* preach one for a pound, but it would not be worth listening to."

TARRY WOO, &c.

" A CONGREGATION of smells, like Wasdale Head Chapel in sheep salving time," was one of Provost Fox's quaint sayings.

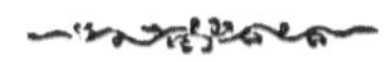

THE WAY TO SPREAD NEWS.

OVER a social glass at Bolton Low Houses, among a few neighbours, one of the company remarked that should the rector drop off, the then curate would stand a good chance of becoming rector of Bolton. " Nut varra likely," says one of the party, " dud ta hear what he's been deein?" " Wey, what *hes* he been deein?" says another. " Wey, he's been committan adultery." " How does ta know that?" " Wey, o 'at I know

about it is he was seen cuttin' nettles of a Sunday, and
if thou dizent co' that adultery I divent know what
it is?"

A POSER.

AT a School examination of boys, at Wigton, after a
long course of questions, the Rev. and self-confident
examiner said, "Now, my boys, I have teased you a
long while and you have answered me well.   Will any
of you ask me a question, and I'll try to answer you?"
After a short interval of silence a boy held up his
hand.   "Well, my boy, what have you to ask?"
" Please, sir, who was it in the reign of King David
that went down and slew a lion among the snow?"—
No answer; and the meeting broke up amid cheers
and laughter. 

SWEEPING DOCTRINE.

A NEW curate at one of the Whitehaven churches
preached a high-flown sermon, consigning all but himself, and a few who thought as he did, to eternal per-
dition.   The incumbent, the Rev. Dr. Huddleston,
heard the sermon, and, waiting for the young man in
the vestry-room addressed him with—" I don't know,
Mr. ——, about this sweeping doctrine of yours.   I
should not like all my pious ancestors who have
not had the benefit of your teaching to be burning in
hell."   From that time the sermons were considerably
modified.

A MISTAKE RECTIFIED.

A YEOMAN'S son who thought himself more likely to make a good clergyman than a good farmer accordingly studied for the Church, and in due time was appointed to the curacy of Buttermere. Like many beginners, he was rather confused on his first Sunday, and began some part of the service out of its turn. On his clerk looking up and reminding him of his error, he said, "Stop, John, let us begin afresh." On leaving, he said, he could not think how he had managed to get through the service, but he would take good care not to commit another mistake in the church. And he never did, for that was his first and last attempt.

FOUNDERED IN A SAWPIT.

THE late Rev. Dr. Huddleston, of Whitehaven, was sometimes made the subject of a sprightly brother clergyman's wit. One day as they and others sat in the public library, the Dr. was provoked beyond endurance by some impertinent remarks, and in an emphatic manner said, " Well, well. 'Nemo mortalium omnibus horis săpit.' " * An allusion to a sawpit near the town that was well understood, and which protected him for the future from his neighbour's wit.

NOT WANTED.

IN a country parish, on a stormy Sunday, the singers did not muster, and the parson leaned over the pulpit

* No man is wise at all hours.

and whispered to his clerk—"John, can we raise a psalm to-day?" John audibly replied, "Hegh! can we raise the divel?" Such was the familiarity allowed in times gone by.

VERY SIGNIFICANT.

A TENANT of a Cumberland clergyman went to pay his rent at the dinner hour, and was desired to wait. A young daughter of the parson begged the tenant might be allowed to come in—he was such a funny man. He came in, and, being directed to sit near the fire, was asked a number of questions about his farm. One of these was, "How was the sow getting on?" "O, she's pig't a barrowful, and yan mair nor she hes paps for." "And how does the odd one do while the rest are sucking?" "It sits and looks on as I do."

A TOO COMMON LOT.

AN aged Cumbrian clergyman, subsisting on a very small stipend, was comparing the hard system of living in his younger days with the way his brethren lived now, and said, that for many years he was summoned to breakfast by his hostess saying, "Priest, come to your poddish." To dinner, by "Priest, come to your tatics (or taties and point)." And to supper, by "Priest, come to your poddish." His later years were softened by a small increase of stipend; but with all his care he never knew what it was to rejoice in plenty.

CHOICE OF TRADES.

PEGGY GORDON, the tinker's wife of Skelsceugh, was asked by the Rev. Joseph Fullerton what line of life was intended for her son Bob. "You see, Sir," says she, "if he turns out a gay sharp lad, we'll keep him in our oan trade ; but if he's nobbet a dulbert, our oald Tom says we'll hev him meadd a priest on."

The parson was highly amused with his parishioner's reply, and spoke of it frequently.

A READING RACE.

THE Rev. Mr. Kirkbride, of the parish of Hesket, found occasion to have a substitute during a Sunday's absence, and was anxious on his return to know how the duty had been performed. Mr. Kirkbride prided himself on his quick reading. and did not like to be outdone in it by any one. On the day of his return he called on a neighbour and inquired how he liked the new parson. "Oh !" says John, "he's t' best I iver hear'd in my life. I niver hear'd a man read so fast." Mr. Kirkbride did not relish this at all ; and, in his excitement, he burst into his native dialect, and said, " I tell ye what, John, he mebby may beat me at t' Lessons, but I'll run him at t' Creed for anything he likes, and I'll give him to Pontius Pilate fore-start."

A GREAT SURPRISE.

IRREVERENT, as it undoubtedly was, it is well known that propriety of speech was too little observed by some few of the clergy of generations gone by.

The late Rev. Mr. Gaskin had a well-known and peculiar knack of exclaiming, "The devil!" on any sudden occasion. The then Bishop of Carlisle happening to meet him, bade him good morning, and the curate coldly returned the salute, not knowing whom he had met. The Bishop, thinking he was not duly honoured, or perhaps not recognized, said, "I think you do not know me, Mr. Gaskin. I am the Bishop." Greatly astonished, he broke out with—"The Bishop! The devil!"

WARSE NER O' TUDDER.

An ecclesiastical official went to Bowness-on-Eden, to make inquiries respecting the alleged misconduct of the clergyman. Making his business known to the parish clerk, that loquacious individual anticipated inquiry by stating that the parson was, "A bad man, Sir! A bad man!" "How do you make that out?" "Wey, Sir, he meade a scàll, Sir, an' he selt t' communion table, Sir." "Indeed." "Ey, an' I can tell ye mair, Sir, for the varra teàble's now in yon public-house parlour, Sir, an' I've drank off't many a teyme sinseyne, Sir." "And have you anything more?" "Ey, amess hev I, Sir. Warse ner o' tudder, Sir. He eb'n went an' selt t' communion claith, when it perlang't to John Hodgson, o' Skinbernees, Sir." "How did you know whom it belonged to?" "It was mark't i' ya corner wid J. H. S., and whea else *could* it perlang te?"

The rest of the inquiry had to be got from a more reliable source; for it transpired that the parson had lent a table of his own to supply the want in the church. The signification of the initial letters J.H.S. are well known in church matters.

SWARMELLING.

THE Rev. Mr. Murphy wishing to cross Bootle beck in a flood, inquired of a ten-year-old boy for a crossing place. The boy took him to a pole hung across the stream; and, on the reverend gentleman not approving of such an unsteady bridge, the boy said, "Wy, my fadder swarmelt it. and I swarmelt it, and càant thaww swarmel't tu?" To swarmel is to scramble or creep over, perhaps, astride of the pole.

A COMPLIMENT.

THE Rev. Henry R—— occasionally preached at Whitehaven, when visiting his friends there.

At a small evening party a lady wished to pay a compliment to his preaching ability, but was much puzzled to concoct a suitable one. At last she expressed the great delight with which she heard him the other morning; for he was "the most *soothing* preacher she ever heard!" It has been said by others that he was one of the quietest of preachers, therefore the compliment was appropriate.

OURSELVES FIRST.

WHEN Bishop Waldegrave was driving over on a Sunday morning to preach at Hesket, he overtook Farmer John Rodgers on foot, and stopped his carriage to desire the man to go to a house not far off to tell the Sebergham sexton he intended to preach there in the afternoon. The man thought the Bishop's horses were able to take their master on his own errand, and said, "Nay, I can gang nin ; I'se gangan o' t' way to Caldbeck till a funeral." In feigned surprise. the Bishop asked if they buried their dead on the Sunday? "Ey," says the man, "we bury them efter they dee, be 't Sunday or warday."

THOUGHTS No. 1 AND No. 2.

A NEWSPAPER tells us that an Edinburgh clergyman of rare and quaint genius, stood gazing earnestly at the mail driven at a thundering pace over the Carlisle bridges. "What are you thinking of?" said a reverend brother. "I'm thinking that next to preaching the everlasting Gospel, I would like to drive the mail."

WHAT AN ANSWER!

IN the newspapers of 1866. it is recorded that, in examining a school of boys, Bishop Waldegrave asked one of them if he had read the Thirty-nine Articles? "No." said the boy, "but I have read the Forty Thieves."

VERY UNGALLANT.

AFTER his marriage in the morning at Workington, the curate of Moresby was called to officiate at his own church. Having performed his clerical duties there, he quietly retired, as usual, to his lodgings at Moresby, in utter forgetfulness of his bride, until reminded by his landlady that he was now a husband.

A SHIFTY CLERK.

A HANDBOOK of the lakes says, the clergyman of Wythburn relates that one Sunday morning, when he came to the chapel, the clerk was quietly sitting astride of the roof-ridge. On asking his business there, Joe said, "O Sir, Jemmy Hawkrigg brak yan o' his car-reàpps tudder day i' t' hayfield, and they gat t' bell reàpp an's forgitten to bring 't back ageànn, seah I've been tworst to git up on t' riggin, and ring wi' my hands; and I thought it was neah use comin' down ageànn between times, and I'se stoppan to give t' third round and than I'se be wi' ye."

FAIRPLAY IS A JEWEL.

IT is said of a parson of old times, when the plunder of a wrecked vessel was a matter of interest to a neighbourhood, that one stormy Sunday he ordered the western door of St. Bridget's Church, at Beckermont, to remain open during service, so that he might see when a vessel, seen in distress off the coast, was driven on shore. His congregation were, perhaps, as keenly intent on the same object, as on his ministrations; and though all might see the ship strike the ground, they had the advantage of ready egress by the door, whilst he was aloft and encumbered with his surplice. When his parishioners began to rush out in a body, as the ship struck, he imploringly called out, " Nay, nay, lads, let us all have fairplay, however."

THE TWO SHEPHERDS.

During sultry summer weather, the mountain sheep are very subject to be blown by the maggot fly, and they require to be closely looked after, to prevent losses in the flocks. One Sunday a Martindale shepherd was returning from his duties on the fell, when he encountered the parson going home from church service.

Parson—"Well, John, I suppose you have been attending to *your* flock, as I have been to mine."

John—"Ey, aa hev. And hed you any in't whicks?"

THE PRIEST AND THE POSTMAN.

An eccentric Buttermere curate of a former day was on his way to church one Sunday, when he espied the village postman clipping a pony and remonstrated with him, as in duty bound, for doing so improper an act on a Sunday. especially when divine service was about to begin. The man pleaded want of time, saying, "It was a lang day's ride to t'heed offish at Cockermouth and back ; and when I's in't town for an hour. I's so thrang liveran out parshels. and laytan in freshans, that I fairly hev nea time else." "But," says the parson, "you are not doing the thing well either, lend me the scissors and I'll show you how to clip your pony." The parson took in hand, and was so much occupied with his cleverness in clipping, that he did not observe the man had slipped away from the other side, and on looking up was astonished to see his congregation approaching in a body.

The wag of a postman had run to the chapel and

announced that " theer 'll be nea sarvice to-day. T' priest's thrang clippin' my powny."

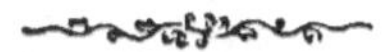

PHILOSOPHICAL.

THE REV. E. STANLEY engaged a raw hand for a man servant. When the man was bringing the roast-beef into the dining-room, his foot caught the door-mat. Down went the man, and the beef rolled forward into the room. Instead of being angry with the man, Mr. Stanley coolly exclaimed, "See, the beef has come, and the man will doubtless follow."

THROWING THE FIRST STONE.

IN a small country parish some of the principal parishioners met together to consider the propriety of laying before the Bishop a rumour, real or unfounded, of some irregularities on the part of their pastor. After much discussion, an elderly man, and rather a wet one, remarked, "Wey, what it's nobbet what yan's done yans-sel, mebby, many a time." The effect of this was silently to melt away the meeting, and with it disappeared the scandal.

A GREEN BAY HORSE.

SOME irreverent young men, wishing to puzzle the parish clerk during service, cut out the word *horse* from a printed document. and pasted it over the word

N

tree in the clerk's book.   When his turn came to read the verse, he read in his sing-song tone, "He shall flourish like the green-bay *horse*."   "Horse!" says he, brushing over the page with his hand—"Horse!" (lower) "Ey, d—n, it is horse"—and read on.

LATING A PRIEST.

A CLERGYMAN, being ill, sent his servant to ask another of the cloth to take his duty.   The man being asked by an acquaintance where he was going to, replied, "Theer a man gitten to be berried to-mworn, and I hev ower to Sannath (Sandwith) to gang to lait a priest."

THE PRINCIPAL PART.

IN the days of "Whittle-geâtts" it was no uncommon thing for the parson to spend a portion of his evenings at the ale house with some of his flock, and the custom was not held to bring discredit on the cloth.

On one occasion a worthy rector, having exceeded his usual moderate libations, was "stiddy't" home by one of his neighbours, with whom the following dialogue took place :—

Parson—"John?"

John—"Yes, Sir."

Parson—"You are a very decent man, John—a very decent man.   But, John, I am afraid you don't come to church so often as you should do, John."

John—"Ey, what than! I pay tithes, and church rates, and Easter dues, and o' thur mak o' things reglar."

Parson (sententiously)—" Aye, aye, John, so you do, so you do. And after all, that is *the* principal part of *the* business, John."

A PARALLEL.

MANY years ago a sexton of St. Bees Church, who had been very intemperate, was left a comfortable fortune. The then Principal of the College, very considerately, undertook to advise him to forsake his bad practices, especially his propensity to drink, and not to be seen tipsy in the street as he often had been. " Ey, doctor," says he, " I'll make ye suer I'll be a better man now when I've got summat to work on. When I want a good drink I'll git some into t' hoose, and drink't theer as you dea."

THE PITCH PIPE.

IN one of our rural parish churches a new pitch pipe had been provided. The clerk had not practised on it before going into his desk on Sunday.

When the time arrived for giving the key-note the instrument could not be drawn out. The clerk tugged at it—thrust it in—tried to pull it out—gave it another thump or two—grinned and pulled again, but move it would not. The parson grew impatient, leaned over the side and whispered, " Stop, Jonathan," and aloud, " Let us pray." " Pray! the hangment! we'll pray nin·till I git this thing to wark."

HARDLY AN AVERAGE.

Not long after the Rev. —— C—— got into pecuniary difficulties a Ravenglass butcher had killed and was dressing the carcase of a pig, and among some casual onlookers was another Reverend of rather wet proclivities, who remarked that the pig was a nice one. The butcher turned aside to whet his knife and was heard to say, "*Hardly* an average like a deal o' you parson fellows." This was duly understood by the party.

VERY HIGH CHURCH.

Before the distinctions of high and low church were much discussed or even known among the rural clergy, a minister from further east called on his acquaintance the late Rev. —— Toppin, of Irthington, and was invited to partake of the mid-day meal. Both were of homely type, and after chatting awhile, the man from the east said in his vernacular, "Aa'm vahha hee choatch." Mr. T. not hearing well and not at all comprehending the purport of the remark, put his open palm behind his ear, and asked, "What is it?" "Aa'm vahha hee choatch." "Hay? what is it?" (Wonder.) "Aa'm vahha hee choatch." "Ey, very well. Sup up yer broth."

HITTING UNDER COVER.

Many years ago a late clerical chief magistrate, of Whitehaven, used to say that if ever he sold another horse it should be on condition that the buyer was to take it out of the county. "For," said he, "I was once walking up towards Hensingham, and on meeting a string of iron ore carts, one of the drivers called out, ' Wo, Jenkins, wo, ye oald feùll ;' and on going towards him he again cried out loudly, ' Jee, Jenkins, jee, ye d——d oald feùll.' On going to him and asking why he used my name in that way, he said, ' I was nut speakin' to you. I was shoutin' to this oald horse.'"

A FAMILIAR BOOK.

A CLERGYMAN was preaching in the quaint old church of Bolton from Genesis xxviii. 20, 21, and remarked that his hearers would all recollect the words of his text, or at least ought to do. To him they were as familiar as the book of his youth—Jack the Giant Killer.

THE MOON INHABITED.

THE late Rev. E. Salkeld had a lively sense of the humorous. Going along the main street at Aspatria on a visit to a sick parishioner with a friend, in passing the Half Moon Inn he heard several voices and much laughter in the house. "Well," said he, "I have heard many people wondering if the moon is inhabited, and now I am convinced that it is."

LOCAL NATURAL HISTORY.

In narrating the following unpublished fragments pertaining to *Local Natural History*, *&c.*, it is not assumed that even a tithe of the facts and incidents relating to this subject of the present and by-gone generation has been collected; but only such as I had some personal connection with, or had received from the principals concerned, or from some well-authenticated source.

It is hoped this effort may stimulate others to hunt up and collect such facts as opportunity may throw in their way, and thus preserve many interesting relics of the natural history of the county, which are now in danger of being for ever lost. Hundreds of local instances might be collected of the faithfulness and sagacity of the dog; the intelligence of the horse; the wiliness and shifts of the fox; and of the extraordinary actions of other animals. And it is not easy to imagine that any boy grown into a man could be indifferent to these; for all have a spice of enjoyment in the adventures of some or other kind of animals and of birds.

THE SLAUGHTER OF THE MILLOM PARK DEER.

About the end of the eighteenth century, the then Earl of Lonsdale, or some one for him, estimated the profit and loss of keeping and preserving the fallow deer, which in a great measure stocked Millom Park. The surrounding wall was scarce high enough to prevent their escape, if so inclined; but being little disturbed and well cared for, they enjoyed their beautiful, undulating home in quiet retirement. Occasionally an adventurous one would break bounds in an evening, and, finding more agreeable pasturage outside, would return to the herd towards morning, to repeat his depredations in the same way, when it suited his pleasure. This began to occur oftener than the neighbouring farmers and landowners found acceptable, and complaints were made. In time the strong deer seemed to mock at the attempts made to confine them within the park; and to prevent their ravages by hounding them homewards with dogs was only play to them; for some grew so bold, if unobserved, as to make their lairs for the day in the corn-fields where they fed in the night time, if the corn was tall enough to shield them from sight. They were too cunning to leave the park beyond an easy run in; and none were suffered to hunt the outlying deer. If the hounds were stealthily laid on the scent or view, the animal made a short run, and a vigorous leap landed him at home where the hounds were not allowed to follow. Or if they did chase within the forbidden limits, the disturbance they caused among the herd was so great, that the hunters were glad to get their dogs beat off as soon as they could, to avoid being prosecuted.

When a hard winter occurred, the animals required an allowance of hay for their sustenance. If this was omitted, considerable loss was sustained in some seasons; a further reason for this provision was, that if the deer were obliged to bite near the ground towards spring, when the May stinting time for cattle arrived, it was found that they kept the pasture so bare that

both cattle and deer were pinched, and no profit
could be derived from either. In every way the herd
must have been an unprofitable stock ; for scarcely
ever could as many be drafted and sold as would pay
the two keepers, besides the cost of the hay. His
lordship having other deer parks better worth maintaining, and this park, being at a distance from any of
his residences, seldom seen by him or any of his
family, was not important enough to be supported at
a considerable annual loss, when the ancient and
lordly towers of Millom Castle (where jurisdiction of
life and death used formerly to be exercised*) had
gone far to decay ; and it was decided that the aristo-
cratic adjunct of a deer preserve should be disparked
and turned to a more profitable account.

The herd numbered about one hundred or a little
over, and, when the order came for their destruction,
a sale was effected with a speculator from Darlington,
at a pound per head.

It was first attempted to take the deer with nets ;
and the neighbours were invited, with their dogs, to
drive them into the nets and witness the sport. In
high glee they mustered from all the neighbouring
vales in great force, well provided with ropes and
cords to bind the captured ; and they succeeded, after
many efforts, in driving the frightened animals within
the ring of nets where the poor prisoners were to be
caught, and secured in any way that could be invented ;
and great sport was anticipated. The nets were too
high for the deer to leap over, and were being gradually drawn closer while the pretty things were admired
as they paced about to find an opening. Finding
none, one of the patriarchs of the herd made a rush

* A stone pillar stands on an elevated bank, where the criminals were said
to be executed by hanging. It is less than half a mile from the Millom
Station, to the east, and about a score yards north of the line, and may easily
be seen from the passing train.

at the net, and, like an arrow from a bow, darted through it, and in spite of the efforts of the hunters in shouting and waving their hats and coats, and the furious barking of the dogs, the whole herd shot through the opening in a few seconds, trampling many a good sheep dog under their feet, and bounding away to the high grounds of the park in seemingly utter astonishment, without a single head being secured.

To make the matter worse, several men and boys, in their endeavours to prevent escape, got toppled over in rather a rough manner; and some were injured by the horns and hoofs of the frightened animals rushing through the crowd and bearing all before them, to the great amusement of those who were out of harm's way.

Some of the shepherds, whose valuable dogs were hurt, declared their dogs were worth more than all the deer in the park; and, though they could enjoy the sport, if they came again to assist, it should be without their dogs, which had been so serviceable on this occasion.

Being often shot at, and some wounded without being killed, the poor animals grew wild, and so exceedingly cautious and watchful, that it was very difficult for any one to get within killing range of them; and people began to tire of the sport which was now becoming laborious and so fruitless. Then, snares were laid in the tracks, with a view to entangle the feet, and others were hung from the branches of trees, under which the deer were attempted to be driven, in expectation of the horns being lassoed; but not a single animal was caught in either way. By swerving, or by stotting movement, the ground snares were passed by or over; and the pendant ones were either broken off or cleverly avoided; and these methods were soon abandoned.

What other means were attempted has not been recorded, but the gun was held to be the only chance of success; and five of the neighbouring yeomen, noted marksmen—"good men and true"—persevered in their self-appointed task till only two remained of the herd. These were long watched until one was brought down, but the other was too wily to allow of being shot.

At last the hounds were collected, and he was hunted and broke bounds, and afforded a few capital runs before the last of the herd was finally torn down.

And so ended the race of the "harts and hinds, wild boars and their kinds, and all aviaries of hawks," reserved by De Boyville * in the reign of Henry the First, when he gave all the parishes between Esk and Duddon to the abbey of St. Mary, at York.

WILD DEER OF ENNERDALE FOREST.

In 1841, the late Mr. John Wilson, of Kirklandhow, told me that when the wild deer inhabited the forest of Ennerdale, their depredations almost ruined the occupiers of the two small farms of Gillerthwaite, at the head of Ennerdale Water. During harvest, the animals were accustomed to come down from the mountains in the night time, and leap into the corn fields to eat what they could; and, on retiring, each of the old deer would take a sheaf of corn in its teeth and run.off with it to the mountains to eat at leisure; and would, in this stealthy way, take nearly the whole crop in two or three nights.

The inhabitants used to place a watchman, with dogs, to drive away the deer, and made use of other

* Lord of Millom.

devices to frighten them ; but the wily animals came so silently that they were seldom discovered in the dark, until each old deer was hastening away with a sheaf in the teeth ; and, when the dogs were let loose upon them, it was mere play for the deer to outstrip the dogs, and carry off their plunder to devour in safety in the rocky fastnesses, where neither dog nor man could safely pursue.

Finding their property taken away year after year, other methods were devised for protection ; the inhabitants collected a number of old scythes and pitchforks, and fixed them in the gaps and open places of the fences, with the points and edges inwards to the fields ; for the deer, in approaching, came leisurely on, but in retreating at full speed, with the dogs at their heels, rushed incautiously on the scythes and forks, and were impaled alive or otherwise cut or disabled, till the greater part was destroyed, and the inhabitants could again enjoy their crops in safety.

THE WILD CAT.

IN 1843, the late Mr. John Walker, of Ullock, told me that about fifty years before, Joseph Pearson, of Ullock, with the aid of his mastiff, killed a wild cat in Watern Woods, Loweswater, after a long chase and severe fight.   The cat weighed seventeen pounds.

These animals had been numerous in most of the wooded and rocky parts of the county, and had been very destructive to poultry and game, and occasionally to young lambs. From their great activity and ferocity they were more than a match for any but a very strong dog, single handed.   Pearson and his dog killed many.

THE EAGLE IN BORROWDALE.

ABOUT the year 1820, I heard the late Mr. John Braithwaite of Millgillhead, relate his encounter with an eagle. In his youth he was shepherd for his father, in Borrowdale; and in returning from the fell one misty afternoon, he heard his dog suddenly cry out as if in extreme distress. He ran in the direction of the sound, and at the foot of a steep crag he found his dog in misery indeed! A large eagle had fastened its beak on the dog's throat, a little below one ear, and one of the eagle's talons was firmly clutched in the dog's flank. The dog was howling at the top of its voice, and snapping at the bird as well as he could, but seldom getting a hold except at the edge of the wing; and the grip of the bird was so painful that the dog soon let go his hold. The eagle held on like a bull-dog, and the pair rolled one over the other, and leaped and flapped and bit and scratched so furiously, that, while their strength held out, it was dangerous to part them. The shepherd saw the danger his favourite dog was in, and was not slow to pull off his long-lapped, home-made, grey duffle coat; and throwing it over the two, they enveloped themselves in its thick folds, until the dog grew weak, and began to falter in its cry. Its master watched his opportunity to tie a handkerchief round the bird's wings and pinion them over its back; and then, with his fell-pole, to wrench off the hold of the eagle, and slip his coat again over it, and to roll it therein, so as it could not harm him. He bore his prize home under one arm, and his disabled dog under the other, and kept the noble bird in confinement many years. His dog recovered with difficulty, and would doubtless have been killed, had he not arrived in time for the rescue. He said, in the days he mentioned, eagles were not scarce in the higher mountains; and were very destructive to the sheep and lambs, as the bird in question had either driven a sheep over the crag, as they were known to do, and the fall had crushed it; or had slain and was feasting on it when the dog was attracted to it, and had quarrelled with the eagle for possession of the carcase.

THE EAGLE ROPE.

IN 1846, the late Mr. Ralph Douglas, of Keswick, said he went to live at Thornthwaite, in 1783, at fifteen years of age. He remembers seeing eagles frequently, and almost daily in the spring. sailing majestically overhead, and occasionally swooping down to the ground, as if seizing prey, and then flying off with it towards Borrowdale, where they usually had nests. At that time a long and strong rope was kept in Borrowdale, by subscription, for the purpose of letting down men into the rocks, to take the nests or young of the eagles. Very many of the inhabitants used to assemble to hold the rope, when a nest-robbing was projected. On one occasion when the man was drawn up, it was with fear and trembling till the man was safely landed with the prize of young birds; for they discovered that two of the three strands of the rope were chafed quite through by the sharp edges of the rocks. However, all was silently effected and the man was safe.

The rope was available for Buttermere, Ennerdale, Langdale, Eskdale, and other dales, but kept in Borrowdale; and was in requisition there nearly every year, and occasionally in the other vales; and the young eagles were sold for high prices. The eagles sometimes shifted their breeding quarters to other parts, when disturbed in Borrowdale. The rope was occasionally used in a similar manner for the release of crag-fast sheep ; that is, when the sheep wandered along the narrow ledges of rocks, where they had not room to turn round to retreat.

MORE EAGLES.

IN 1851, Mr. Fletcher Greenip, of Portinscale, told me that. a few years before, he saw three eagles in company, near the head of Bassenthwaite lake, during frost, apparently hunting the springs and unfrozen ditches for waterfowl ; and that Joseph Summers, of Castlerigg, saw seven eagles in company about the same period. Mr. Greenip would hardly be mistaken, for at that time he had a good collection of living birds of prey, including two or more eagles. The *Field* newspaper records three other instances of eagles having been seen, viz. :—In Little Langdale, in 1859; Newlands vale, in 1863 ; and Uldale, near Egremont, 1864.

THE MART IN BORROWDALE.

THE same old gentleman, Mr. John Braithwaite,* used to relate, that, while he acted as shepherd, he had occasionally missed sheep, one at a time ; and that when found they were invariably dead.

They were always found at the foot of some high rock, much mangled and bone-broken, and had been

* Vide p. 188.

bled by a bite in the throat. This was thought to be the work of a dog; and other surmises prevailed, without any certainty as to what was the real offender.

One day he had a clear proof of the mode of destruction, and of the culprit too. In scrambling through a rocky region he was surprised by the carcase of one of his wedders tumbling from ledge to ledge of the rock very near him, and falling with a heavy thud at the bottom. Hearing no dog bark or other sound leading to discovery, and suspecting foul play, he stood listening, and kept his dogs in. In a very short time he was still more surprised to see a yellow mart come hurrying down round the end of the crag, run direct to the mangled sheep, and fix its teeth in the jugular vein, and begin sucking the blood. He took time to be quite sure of the circumstance, and then let his two sheep dogs off in pursuit of the mart. They had seen it come to the dead sheep, and were with some difficulty kept quiet till leave was given, and then were down on him in a moment ; but he was too quick for them, and managed to get up into rough ground, where he had a great advantage over the dogs, as he could glide along narrow ledges where the dogs could not follow ; and, with his swift and peculiar snake-like motion, soon distanced them and effected a safe retreat.

After this discovery, he was hunted day after day till caught, and much rejoicing followed his death ; and many misdeeds were laid to his charge, which no animal of his kind was, till then, thought to be capable of accomplishing.

This sagacious animal, then, had been the sole depredator, it was believed, in all the previous instances, by chasing the sheep over precipices for his luxurious feast of the warm blood ; for after his capture no more were destroyed in the same way.

PIKE AND BUZZARD OR GLEAD.

WHETHER driven by hunger or impelled by a habitual propensity to take life, with which the buzzard is credited, an incident of one or the other occurred about the beginning of the nineteenth century. A large, dead bird of this species was found at the edge of the water in Ullock mill dam, on the Marron, having its claws firmly fixed in the back of a pike of a few pounds in weight; the fish being also dead. It would seem that the fish had been basking in a shallow; perhaps with the back out of water, as they sometimes do, and had been discovered by the bird, which had pounced upon it and fastened its hooked talons into a fish heavier than he could lift out of the water; that the pike had been so strong as to drag the prisoned bird under water and drown it, but could not liberate itself from the dead clutch of the buzzard, and both had come to an untimely end. Very rarely is a pike found in the Marron; and it was supposed the twain had been floated down the stream from Mockerkin Tarn in time of flood.

THE DOG'S REVENGE.

A BUTCHER, named Fearon, residing at Dean, was driving sheep over the open commons, to Whitehaven, for slaughter; when near Studfold, between the commons of Dean and Distington, the dog misbehaved and was chastised by his master, and slunk away, refusing to assist in driving the sheep. When Fearon was returning in the evening, the dog, a mongrel mastiff, rushed out of a ling-bed on Freerbank, and savagely attacked his master. The free use of the walking stick availed nothing, but the butcher's knife was fortunately at hand, and its assistance settled the matter; the brute was left dead on the moor.

Fearon was strong in the opinion that had he not been so well provided, or had refrained from the use of the knife, he would have been the victim of the dog's revenge.

BADGERS.

THESE animals are now extinct in the wild state in Cumberland, but were not scarce till about the end of the 18th century. The localities of their burrows and places of resort are still preserved in the many names of Brock hole, Brock stone, Tod hole, Tod hill, Tod dale, &c. The situations of many of these places seem more likely for the den of the badger than the bield of the fox; and though the fox was often called the Tod, there are good reasons for believing that name to have been applied to both the fox and the badger.

The badger inhabited the lower grounds where these names are mostly found. The range of the fox comprises both high and low; and both animals used similar burrows in the low country.

There were brock holes in a sand bank in Eskat woods near where the cottage now stands; and these animals being fond of basking in the sun, a hedger came suddenly upon two of them sleeping, and making a quick stroke with his bill hook he wounded one, but both got into their hole and were never seen again. These were the last known in that part.

FOX-HUNTING.

ONE of the natural born propensities of the Cumbrian is a love of the chase ; and though it may be less indulged in modern times, it is inherent in all.

Threescore years ago the enthusiasm of fox hunting was kept up as it was wont to be in times gone by, and was now and then exercised and celebrated in a peculiar manner. But a true picture of the fox-hunters of that day cannot be given without introducing a little of the rough and disagreeable side of it.

A credible hunter, who formed one of the party, related that after a very exciting run from near the Dash Waterfall, in Uldale, to Swineside in Mossdale, the fox was run into and killed by the hounds in a dairy, amid a great destruction of pottery and a plentiful splashing of milk and cream. The hunters adjourned to an inn near at hand, and, after a glass or two each, cut off the dead fox's feet, dipped them in a bowl of punch, and drank it to the success of foxhunting ! As their enthusiasm rose with their libations, they cut off the brush and stuck it in a candlestick to ornament the table; then castrated the dead animal and seasoned the next bowl therewith, drinking that too !!

What would modern foxhunters think of such endings as these? Such were not unusual then.

INSTINCT, OR WHAT?

WHAT an extraordinary faculty some animals possess of finding their way home when conveyed to a distance without being able or allowed to see the road they travel, or the objects they pass on the way !

Several years ago, a family of miners removed from Alston to Whitehaven, and stayed all night on their way, at Keswick. Their cat was taken the whole way in a covered basket, and was let out on arriving at their lodgings in Whitehaven.

For two days it remained quiet and appeared settled in its new abode ; but on the third day it was missed, and not heard of again for some months, until the owner had occasion to visit Alston, and there found his cat at the house he had left. On comparing dates it was found that the animal had only been a week on its return journey—a distance of about seventy miles by road.

This was related by the person at whose house the family had stayed at Keswick, and where the man slept on his second trip.

The cat could not safely travel by daylight, and even in the night time she would be liable to meet many interruptions from dogs and otherwise, and be obliged to frequently swerve from her course and take circuitous routes. It is likely she would have to traverse the indirect streets of Keswick and Penrith, and to surmount the bleak heights of Whinlatter and Hartside.

Could instinct be the guide that unerringly led her by the way she could not know, to her old home?

THE DOG AS A SHEEP WORRIER.

It may be remarked that each kind of dog, if of pure breed, has a peculiar and distinct mode of attacking other animals, and especially sheep.

The mastiff is now scarce and commonly chained, and is little known as a destroyer of sheep; and the bull-dog is not often accused of that crime, because it is seldom allowed to ramble from the house or heel of the owner; and, unless roused for a short course, both these are too slow of foot to do much harm. They stop their prey by grasping the nose or some part of the head.

The greyhound is more known as a destroyer of lambs than of sheep; and, with speed at command, its mode of attack is similar to that applied when in pursuit of the hare—that is, grasping the loins, or pitching the helpless animal into the air and seizing it by the back as it falls, and at once disabling it.

The pointer and setter usually fasten on the sheep or lamb by the flank, and hold on till the victim can be overturned or brought to a stand-still, when the operation is soon over. These commonly make their attack in the daytime, and are, generally, the most destructive dogs among sheep when they acquire a propensity for such tempting amusements; for their speed and endurance enable them to hold out for several hours at a stretch in their destructive career.

The sheep dog is entitled to the credit of being the cleverest of the dog tribe as a destroyer; for he goes about his work with more cunning than any other of his race, and it is seldom found out before much harm is done. In some cases many months have elapsed ere the true culprit could be detected, so wary has he been in all his proceedings. He takes his victim by the throat; overturns and throttles it at once. In his mad excitement he often leaves the poor animal struggling in the throes of death, and hurries off to add other unfortunates to his crime.

This dog, when at maturity, is seldom known to worry near home, or among the flock of his owner.

When once blooded he will sneak two or three miles away in the dark to a strange flock, and will sometimes entice a youngster along with him ; after a little play together, both attacking the same sheep, the older criminal at the throat, and the other wherever it can lay hold of, they soon make an end of the matter.

In the excitement of the chase the young dog is apt to give an occasional bark or *wilk*, as it is termed, and to cause detection. The old one never barks.

It seldom happens that the hound takes to worrying sheep. In the winter months he has his special duties to attend to, and these are more fascinating to him than the chase of a tar-coated sheep. During the rest of the year he indulges in a habit of laziness ; and, if liberally fed, his habit partly unfits him for preying on live mutton. There are occasional exceptions to all these, but they are rare.

Cross breeds and mongrel dogs have no settled mode of attack until well practised in the business, and then each adopts a system of its own or varies it to suit the whim of the moment.

The sheep dog commonly begins his sport about midnight ; and after a lively hour or so of destructive amusement, rolls and rubs himself on the grass, and is found at home in the morning, as clean and tidy, and as unconcerned and ready for his breakfast and work, as if he had been all night in his kennel, or sleeping at the foot of the straw stack. He seldom worries for a livelihood, or even partakes of the blood or flesh ; and all his energy, for the time, seems to be expended in sport or excitement. A clumsy whelp may come home towards morning with bloody marks on his head or legs, but he soon learns to know better, if not detected and hanged.

When a lad, the writer assisted in collecting and throwing into a disused pit more than forty dead lambs in one morning. This was the previous night's work of an idle cur, kept by a labouring man who had no use for it. The miscreant was detected at his work in early morning by the writer's father, who was on horseback, and followed the dog over hedge and ditch for a two-mile course to its home, and had it grudgingly destroyed. Three or four lambs had been worried on the same ground a few nights before, and all were bitten in the neck, doubtless by the same dog.

About two years previous to the above chase, the same horseman was inspecting his flock one morning on another heaf (Dean Common), when he saw the sheep violently disturbed; on galloping up to them he found a strong pointer dog, so earnest in its work of destruction, that he could not beat it off while in the saddle, and on alighting to thrash it, the furious creature turned to attack him; and, during his momentary act of remounting, it fell to its bloody work again. He then, in his excitement, attempted to ride it down, but it slipped aside from the horse's feet; and in its extreme fury would have continued to worry, but he chased it so close that it made off towards its home, and he followed it a distance of five miles, where he found its owner, who, being a surgeon, applied a safe and speedy remedy to it.

On his return he found it had destroyed some and greatly injured several of his own sheep, and some belonging to his neighbours. All of these were savagely torn in the flank, and some of the dead had their bowels protruding. These were all old sheep, but no match for the infuriated dog.

Instances might be multiplied of extensive sheep worrying, and scarce a vale can be found without its tale of destruction; some may enumerate several. These more often occurred on the low moors than on the mountains. On the fells large flocks were depastured; the dogs were fewer in number, were well broke, and had plenty of legitimate employment. The low commons were stocked with a few sheep belonging to each small farm around ; and each small farm kept one or more ill-trained curs, with little work for them to do. These, if not closely watched, found sport in chasing sheep occasionally, and sport led on to mischief. Happily such instances are less frequent now than fifty years ago.

It is somewhat rare to have a dog possessed of the faculty and inclination to *mark* sheep that are buried under a deep snow drift. Such dogs are of great value for that special purpose, but they become so wild with joy, in the act of releasing the sheep, that they would worry the excavated animal there and then if suffered, and are too apt to take up the business of worriers after their snowy duties are ended.

ENNERDALE PILLAR STONE.

In the early part of the present century, a reliable old dalesman told me that before the red deer were destroyed in the Crown Forest of Ennerdale, sheep used occasionally to venture upon the Pillar Stone in search of a chance bite of grass, while the deer occupied the surrounding forest, during the latter half of the previous century. Some of the old stags also chose the same elevated stand as a look-out. If they found a sheep or two in possession, they invariably forked them over the side, treating them to a fall of about 200 feet. To prevent such losses, the shepherds assembled at the place, and handed stones from one to another along the dangerous entrance neck, and had a wall built high enough to prevent the ingress of sheep and deer.

THE WILD DOG OF ENNERDALE.

A RECENT occurrence recalled to my memory the misdeeds of the Ennerdale dog.   These were so numerous and audacious, and so unusual, that whatsoever mischief other dogs might have done in other years, their deeds of destruction were all greatly overshadowed by the doings of this animal in the year 1810. "T' girt dog" was talked about, and dreamt about, and written about, to the utter exclusion of nearly every other topic in Ennerdale and Kinniside, and all the vales round about there ; for the number of sheep he destroyed was amazing, and the difficulties experienced in taking him were beyond belief.   The tiger of India seldom undergoes more than two or three short chases before he is destroyed ; and the wolf of the Russian forests is usually taken after one long-winded run, when he can be singled out from his pack.   But this creature frequently tired out the fleetest pack of hounds selected purposely for their endurance, and for a long time his cunning baffled all attempts to entrap or destroy him.

It is upwards of half a century ago, but many of the incidents in connection with the depredations and exciting chases of this wonderful dog are fresh in my memory, and were recorded as well soon after their occurrence ; others have been related to me by persons who suffered losses of sheep by him, and who took active part in the watchings for, and ultimate capture of the animal.   Amongst the rest, Mr. John Steel, of Asby, who fired the fatal shot, has carefully written his recollections of the affair to me ; and, though he is now turned of four-score, can narrate circumstantially the incidents of the year so eventful to the welfare of his flock and of every flock in the district.

No one knew to whom the dog had belonged, or whence he came ; but being of a mongrel breed, and excessively shy, it was conjectured he had escaped from the chain of some gipsy troop. He was a smooth-haired dog, of a tawny mouse colour, with dark streaks, in tiger fashion, over his hide ; and appeared to be a cross between mastiff and greyhound. Strongly built and of good speed, being both well fed and well exercised, his endurance was very great. His first appearance in the district was on or about the 10th May, 1810, when he was seen by Mr. Mossop, of Thornholme, who was near, and noticed him as a stranger. His worrying exploits followed soon after ; and from that time till his being shot in September following, he was not known to have fed on anything but living mutton, or, at least, the flesh of lambs and sheep before the carcases had time to cool. From one sheep he was scared during his feast, and when the shepherd examined the carcase, the flesh had been torn from the ribs behind the shoulder, and the *still beating* heart was laid bare and visible. He was once seen to run down a fine ram at early dawn ; and, without killing it, to tear out and swallow lumps of living flesh from the hind quarters of the tortured animal while it stood on its feet, without the power to resist or flee, yet with sufficient life to crawl forward on its fore legs. He would sometimes wantonly destroy seven or eight sheep in one night ; and all his work was done so silently that no one ever heard him either bark or growl.

At other times, when a lazy fit came over him, or

when he had been fatigued by a long chase, a single life and the tit-bits it afforded would satisfy him for the time—taking his epicurean meal from a choice part of the carcase. He seldom fed during the day; and his cunning was such that he did not attack the same flock or sport on the same ground on two successive nights, often removing two or three miles for his next meal. His sagacity was so matured that his choice often fell on the best. or one of the plumpest, of the flock; and his long practice enabled him to dexterously abstract his great luxury, the warm blood, from the jugular vein; and if not with surgical precision, it was always with deadly certainty, for none ever survived the operation. The report was current at the time that he commonly opened the vein of the same side of the neck.

He was often chased from the fells by the shepherds and their dogs, as well as by hounds; and many an enlivening gallop has been enjoyed at the unusual season of summer, by occasional horsemen who have been crossed and surprised by the chase in full cry. So exciting did it become, that when the cheering echoes gave notice that the game was on foot, horses were hastily unyoked from carts or ploughs, and mounted bare back, and ridden as long as they could go, and then left to take their chance whilst the riders continued the chase on foot. It was no uncommon sight to see a score or two of men running at the top of their speed after the hounds, without hats or coats, to the wonder of the inhabitants of the districts they passed through; and many well-to-do yeomen have been obliged to strangers for hospitable refreshment at the end of an unsuccessful chase, ending many miles from home or the starting place, having joined the hunt in their hurry with empty pockets.

All through his career of depredation he was exceed-

ingly cautious and provident in the selection of his
resting places ; most frequently choosing places where
a good view was obtainable, and not seldom on the
bare rock, where his dingy colour prevented him being
descried on stealing away.   For a few weeks at first,
it was thought, from his shy habits, that it would be
easily possible to drive him out of the country.   But
this was an entire fallacy ; for he seemed to have
settled down to the locality as his regal domain ; and
though many a time chased at full speed for ten or fifteen miles right away, he was generally discovered by
his murderous deeds to have returned during the first
or second night following.

A few hounds had been usually kept in the neighbourhood to aid in the destruction of the fell foxes,
which took tribute of lambs in the spring, and of geese
and poultry at other seasons.   These hounds, distributed among the farm houses in the vale of Ennerdale
and Kinniside, and being allowed to run at large, were
easily assembled by the halloo of any shepherd espy-
ing the dog, and were often available in chase though
of no real use ; for the dog got so familiarised with their
harmlessness, that, speedy and enduring as they were,
he has been known to wait for the leading dog and
give the fore-leg such a crushing snap with his powerful jaws that none of the pack would attack him twice.
From the unequal speed of the local hounds, he seldom had more than one dog to contend with at a
time, and his victory was quick and effectual.

The men of the district volunteered to watch in
turns on successive nights, armed with guns or other
weapons ; and when these were wearied out other
volunteers came in from a distance, or were hired to
watch on the mountains through the nights, rain or
fair ; and the hounds were distributed in leading
among them, covering many miles of the ground

nightly. If any one fired a shot, or gave the view
halloo, the dogs were let loose, and were soon laid on
the scent, pursuing it with the same bristling energy
that accompanies the chase of the fox. But no dog
had any chance to engage him singly in battle till the
rest came up. Various schemes were tried to entice
him within shooting range, such as tethering bitches
in heat on his domain ; but though the cunning brute
was often seen to hover about them, yet he took especial care to keep out of harm's way. Poison was tried,
but soon abandoned, on account of the risk of injury
to other dogs. The bait of the sheep already destroyed
had no effect on him, for he was too well versed as an
epicure to touch a dead carcase if ever so fresh. Week
after week, the excitement was kept up. The whole
conversation of the neighbourhood, and of adjoining
vales, was engrossed by the interesting topic of the
" worrying dog." At home or abroad, at church or
market or fair, if an Ennerdale or Kinniside man was
met with, " t'girt dog " was all he could talk about or
think about.

Newspapers reported his doings, and friend wrote to
distant friend about him, but no one took time to
write a song about him. If any songs have been
written, I trust that either John Steel, the slayer of the
dog, or some one else, will send them to the publisher
of this work whatever the quality may be.

Every man who could obtain a gun, whether capable of using it with effect or not, was called out, or
thought himself called out, to watch or pursue, daily
or nightly ; and many an idle or lazy fellow got or
took holiday from work to mix with the truly anxious
shepherds, and to snoozle under a rock in the night,
or stretch his lazy carcase on the heather in the day,
with a gun, or a pitchfork, or a fell pole in his hand,
under pretence of watching for the wild dog.

Men were harassed and tired out by continuous watchings by night, and running the chase by day. Families were disturbed in the nights to prepare refreshments for their fatigued male inmates, or for neighbours who dropped in at the unbarred doors of the houses nearest at hand at all hours of the night. Children durst not go to school or be out alone, and they often screamed with fright at the smallest nocturnal sounds, or in their dreams; while women were exhausted with the toil of the farm their husbands and brothers were obliged to abandon to their care. The hay crop and all field labours were neglected, or done by hurried and incomplete snatches, no one attempting jobs that could not be performed in an hour or two,—every eye on the look out, and every ear listening for the alarm of the frequent hunt, which every one was ready to join in. Property was disappearing in the shape of sheep worried, crops wasting, wages paid for no return, time lost, and work of all kinds left undone. Cows were occasionally unmilked, and horses unfed or undressed. Many fields of haygrass were not cut, and corn would in all likelihood have shared the same fate if an end had not opportunely come.

There are few dogs that do not occasionally indulge in a long and melancholy howl, when quite alone, and listening to the distant howl of other dogs; but " the Worrying Dog of Ennerdale " was never known to utter a vocal sound. And, along with this remarkable trait, his senses of sight, hearing, and scent, were so acute that it was rare indeed for any one to come upon him unawares in the day-time. On the few occasions when he was accidentally approached in day-light he exhibited nothing vicious, and always fled hastily.

On one occasion the late Willy Jackson, of Swinside (the respected father of the celebrated wrestler), was leaving his house with his loaded gun, when, quite unexpectedly, he saw the dog in the act of lifting his hind leg against a tall thistle, within about thirty yards of him.   He raised his gun and took steady aim, with a strong determination to end the life of the dog and the present troubles of the district, but on pulling the trigger his untrusty flint gun missed fire, and away went the dog.

The protracted excitement became so great and annoying, and the losses so heavy, that when the July sheepshearings or clippings came on, a subscription was determined upon for collecting and maintaining a more efficient pack of the swiftest and most vicious hounds that could be found; and a very fine lot of swift and spirited dogs were procured, thought to be equal to any emergency of the kind.

In that year the late Mr. John Russell, who had a brewery in Whitehaven, and a sheep farm of some three thousand acres in Ennerdale, whose flock suffered with the rest, offered ale to the watchers, and a reward of ten pounds for the capture of the dog, dead or alive.   The other sheepowners raised about twelve pounds among themselves as a fund for refreshments, and a free whittlegate was the order of the day to all who professed to be watchers or pursuers.

These measures caused much enthusiasm, and great numbers of men assembled, sometimes by request or appointment, and sometimes voluntarily.   On a fine July morning about two hundred men and a number of hounds in couples were spread over the Kinniside fells to search for the dog, and were not long in rousing their game about the part of the mountain called Hope-head.   The view halloo by forty or fifty men soon brought the hounds to the place, and the scent being fresh a quick and hopeful run took place towards Wasdale-head ; but the destroyer found his carcase too heavy to make good way over the crags and rough fells, and turned his course back by the heights overlooking Wastwater—the echoes of the hunt ringing across the lake and reverberating from the Screes —to the smoother ground of Brownyedge and Stockdale Moor, and took shelter in a cornfield at Priorscale, having thrown the hounds and most of the men off his track for a time by his crafty turnings, and only about forty of the two hundred men coming down to the field where it was expected the dog was resting. Watchers were set round the field till more hounds were collected by the present Mr. Mossop, of Thornholme (" merry Charlie "), who on his fast pony scoured the district where dogs were kept, and soon had a reinforcement ; but it was too late — the dog had stolen away without resting. He was traced by a slow hunt, and heard of now and then through Calder and Seascale, till night coming on he was finally lost in Drigg, and the weary hunters had to return unsuccessful.

Seldom a week elapsed without the dog being once or twice chased out of the district, most frequently down into the lower country where the level land better suited his running, and where the softer ground of the fields did less harm to his feet.

On one occasion he was run across the vale of Ennerdale through Loweswater, and lost in the mist and night. Next morning his traces were found on his old ground by two or three fresh carcases. On another occasion he was run from Kinniside fells through Lamplugh and Dean, crossed the river Marron several times, and rested in a plantation near Clifton, till a number of horsemen and some footmen came up and the hounds again aroused him and ran him to the Derwent and there lost him, after an ex-

hausting run of nearly twenty miles. This chase was
more severe than usual, and he took two days to rest
and return in.

Many times he was run in the same direction, and
always found means to escape.   One Saturday night
a great number of men was dispersed over the high
fells, watching with guns and hounds, but he avoided
them and took his supper on a distant mountain ; and
the men not meeting with him, came down about
eleven o'clock on Sunday morning and separated about
Swinside lane end.   In a few minutes after, Willy
Lamb gave the " view halloo."   He had started the
beast in crossing the wooded gill, and away went the
dog with the hounds in full cry after him.   The hunt
passed Ennerdale Church during service ; and the
male part of the congregation, liking the cry of the
hounds better than the sermon, ran out and followed.
It has been said the Rev. Mr. Ponsonby could not
resist, and went in pursuit as far as he was able.*
This run ended at Fitz Mill, near Cockermouth, in a
storm which the wearied men and dogs had to encounter in a twelve-miles return.

Next morning the dog was seen by Anthony Atkin-
son to steal into a grassy hedge and lie down to rest.
Such an opportunity seldom occurred and was not to
be lost.   Anthony charged his gun with swan shot
and crept cautiously towards the place, with a determination to have as close a shot as he could ; but the
wily animal was on the watch, and stole away at a
long-shot distance with three of Anthony's pellets sticking harmlessly in his hide, as it proved when the skin
was taken off some weeks after.

Once he led his pursuers a weary chase to Seaton,
or Camerton, and was lost in the whinny covers there;

* The discipline of the Church was not strict at that period, and the excitement of the time and district might well have caused such an act, but it
is not confirmed

and I well remember the hunters, some on foot and some on horseback, returning late and weary; some without hats, and some without coats, which they had thrown off to lighten their burdens in the hot pursuit. At another time, John Steel, of Birkmoss, was leading two noted hounds from Gosforth over the Kinniside fells, and when near Swarthgill head. about one in the morning, his dogs struggled violently to get away although he could not see or hear anything to excite them. Not long after he met the other hounds on the drag of the wild dog, which they ran almost direct to the place where his two hounds had been so difficult to restrain, and there were found three sheep newly killed—so quietly was the work of destruction done. That morning the dog was run to and lost at Irton.

He was once run from the head of Ennerdale lake over the tops of the Kinniside range by Dent and Egremont to St. Bees, where he avoided capture. The same evening he was seen to steal away from a garden where he had secreted himself till danger was over, but no one had then the means of capture or pursuit ready. This day a violent storm came on, and many of the pursuers, having left their coats and waistcoats on the fells, were soaked and battered by the rain and wind on their return, till some of them took colds which remained with them till death.

A Mrs. Russell, visiting at Birkmoss, went to pull a few apples in an orchard near the river Ehen, and returned immediately in great alarm, saying she had seen "an awful looking wild beast" resting in the long grass under the very tree she intended to take apples from. John Steel had just returned from his watching on the fell, and well knew what the wild beast would be; so he speedily placed a person to watch the dog and hallooed for the hounds. In half an hour the pack had assembled, with some scores of men, but

P

the beast had crept off unseen by the watcher, and was hidden in another place. He was quickly found, and started, with the hounds at his heels and the shouts of the many hunters ringing around him. So puzzled was the animal to get outside the gunless crowd, that he bolted between the crooked legs of Jack Wilson, a deaf old man who was stooping to gather sticks, and quite unaware of what was going on around him till the dog glided under his nose and made its escape. Jack was sure it was a lion ! The hounds again ran him near to St. Bees, and again he foiled them.

On another occasion the dog had been seen, and a number of men soon mustered, thirteen of whom were armed with loaded guns and stationed at different parts of the wood and fields where he was believed to be lurking. The halloo was soon heard, and every armed man was in hopes of earning the ten pounds reward. The dog ran in the direction where Will Rothery was stationed with gun in hand ; but so much was Will overcome by his near and first view of the creature which had become so fearful a scourge in the country, that instead of lifting his gun to take aim, he quietly stepped back and suffered the dog to pass at a short pistol-shot distance, without attempting to do him any harm ; merely exclaiming, with more fear than piety, " Skerse, what a dog !"

Many other long and arduous chases took place, but, the incidents not varying much, a full recital might become tedious.

As the summer advanced, and the crops got full on the ground, it was found useless to continue chasing the dog ; for, if run up to, no dog hitherto laid on could match him, and he got so well acquainted with the country for many miles around the district chosen as his home, that, after leading his pursuers many a long and weary chase, he always threw the hounds off the scent by some clever manœuvre ; often gliding from one cornfield to another, where the hunters would not go in lest they should injure the growing crops in assisting the hounds. In this way it was found he sometimes doubled and passed his pursuers, but more often led them a headlong course.

At last it was thought better to waste less time over him till some of the crops were cut, and then one available source, at least, of his deceptions, would be taken away. And people began to find out that the loss of even three or four sheep in a night, for two or three nights in the week, was not so much as the additional loss of their ripe crops would be, if they continued the earnest play of hunting an animal which hitherto had baffled all their skill and exertions. So it was agreed that a cessation of arms should take place on the side of the pursuers, for two or three weeks till the land was partly cleared, and the crops saved ; and then to resume offensive operations with increased vigour.

A chance incident soon overruled this determination, for, on the 12th of September, the dog was seen by Jonathan Patrickson to go into a cornfield.

Jonathan quietly said, "Aa'l let ta lig theer a bit, me lad, but aa'l want to see tha just noo."

Away went the old man, and, without the usual noise, soon raised men enow to surround the field ; and as some in their haste came unprovided with guns, a halt was whispered round to wait till more guns were brought and the hounds collected. When a good muster of guns and men with dogs were got together, the wild dog was disturbed out of the corn ; and only the old man who had seen him go into the field was lucky enough to get a shot at him, and to wound him in the hind quarters. This took a little off his speed, and enabled the hounds to keep well up to him, but none durst or did engage him. And, though partly disabled, he kept long on his legs and was often headed and turned by the numerous parties of pursuers, several of whom met him in his circuitous route from the upper side of Kinniside, by Eskat, Arlecdon, and Asby, by Rowrah and Stockhow Hall, to the river Ehen. Each of these parties he shied, and turned in a new direction till he got wearied. He was quietly taking a cold bath in the river, with the blown hounds as quietly looking on, when John Steel came up with his gun laden with small bullets, but durst not shoot, lest he should injure some of the hounds. When the dog caught sight of him it made off to Eskat woods, with the hounds and John on its track, and after a few turnings in the wood, amid the greatest excitement of dogs and men, a fair chance offered, and the fatal discharge was made by John Steel, when the destroyer fell to rise no more, and the marksman received his well-earned reward of ten pounds, with the hearty congratulations of all assembled.

After many a kick at the dead brute, the carcase was carried in triumph to the inns at Ennerdale Bridge; and the cheering and rejoicing there were so great that it was many days ere the shepherd inhabitants of the vale settled to their usual pursuits.

The dead carcase of the dog weighed eight imperial stones.

Since that eventful year, no extensive worrying of sheep has occurred there.

The stuffed skin of the "wild dog" was exhibited in Hutton's Museum, at Keswick, with a collar round the neck, stating that the wearer had been the destroyer of nearly three hundred sheep and lambs in the five months of his Ennerdale campaign.

THE CORNCRAKE.

THIS bird has the reputation of being a ventriloquist, and it possesses the instinct to feign death when in danger.

My son heard the scream of a bird as if in distress. Proceeding in the direction of the sound, and cautiously peeping through a hedge, he saw a young corncrake in the bottom of a dry gutter, crying out as if it wanted help. It caught sight of him, and with a despairing shriek it toppled over and lay as if dead —its wings spread and its head down among the weeds. He was trying to turn it over with his stick, when it quickly sprang up and ran off, evidently a sound bird.

ANIMAL SYMPATHY.

A FARMER in Loweswater had a horse which was apt to kick or bite any one but a son who was of weak intellect. A friendship had been established between the two, and the horse submitted to the lad in perfect quietness, the lad treating his friend with uniform kindness, which perhaps the rest of the family had not always done. One day a neighbour remarked to the father that it was scarcely safe to trust the young man with such a horse. The old man was of few words and very seriously said, "A mad horse 'll nut strike at a feùll!"

PLAYFULNESS IN HORSES.

MOST horses are of a playful disposition among their own kind whilst young, but not many attempt to play with other animals.

A two-year old colt I had was an exception. Having no horse to play with or tease, he took a delight in singling out a sheep or a cow, and would chase it in a canter, threading through among the others, still keeping to the same.

When the animal became blown and attempted to slack or stop, the colt would nip its rump and make it go till it was exhausted and obliged to lay down. If the lively colt had satisfied its craving for fun and action, it would stand near its victim ; but if not, another was selected and the process repeated. Once it chased a fine Leicester ewe to death, and then was punished by imprisonment. Another, a small pony which had been foaled in the workings of a ninety fathom coal pit, began this trick on being let loose on the green sward ; and in the exuberance of its enjoyment of companions in the daylight, ran a heifer till she laid down and died. These are not solitary instances. I have known several, varying in parti culars but all tending to shew the delight the chaser had in his pastime irrespective of consequences to others. Sometimes the horse, impatient of the slow canter. would throw up its heels and tail and take a furious galloping circuit—now and then rearing and kicking, by way of getting rid of a part of its super-abundant energy; then return and select the same or another animal to begin a like course of teasing and chasing, repeating the performance till the chased gave in or the chaser was satisfied.

INTELLIGENCE OR REASON ?

WE hear and read of many instances of intelligence among horses, and some approaching the verge of reason.

I had a fine little bay mare which had been a doctor's saddle beast for three or four years at Caldbeck. I bought her solely for the saddle, riding to fairs, &c., and occasionally taking part in driving cattle. One day when about two miles from home and having a score of heifers before me on the road, I alighted, and throwing the reins over her neck, let her go, believing she was so quiet as to be trusted to go gently along. In a few minutes she suddenly trotted forward to near the head of the drove and fell in behind the foremost three or four, drove them at the ordinary pace and allowed none of them to drop back. If any of the followers attempted to pass her in order to join the leaders, her ears were laid back and she sprang forward to intercept their advance. To my surprise she kept her station till reaching home.

On previous occasions when riding behind a drove I had been much amused at her acting the dog and crossing the road without my guidance to nip the rump of a loiterer. It is a great help in driving a number of cattle, for a man to go forward and take a few before him by way of leading the rest onward. How the intelligent animal got to understand driving cattle without experience or training is very singular; and she was equally ready and able to take the leading part or to drive behind, being very patient with all that were tolerably tractable, but generally impressed her first nip so vigorously that if only her ears were laid back and her nose poked towards the offender no further reminder was needful. Although so quiet when on what she seemed to think her duty—being always in good condition she was as playful as a kitten when clear of saddle and bridle and turned loose in the field, where she would play a variety of antics indicative of great enjoyment. People commonly deny the power of reasoning to animals, but this one must have been an observing and thinking creature, and capable of drawing conclusions altogether different from the promptings of instinct.

Later I had a strong grey horse, Jerry. While out at grass a painful swelling began on his brisket, and a veterinary was called in. The horse was brought and backed into a shed, where relief was given by an operation which had to be repeated daily. Next day he was brought and backed in about the same hour as before, the operation performed, and relief appeared to be felt.

On the third day, and on every succeeding day till a cure was effected, Jerry came and very orderly backed himself into the shed at the usual hour; was duly attended to and shewed the same symptoms of anxiety to be dressed as he would for an expected feed of corn. Before the swelling entirely disappeared he ceased to come, for evidently the pain was gone and he had no further need of assistance.

ILLUSTRATIONS OF CUMBERLAND WORDS.

THE DOUBLE MEANING.

Two frolicsome young men called on the late Mrs. Braithwaite, who kept an inn at Ravenglass, for refreshment; and as eggs were to form part of their meal, Mrs. B. inquired if they would have them boiled hard or soft, or how? Expecting some fun would arise out of it, they chose to have them *how*—not thinking the word meant hollow or empty. The good landlady was as wide awake as the young men, and met their saucy answer by blowing the contents out of the eggs and serving up the empty shells.

LEAH WOOD.

A poor old woman, who enjoyed the now almost extinct Christian name of Leah, resided in one of the last of the cottages connected with the Roman encampment at Old Carlisle. She had a strong idea regarding a future life; and, with a little play upon words, used to say, " I'll 'peer hee if I dee peer,"—meaning that she hoped to appear high though she might die in poverty.

TWO LITTLE MISTAKES.

A cow-doctor went to see an old woman's sick cow at Grinsdale, and prescribed a certain quantity of Bole Ammoniac to be boiled in new milk and given to the cow.　On his next visit she said to the doctor, "I cudn't git a oald alminac in o' Grinsdale, seah I boil't her a oald Chivvy Chess and gave her, and that dud reet weel."　"Reet, my bairn, reet," says he.

STICKING AT K.

Tommy Stamper, of ——, near Penrith, sent his twelve year old son to school.　After a few months, a neighbour asked the schoolmaster how the lad got on in learning.　The reply was, "He's stickin' at K.　I knew he wad be a dulbert, for his fadder was yan."

PRIEST'S WALKING STICK.

A clergyman who had mislaid his walking stick made inquiry about it of his landlady, who called to her daughter, "Jane Ann, whoar t' priest's kebby?"— walking stick.

THE POWER OF LANGUAGE.

Doctor to sick child—"Open your mouth, child, and put out your tongue."　No response ; but a vacant stare. "This must be a very stupid child of yours, my good woman." "It's ye 'at's stupid. Neabody but a feull wad talk tul a bairn that way. Oppen thy gob, hinny, an' put out thy lolly." The child was all obedience when addressed in a language it understood.

JACK ROBINSON.

A LOCOMOTIVE engine having got off the rails of the Cockermouth line, a gang of men were busily employed in endeavouring to replace it. An officious Newcastle by-stander suggested that if they would do so and so, they would get it on the rails " afooa yan could say Jack Wobison," when a Cumberland platelayer replied, "If she bides off till *thou* can say Jack Robison she'll hev a lang wait."

THE ROAD TO HENSINGHAM.

EARLY one morning a gentleman met a young man from the country, in Whitehaven, who, pointing up Lowther-street, inquired, "Is that t' bainest rwoad to Hensygem?" The gentleman, very sensibly, replied in the dialect the querist best understood, " Ey, thoo mun gang reet forrat and hod up t' brow, an' it's theer reet eb'n fornenst tha."

HEG OR EGG.

A WELL-TO-DO mason of Whitehaven about to sit down to breakfast, said to his daughter, in the vernacular of most of the seaport towns of Cumberland, " Bessy, boil me a heg."   Bessy had learnt more of the proprieties of speech and ventured to say, " Father, you should have said an egg."   John, not seeing his error, and not relishing to be corrected by his daughter, retorted, " Than gang and boil me two negs."

THE LAWYERS PUZZLED.

In a recent trial at the assizes at Carlisle, a genuine Cumbrian was under cross-examination relating to a quarrel and disturbance which occurred near Hawksdale bridge end, near to the sluice which supplies the Bishop's mill, &c., with water, when the following colloquy took place :—

Counsel—" Now, my man, did this happen on the North or South side of the river?"

Witness—" North or South?   'T was t' *cloor heed* side aa tell ye."

The Court and Bar were amused, and were alike at sea, until a grey-headed juryman explained that Solomon, the witness, referred to the side where the sluice was.

The witness was a native of Matterdale where the word still survives.

SCHOOLMASTER ABSENT.

The following is a literal transcript of a note received by a medical gentleman of Keswick, in 1860, from a patient.

Barkesole Jen

" the sick nume of her lims an no
" hopitite and cold and shiviry and
" fosht of wind and no tost in my
" mouth."

Translation attempted :

B———e, January.

The sick person is benumbed in her limbs, has no appetite, is cold and shivering, and troubled with flatulence, and has no relish for anything.

HORS DE COMBAT.

SCENE, river Derwent. Very patient angler to his friend —" Aa've fisht this whol in o' weather for a fortneth successfully widout gittan a bite, and to mend o' I heukt a stob and lost my strop and iver so mickle tackle; and o' togidder I was putten horse de contract."

ANECDOTES OF THE FARM.

As many items in this volume have had their origin amongst the rural population, a number of them are given in a collective form to show a little of what has occasionally occurred among the agricultural community in the past and present generations, as affecting their habits and manners ; and as contrasting with the rapid transition now taking place in the education and acquirements of that class by the general spread of information.

THE EFFECT OF UNBELIEF.

THE old aphorism that the buyer ought not to be ignorant of anything the seller knows is too seldom acted upon.

A Quaker standing in the fair, with a milk cow for sale, was asked by a farmer if she gave much milk? " Yes, friend ; but thou seest the milk goes in at the mouth." John took this to mean that she would milk well if fed well. Eventually a bargain was struck. Next week the Quaker met with John exposing the cow for sale in another market, and exclaimed, " What, tired of thy cow already, friend ?" " Ey, d—n her, she sooks her sel." " Well, friend, I told thee the milk went in at the mouth, but thou would not believe me."

SLORPING.

A century ago, many sets of farm buildings consisted of oblong blocks adjoining the farm yards. The dwelling at one end of the block was separated from the out buildings by a covered passage. There was an inner door opening out of the passage into the kitchen or living room, and another on the opposite side into the byre ; and the passage was a common thoroughfare for men and dogs, horses, cattle, wheelbarrow, poultry, &c. It occurred one morning, at a house of this description, near Wigton, that one of the farmer's sons was endeavouring, unsuccessfully, to conduct a mare and young foal through the passage while the father was labouring at his porridge and milk in the kitchen, and making a very audible noise in the act of clearing the spoon of its contents. The foal would not enter the passage and the mare refused to go without it. The son called out, "Slorp easy, fadder. T'meer kens tha, bit t' fwoal dizzent." No doubt the foal would gain courage when the noise ceased.

<hr>

MERITED DISGRACE.

Joseph Sibson, when farming at Canonby Hall, placed great confidence in the indications of his barometer. On retiring to bed one night during hay time, he remarked that they would be able to take in a great quantity of dry hay next day as the mercury was rising.

Next morning rain was falling plentifully. In his passion he took down his weatherglass, and spitefully threw it on the midden—"Thou's a leer, and I'll hev nea leers about my house."

WATER STRONGER THAN RUM.

THE same Joseph Sibson was as staunch a teetotaller all his long life as any in this professed age of abstainers.

One day while exhibiting his grain, noted for excellence, in Cockermouth market, a neighbour offered to treat him with a glass of rum, saying it would strengthen him. "Nay, nay," says Joe, "I'll hae nin on't; my coald water's stranger nor thy rum." They parted and met no more that day till Joe was driving homewards, about a mile out of Cockermouth, when his neighbour staggered out from the hedge-side and asked to be allowed to ride home in the cart. "Ey," says Joe, "and I'll help thee to get in. I telt thee my coald water was stranger nor thy rum, and thou sees I can gang heamm without help, and thou cannot."

"BODDERMENTS" OF FARMING.

ILLUSTRATIVE of the low scale of intellect possessed by some (fortunately few) of the Cumberland peasantry, and of the imperfect knowledge of their duties by others who bargain to be paid for what they know they cannot perform, and of the difficulty and trials of patience a master has to experience in training such lubbers, the following may be recorded:—

The late Mr. R. Jefferson, of Cunningarth, hired two men from Bewcastle, on the same day, as competent ploughmen. On the first morning after entering service, they were sent, each with a pair of horses, to plough. The head man followed soon after to see how things went on, and met one of the men returning with his horses. "Well, Tom, what's the matter?"

"O Wully!" said the ploughman, "the plugh ran into the grun', and the horses couldna poo her oot ageann." The bolt of the plough bridle had slipped out, and the ignoramus had fixed it in the bridle *below* the beam, giving the plough such hold of the ground that, had the horses been strong enough, they must have drawn the plough bodily into the earth! After getting this team into working order, the bailiff observed some zig-zag movements going on with the other ploughman. He was amused with the blunders of the first, but a sight of the second tried his patience very hard, and caused him to remark sharply—"Now, Alic, you're making queer work." The apologetic remark was, "Weel, Wully, the plugh grippit the grun' better i' the mwornin ner she diz the noo." On examination, the sock or share had come off, and the blunderer number two had never missed it, but was scratching away under an impression that something must be wrong; as he did not know what ailed the plough, he persevered in the idea that if the work went on he might be right in the end. Such are part of the "bodderments" of farming.

Another instance may be quoted. Mr. Jefferson, of Preston Hows, had a lad from the workhouse as servant. The lad had been pretty well drilled in the rudiments of education; but his ignorance of the ways of the world, and of common things around him, was more than might be expected even from the limited experience of workhouse life. One day the chief business of the farm was carting manure to a distant field, and having had some little training on the farm, the lad's job was to meet and exchange the laden and empty carts on the road, that is, to "lead between." Mr. J. saw him safely out of the yard with a full cart, and followed in a few minutes to see what progress was being made in the field. He had not gone far when he met the lad whistling leisurely homewards with his hands in his pockets, without any signs of hurry or alarm.   No inquiry was made and no explanation given, until the lad came close up to the master and quietly said, " Please, master, Beauty's tottled over."   He had left the mare and cart, heels uppermost, in the dyke gutter, and it did not occur to him that haste was necessary to have the poor animal relieved.   This lad's good humour and innocent ways were often amusing, but sometimes of a costly nature to the master.

A TENANT'S GOODWILL.

A CUMBERLAND landowner had a deaf tenant in arrears with his rent.   The tenant came in high glee, saying he had come to pay all he owed.

Landlord—"I am very glad of it John, but they tell me you have been selling straw from off my property, which you had no right to do."

John—Putting his hand behind his ear—"Haye?"

Landlord (loudly)—"They tell me you sell straw off the farm."

John, after some difficulty in understanding what his landlord meant, or in framing his answer, said, "Sell strea!   Ey, I wad sell yan o' t' fields, landlord, rayder ner you sud gang widout yer rent."

BUILDING WITHOUT A PLAN.

A ROUGH-AND-READY one was Jonathan Sewell.   He was set to making a haystack when living at Stockhow Hall; and William Fearon, who had been some years a sailor, was ordered to fork the hay to him. When the stack was rather more than half built, down it came and Jonathan with it. Foaming with rage and sputtering tobacco on all sides, Jonathan roared out, "D—n tha, Will, cuddent thou ha' telt ma t' stack was cumman down?" Very coolly and sarcastically Fearon replied, "Jonathan, if thou had told me what thou intended to do I could have told thee long since, but no man in England could guess thou was building a haystack."

In Jonathan's day, money transactions frequently took place without security or even written memorandum, and repudiation was scarcely known. He lent a few pounds to a neighbour who fell into difficulties. On asking for payment, he was told he had got all he was likely to get. "Than I'll gi' tha a resate," and knocked him down.

PROFIT OR LOSS?

A FARMER having indulged too long at Wigton market, was returning homeward sleeping in his cart. He was met by a wag who unloosed the horse and drove it towards home, leaving the unconscious sleeper in his cart by the wayside. Awaking sometime after, he rubbed his eyes, scratched his ears, and thus logically addressed himself : "If aa be the real John Thompson, I've lost a horse and a set of car gear. If aa's not the real John Thompson, I've fund a car and a basket o' marketin."

A PEDIGREE.

MR. TROUTBECK used to tell a story of a neighbour who took a bull, and not of the best, to Penrith fair for sale, which had been reared because of the milking qualities of its dam. When quizzed for a pedigree, well knowing the ungainly figures of both sire and dam, he replied, " He hed a fadder I'se warrant ye, and for a mudder, presarve us o'."

MORE HASTY THAN DISCREET.

A FARMER'S wife, on entering her dairy, found a cat sitting on the rim of her well-filled cream pot busily lapping the cream. More hasty than discreet, she struck at the cat and toppled it head over heels into the cream, saying, " How likes ta that by lickin' o' cream ? "   It is not recorded how the cream was afterwards used, but the saying got current and is often used in the west of the county.

TWITCH OR FIORIN?

THE late J. C. Curwen, M.P., was once lecturing to his tenant farmers on the high feeding properties of Fiorin Grass introduced and so much praised by Dr. Richardson.   He handed round a sample for inspection, when Walter Wood, the shrewd old Scotch banker, came into the assembly room, and asked to look at the grass.   After eyeing it over he handed it back, and to the great amusement of the farmers said, " It's just twutch, Maister Curran, and d—d bad twutch tue."   Few durst speak so freely to the M.P., but old Walter was a Galloway man and thought to be a man of money, so was privileged.

WILFUL WASTE.

A WELL-TO-DO farmer of an economic turn was invited by the late William Blamire, Esq., M.P., to dine with him at Thackwood Nook. The man was seated next his landlord, and after other substantials, was helped to pudding. Before he was well aware, Mr. Blamire poured a glass of wine over the pudding on John's plate. This was an act which John could not reconcile with his ideas of saving, and he exclaimed, " Nay, ding, landlord, but this is *fair* extravagance. "

FELL *versus* FIELD.

AN old lady at Caldbeck was in the habit of using mutton of her own feeding, for when the sheep were fed in the fields the mutton was too fat for her, and when fed on the fell it was too lean. In order to have it duly mixed, the sheep were changed each alternate week from field to fell, and from fell to field.

When killing time came the lean predominated, and she wonderingly exclaimed, " Whea *wad* ha' thought it ! t' fell 's bang't t' fields ! "

HORSE DEALING.

A FARMER near Brampton bought a mare from a Quaker, who spoke highly, but guardedly, of her good qualities. Amongst other inquiries, the farmer asked if the mare would draw? " Friend," was the reply, " it would delight thee to see her draw."

The buyer would indeed have been delighted to see her draw, for she entirely refused it.

UTILISING THE BULL.

Capt. John Tickell had been a strict disciplinarian when in command of a vessel at sea; and when he went to reside on his estate of Brighouse, in the Vale of St. John's, he continued his dislike to keeping idle hands or idle cattle. He said horses worked, and cows gave milk, but the bull was more of a gentleman than even the pigs or himself, and was not so good eating as the pig at the last. Carrying out this idea, he ordered his men to harness the bull and yoke him to a cart, and he should be made to work for a maintenance. The bull was untrained for work and soon broke away ; and after galloping about the field with the cart sometimes on its wheels, but oftener on its side or bottom uppermost, he plunged into a deep pool in the river. Being much hampered with the gear and the cart dragging among the large stones in deep water, the animal would have been drowned if the men had not rushed into the water and cut the harness, at no little risk to themselves from the frantic exertions of the bull to free himself. The Captain looking on, said he now believed the bull was not made to work in the cart, and did not try him again.

TEACHING MANNERS TO THE PIGS.

Capt. Tickell kept a great many pigs of various ages in the same yard, and, observing the strong animals to get the best share of the food given to them, said he would teach the big brutes manners. He gave orders for potatoes to be boiled and given entire to the pigs whilst hot from the boiler. As usual, the older swine rushed in and shouldered the young ones to a side. Each of the old ones seized a potato in its mouth and ran to the outside of the crowd; but finding a hot mouthful, on crushing the potato, he would drop it and run in for a cooler one; and then the smaller pigs fed on what the larger ones brought for them, ready crushed and cooled.

His attempts to teach manners to the herd did not succeed well; for occasionally hot potatoes were swallowed, causing inflammation and death to some of his largest and best swine.

DEVIL JACK.

At the time this sobriquet was obtained Jack was a raw lad acting for his mother who had a farm.

He was offering butter for sale in the market, having a shrewd guess it was deficient in weight. Observing the weighing officers approaching, and while others might be thrusting pennies or half-pennies into their pounds of butter, he, more thriftily, quietly slipped into a shop and squeezed his pounds into shapeless lumps, and went out to take his chance in the market again. On returning home the old woman inquired how he had got through with his butter. "Wey, mudder," he said, "when t' weighers com aa squeezt it up, and when they axt if aa selt it i' punds—nay, sez I, my mudder's lost t' weights and aa sell 't i' lumps and dozzels."—"Thou is a divel, Jack, wi' thy lumps and dozzels."

A DAY DREAM.

A tenant on an extensive farm belonging to the late Sir Wilfred Lawson, Bart., dealt largely in sheep, and made frequent bargains both at home and at various markets. One day, armed with bill hook and mittens, he was busy repairing a hedge. A heavy shower coming on, he sat down under the shelter of a bush and indulged in his day dream of selling a lot of sheep. One of his men servants was sheltering, unknown to his master, and near enough to hear the one-sided dialogue of a hard bargain going on. The bargain began to draw to a close, and the man heard his master say, " Here thou sal hae them." Immediately after he heard the sound of a sharp stroke, and his master uttered a loud oath. Fearing some ill, the man started up and found his master had closed the imaginary contract by nearly chopping off the fingers of his left hand with the bill hook.

IT IS GOOD TO BE THANKFUL.

About the year 1800, James Lacklinson, who lived at the High in Moresby, was walking in one of his fields among whins and briars, when he stumbled forwards and fell across the mouth of an old unprotected coal-pit, grown over with briars. Fortunately, his length of six feet four inches stretched across the narrow mouth of the pit, and saved his life. In his constant family worship the grateful man used devoutly to thank God for making him so tall, or he would have come to a sad end.

CAT IN CREAM POT.

Mr. Birkett, of Penrith, had a property at Lazonby, and went there occasionally to shoot. On one occasion, after a good day's sport, the farmer's wife set a nice looking pie before him. Exercise had whetted his appetite, and on finishing his hearty meal, he said it was the best pie he had ever tasted. The good wife was pleased with the compliment, and said, "Well, you see, Mr. Birkett, we hed a bit of a misfortune. Our thief of a yellow cat fell into t' kurn, and we niver knew till we com to tak t' butter out, and t' cat was kurnt to deeth, peer thing! We could'nt sell t' butter, seah we meadd it into pie crusts."

❦

A PERFECT CURE.

A LONG time ago Frank Graham came from Bewcastle to reside at Caldbeck. He kept a sow and allowed her to maintain herself as best she could. She soon took to invading the property of others, had especial delight in rooting up potatoes when they were to be had, and had learned to lift a neighbour's gate off the crooks with her nose, and to indulge in her favourite feast, many times a day, without shame or compunction. The owner of the field, grown tired of this, went to Frank in great wrath and threatened an action. Frank, in reply, says, "Wully, dinna put yer-sel in a passion about the puir beast, she's no to bleame. It's yer oald bad yett that's no fit to turn a sookin' pig." "Wey mebby," says Willy, "t' yatt's nut a good un, but she's nea business theer. It's nut a quarter of an hour sin I put her out, and gev her a good yarkin, and now she's been in ageann. She mun hev a verra bad memory." "I ken nought about her memory, Wully, but I ken she's the maist forgiven beast alive, and bears nea malice, and that shews a guid disposition." Willy turned away an unbeliever,

and nailed bits of an old scythe along the bottom rail
of the gate; in less than an hour after the sow was
minus the end of her nose—having herself cut it off
in her attempt to lift the gate.

This gave rise to a common saying at Caldbeck, that
such a person "bears no more malice than Frank
Graham's sow."

LING BESOMS.

THE late Mr. Joseph Roberts, of Egremont, who
farmed high, had a field on his Marlborough farm
which grew little but heather, and that only weak, but
he top-dressed it heavily with farmyard manure. The
late Mr. James Miller, also a good farmer in his way,
could not conceive the utility of such an extravagant
application upon what he called only moor land, and
exclaimed to a friend. "Zooks lad! aa doont know
what farmin's gaan to git tull next. Yonder Joe
Roberts muckin his field for ling besoms." But the
muck did its duty, and never another ling besom was
got from that field.

THE RAID ON THE CAULDRON.

THE late Laird Stalker, of Lambfield, near Dalston.
was a worthy man, of very large size, and somewhat
eccentric as well as humorous. He claimed descent
from William of Wykeham.

He went annually to the northern fares to purchase
sheep for winter stock. Before railways were in use
he travelled by mail and on one occasion went with a
number of his Dalston and other neighbours to one of

these fairs. The time of the mail had lately been accelerated to ten miles an hour, with no stoppages for refreshment.   Mr. Stalker was noted for his healthy appetite, and was unprepared for a ten hours' fast, so he watched his opportunity while the horses were being changed at a farm house, where he noticed a cauldron boiling in a cellar, and dived down to inspect its contents.   He whips off the lid and found it full of fine potatoes ready for use.   Without a moment's hesitation he filled both his large hands with the roots and ran for the coach.   To relieve his hands from the heat, he pitched the potatoes to the roof and began to ascend, when a brawny bare-legged girl ran out and seized the tails of his coat, screaming — "Hegh ! haud him ! haud the muckle southron ! he's grabbit twa nievfu' o' the pig taties an' aa wush they may choke him."   He managed to scramble to his seat and the mail started, leaving the guardian of the cellar to witness him and his friends enjoying the raid on the cauldron.

VERY LIKELY.

A lad, returning from an agricultural show with a horse he had been exhibiting, was asked if he had got a prize.   "Nay," he replied, "I've gitten nought, but iverybody said if our maister had been t' judge, I wud hae gitten t' heed prize."

NEW WEIGHTS AND MEASURES.

People may occasionally be put to extraordinary shifts, but, generally speaking, where there is a will there is a way.

The late John Cook, of Middletown, had sold some seed oats and soon after met the purchaser who told him the corn was short of the weight bargained for. John very innocently replied, " You see we isn't seah varra weel off for weights at our house ; we hev yaa fifty-six, and we hev a cobble and a lump of a car wheel 'at we know t' weight on ; and than we put in t' sarvent lad. But I've just bethought me 'at t' lad had been badly for about three week, and mappen he'd lost a bit o' weight; seah I mun send ye a bow-sterful to mak't up."

In times gone by it was no uncommon thing to see incongruous weights of the above description, with the exception of the lad.

Cobbles were in great use, and many had rings let in and were marked 7 or 14, &c.; and other singular devices were resorted to which the Inspector has now set aside.

MEMORANDUMS OF OLD TIMES.

In Mid-County Dialect.

Fwok tells of oald times—sek good oald times,
   They hed when they were o' young ;
And niver sek times sen them oald times,
   Was read on, or hard on, or sung.

I' winter time when t' weather was coald,
   They hardly stirr't out o' t' neuk ;
Bit to fetch in a trugful o' peats 'cross t' foald,
   And sledder about and smeuk.

They wad thresh a bit, mebby, and fodder their kye,
   And poo a lock out o' t' hay mew ;
And at neet after milkin', and supper put bye,
   Mak swills, or wad card skin woo.

Or mappen wad beetle a carlin sark,
   On t' beetlin' steann at t' door ;
Or plet a few strings o' hemp efter dark,
   Or caper about on t' clay floor.

A carlin sark, new, was rumplement gear,
   To wear next a maisterman's skin ;
So he lent it to t' sarvent to beetle an' wear,
   By way of a brekkin in.

T' oald fwok were drist in duffel blue,
   And t' youngsters in heàmm-spun grey ;
And nowder were often ower clean or new–
   Bit darn't frac day to day.

And o' wad hev brackins or strea in their clogs,
   Or stickin' ower t' edge o' their shun ;
And wad clammer up t' fell, or striddle through bogs :
   Od, man ! but this was laal fun.

And still you believe they were rare oald times,
   Far better nor any 'at 's now ;
So I'll put summat down in canteran rhymes,
   And than you may judge if its true.

Their habit o' leevin was poddish at mworn,
   And taties and point at neunn ;
To let thersels down wi' tea they wad scworn,
   So they poddish't at eebnin seunn.

They kilt a fat cow at Martinmas time,
  And quartert wi' neighbours three;
And except at Kersmas or clippin' time,
  Fray flesh they wer nar about free;

Unless it was bacon, o' reesty and smeuk,
  And kizzent and dry't like a sneck;
Till if it fell down on ta t' flags off t' heuk,
  It wad ring like a pot, or med brek.

And than they wad frizzel 't in t' sotteran pan,
  And fry't till as brown as a peat;
And conny laal bits wad be gien to ilk yan
  On truncheons, to girn at and eat.

Their bread was clap-keakk, meadd o' barley meal,
  Or hard havver bannock so thick;
Their cheese wad rowl down a fell side like a wheel,—
  Mappen hack't it to bits wid a pick.

For drink wid their dinner, they'd sour milk or whey,
  Or else, for a treat, treacle beer;
And if any indulg'd in ought better, they say,
  'Twad be talk't on for nar on a year.

And o' fare't alike—beàth maister and man,
  In eatin' and drinkin' or wark;
They turn'd out at morn and togidder began,
  And left off togidder at dark.

And thur was their ways in them oalden times,
  (For evidence stark we can bring;
That'll testify strang to t' truth o' my rhymes,)
  When George the Third was king.

Nowder oald man nor young weàrr beard or moustache,
    Bit they warn't slape feàsst ebn than;
For atween two Sundays they niver wad fash,
    And afoor church-time they began

At week-oald beard to hassel and hack
    Wid razor as blunt as a saw;
If ya side gat off theer was nea gitten back
    Till tudder was stubbelt an' o'.

Bit theer two sides to this, as to meàsst other things,
    And it's fair 'at they beàth sud be known;
Aa'll jingle a bit (while t' rest on ye sings,)
    And set it o' down as my oan.

And month efter month for a heàll year lang,
    To tell ye how o' things went;
Aa'll bodder my brains for a kind of a sang,
    And mebby may send it to prent.

JANUARY.

Kersenmas turn'd, and some feastin' gaān on,
    Fwok up leàtt at neet and sair tue't
To git till o' t' furthneets, and hevvin to don
    Two sets o' duds, and they rue't.

For they say next Kersmas is far off to fetch,
    And now-for't or niver, is thought;
They kevvel and swing, and dance ledder-te-spetch,
    And royster and swatter like ought.

They feast on roast beef, and on raised geùss pyes,
    And giblet, and mince pie, and sweet ;
And many good things—Lamplugh puddin',* for bye,
    Smooks on a broad teàble that neet.

They woken next mwornin and find ther-sels queer,
    And o' out o' sworts for hard work ;
Bit Kersmas comes nobbet yance in a year,
    And meàsst on 't is kent efter dark.

Wi' snow a feùtt thick—mebby clean out o' cwols,
    " Keaà fetch a pack-leàdd on a horse ;
" Pick t' best rwoad ther is, and mind keep out o' t' whols,
    " Lest thou torfor on t' moor and 's a corse.

" If lang at t' cwol greùv thou's to wait for thy bout,
    " Or it's mist, or thou's thrown into neet ;
" Thou mun put up a shout and we'll raise a turn out,
    " And on t' foald yat will hing out a leet." †

FEBRUARY.

Now down wid a buryin skin onta t' leāth floor,
    And thresh a lock bigg for a batch ;
To t' deetin hill carry't, but forter't afoor,
    Than throw't up for breezes to catch.

Some wheat mun be crec't for a frummety dish,
    In t' creein trough, 'back o' t' leāth door ;
A piggin o' that wid a bit o' sote fish,
    Maks a dinner for rich or for poor.

---

* Lamplugh pudding consists of a large bowl of hot ale with biscuits steeped in it, all well spiced.

† Often in use before commons were enclosed, or roads were made.

Now fit up a pillion for maister and deamm,
  To hotch off to t' town amang t' rest ;
Top cwoat till *his* heels—*she* at startin' frae heàmm,
  In starch cap, wi' lugs, for her best.

For debts sud be paid, and credits brought in,
  (This was seldom but yeance in a year :)
And at Cannelmas time they meàdd a girt din,
  Ower payin' and scrapin' up geer.

Now set t' parish prentice to cardin' o' woo,
  To keep him at heàmm efter dark ;
Theer scutchin' o' line for men fwok to do,
  For that's mair a man-body's wark.

And woman-fwok, they mun be whirran t' woo wheel,
  Or spinnin' a web frae their lint ;
Or plyin' their teuls—their rock and their reel,
  And singin' o' t' while without stint.

It's canny to hear o' so cheery gang on
  Of a neet when it storms and it blows ;
For whatever's outside, wid a good fire on,
  It's a comfort inside yan weel knows.

Some on a lang back't settle are sittin',
  Some choose a steùll wi' three legs ;
Or a sheepform, and yan may be knittin',
  Another at sowan she pegs.

MARCH.

Now out wid a heàmm-meàdd roan-tree plue,
  Wid ironin' scanty eneuff ;
Lait up strea braff'ns—reàpp traces enue,
  And see 'at they're o' draft preùff.

R

Next yok in o' lang-horn't owsen two pair,
　Two lang-tailed horses unshod ;
Co't' plue-hodder, plue-co'ers—two or three mair,
　Wi' speadd, and wi' pettle, and prod.

Now t' bullocks nit yok't sen plue-time last year,
　His horses out-liggan, and lean,
And kaim'tly—and t' trappins o' flimsily gear,
　And t' ley fur stark as t' town green.

"Jee hop and away, my lads," t' plue-hodder sings,
　And they striddle and start for a try ;
A cobble flings t' plue out, and "wo-oy," he rings,
　And his team is n't wont to comply.

He gangs on a bit and he sticks in ageànn,
　And mebby gits on to t' land end ;
And turns and gangs yark on another girt steànn,
　And fin'ds 'at his team duzzent mend ;

For yan is coald shoudert ; another is tetch't ;
　And some poos as hard as they can ;
And t' co'ers hes use't up o' t' patience they fetch't,
　And nit mickle better is t' man !

He roars and he sweers, and yarks wi' his cwords,
　And he scops at his drivers wi' clods ;
They whack wi' their yedders—shout uncanny words—
　He batters away wi' hard sods.

Now t' oxen gits kysty and kevels about,
　Gets legs ower t' traces and o' ;
His hoaf-brokken horses seùnn kick thersels out,
　And poos him by t' neck,* gayly low.

* It was the custom for the ploughman to wear the guiding cords in one
piece, the middle being behind his neck, that he might not drop the cords
whilst his hands were engaged in holding the stilts and throwing sods at his
team.

A plue-coer lad is amang t’ bullock feet,
    Two lasses rin skirlan heàmm ;
T’ curs fo’ to barkan and baitan out-reet,
    Na wonder if some git a leàmm.

For sek a tow-lowe, and sek crashin’ about,
    Sek capers o’ bullocks and men ;
Med set them to yope and to yernestly shout,
    They wad niver plue mair wi’ t’ *lang ten.**

Then heàmm to cow’t lword and het piggins o’ keàll
    O’ masselton pez o’ dark grey ;
Wi’ groats and round haver-meal stir’t—sek a meàll
    Was nit to be hed ivery day.

And snug may they mak ther sels round a hearth fire,
    While t’ wind roars and brullies outside ;
And sleet brings down t’chimla scut-drops thick as mire,
    And they couldn’t keep’t out if they try’d.

Bit storms o’ git ower and whietness comes,
    And mishaps may seùnn be forgitten ;
Efter sleepin’ o’ neet as sound like as drums,
    A new job for mworn mun be hitten.

And now for pwok-mittens on dinnellan hands,
    And dykin’ mittens and swatch ;
To mend up some gaps round plewin’ lands,
    And waik spots, and creep-whols to patch.

APRIL.

When frost gits away, theer haver to sow,
    And a heedlin’ o’ hemp or line ;
And mebby a lock mair in t’ hempgarth an o’
    For winter-neet wark to plet twine.

---

* The set out consisted of ten individuals without the dogs.

Now muck's to be cary't in hots and in creels,
    To cover some scraps of oald land ;
In side-back fields whoar cars on clog wheels,
    Wad hardly be seàff to stand.

A smo' lock o' taties will hev to be set,
    In lazy-bed fashion I trow ;
Nea miss or disease hed than to be met,
    For e'en t' varra peelins wad grow.

Bit peelin' o' taties was thought a girt sham,
    And t' prentice was setten to scrapin' ;
Nea doubt he thought scrapin' was nought bit a " bam,"
    And was laid onta him as a snapin',

Than he wad git drowsy, and noddle and scrape,
    As an unpaid prentice wad dee ;
His knife and his tatie wad seun git so slape,
    They wad rowl out o' hand off his knee.

And than for a clout ower t' lug, or a skelp,
    That he thought nowder music nor rhyme ;
For he was install'd as a farmer's help,
    In that far away good oald time.

MAY.

Now lambin' time's on, beàth in April and May,
    Now up seun and leàrt, or o' neet ;
To suckle laal starvelins by neet and by day,
    And see them get on to their feet.

If yance they git milk and can wander about,
    They care not for frost nor for snow ;
For it's plenty o' suckle 'at gars them git stout—
    To skip, and to lowp, and to grow,

No cleanin' o' land, nor pickin' o' weeds,
   Let iv'ry thing prosper 'et can ;
For o' plants were sent us to ripen their seeds,
   And mak ther sels useful to man.

Dry thissels mak capital eldin for t' fire,
   And dockin-stalks narly as good ;
For hettin a yub'm or beddin' a byer,
   Seah thought our fworelders—they dud !

And t' mother o' girse was that lang reutit twitch,*
   Girt plenty they grew—dunnot doubt it ;
If any amang them was keen to grow rich,
   They niver could mannish without it.

And cleet-leaves for smokin' in black scutty pipes,
   Wid bacca a varra smo' matter ;
Wad raise a girt reek, when a sup o' yal swipes
   Or smo' beer wad help a smo' chatter.

That wish-weshy tea now so mickle in use,
   (Co' it "spend-time" or "trash" for you may ;)
Was a treat for our girt fwoks, and nit for abuse,
   By usin' it three times a day.

JUNE.

While girsins is bare efter lambs and their yowes,
   Milk kye hes n't mickle to eat ;
Than croppins of esh mun be foddert on t' howes,
   To give to t' oald milkers a treat.

* The use of the feather of the sock was abolished lest it should cut and destroy the roots of the twitch or couch grass.

Now joggan to market on butter-kits two,
  And basket wi' garn and eggs
Packt seàff in a wallet o' drab stripe and blue,
  And slung onder beùtt-stockin't legs

Waggan lowse widout stirrups astride of a pad,
  And hotchan through swang and through syke;
Plodan away on a cwornless yad,
  Cross t' moor widout rwoad or dyke.

No dinner, no nought, bit three hoperth o' yal,
  And horse in a foald at sneck hay;
Scrapan and seàvvan t' days takkins nar heàll,
  And—map'm gang swober away.

Now grund up a flay-speàdd to cut toppin peat,
  Wid lang speàdd for black peats forbye;
And spreed them weel out, to git wind and sun heat,
  And stirr them sometimes till they dry.

Than hey for good spwort when comes peat leadin' time,
  And gittan them seàff into stack;
For wet-weather peatin' wad spoil any rhyme,
  And poverty bring on its back.

JULY.

Now gedder in t' sheep and wesh them in t' dem,
  And swing them and sop them in t' watter;
If a waik an sud torfer it's nobbet t' oald gem (game),
  And mebby it's nea girt matter.

Sek bleatin' o' lambs, and sek barkin' o' dogs,
  Sek jybin' and jwokin' o' men;
Sek clat'rin' o' lads in their oald cokert clogs,
  Sek drinkin' o' whisky.   Amen!

Let sheep run a fortneet and than comes on clippin',
    And bleatin', and fleecin' o' woo;
They submit, without whimper, to tying and strippin',
    And feel leetsome they hardly know how.

Sek a ged'rin' o' clippers and helpers and that,
    Sek elbows, and clinkin' o' shears;
Sek sweatin', sek crackin' o' dogs, and o' what
    An income some woo-buyer clears.

Now clippin' o' done, comes weshin' o' hands
    And kestin' off scoggers and brats;
A fleece is hung up on a powl in t' lang-lands,
    To be run for without shun or hats.

The prize is awarded, to feastin' they wend,
    At a plain but a plentiful spreed;
On broad pewder dishes, weel leàdden at t' end,
    Wood trunchers off whilk they can feed.

Next out wid a punch bowl, and yal i' girt plenty,
    Wi' horns and glasses to drink frae;
And piggins, and mugs, bit nought varra dainty,
    And nought 'at a clipper need shrink frae.

Than a whyat laal crack for about hoaf an hour,
    And a buzz—seun to rise till a chang;
Than somebody knattles on t' teàble befoor
    He says, " Lads, you mun join in my sang."

* " Here's a good health to the man o' this house,
    " The man o' this house, the man o' this house;
" Here's a good health to the man o' this house,
    " For he is a right honest man.

* A very old clipping song   The guests in turn obey the commands of the third and last verse, and if the glass is not emptied by the end of the refrain, the penalty is enforced a second time.   And if a man was desirous to get quickly drunk, he would incur the penalty till his end was accomplished.

" And he that doth this health deny,
　" Before his face I justify [or just defy];
" Right in his face this glass shall fly,
　" So let this health go round.

" Place the canny cup to your chin,
　" Open your mouth and let liquor run in ;
" The more you drink the fuller your skin,
　" So let this health go round."

Than " O good ale thou art my darlin',"
　And t' shepherds' " Tarry woo ;"
" The Raven and the Rock Starlin',"
　And many a ringer too.

And than they depart in good humour and peace,
　To heàmm for a few hours' sleep ;
While clippins' hod on their labours weent cease,
　They mun rise wid mwornin's first peep,

To help a good neighbour at his merry meetin',
　A heàll country side to employ ;
In housin' and clippin' wi' much friendly greetin',
　For clippin's are meetin's o' joy.

AUGUST.

Now mowers can't work through t' middle o' t' day,
　For t' bitin' o' clegs, and for heat ;
So they snoozle some hours on t' new gitten hay,
　And mak't up by workan at neet.

'Till t' glowworm leets up, than to blanket they stakker
　To snatch a laal sleep, and then rise ;　　[chatter,)
And at it (while t' white-throats in t' dykes cherr and
　And whittle-te-whet their lang scythes.

Than skalin' and turnin' wi' fork and wi' reàkk,
   And skewin' t' about to dry;
And cockin', and brekkin', for good hay to meàkk,
   And rake into plat forbye.

Neist dress up in trusses and tye wid a reàpp,
   Or cram, if it's short, into sheet;
For if it be windy a part med esceàpp,
   And waste a girt lock afoor neet.

Than up wi't on horseback and loup on ahint,
   And away to t' leàtth door in a crack;
Hitch't off onta t' peazz, and about, sharp as flint,
   And gallop like mad o' t' way back.

Now t' main weight o' t' hay crop sudd be geddert in,
   And t' fag end 'll follow in time;
Theer still a few slaggarts to saunter ahin',
   And niver wi' t' foormest can shine.

Bit no idle time need be spent on a farm,
   If a man's nobbet mindit to work;
He may pettle about, keepin' o' things frac harm,
   And at it frae mwornin' till murk.

And if he sud slack for a day or for two,
   He's seaff to find summat geànn wrang;
And then he mun fettle and be in a stew,
   And find his sel double-ly thrang.

His reuf may want patchin', and he out o' thack,
   He may out onta t' moor and poo ling;
Or bring in a burden o' seaves on his back,
   For strea's ower costly a thing.

SEPTEMBER.

Now shearin', and bin-din', and stookin' is rife,
　　And workin' frae dayleet till dark ;
Ey, workin' as if they were workin' for life,
　　As hard as they fairly can yark.

Beatth maister and men wear beards a week oald,
　　And shave, if they've time, at t' week end ;
They mun stick to their sickles be 't het or be 't coald,
　　Nor straight their backs out of a bend.

Harvest gets endit like meàst other things,
　　And kern-supper follows as sure ;
A thanksgiving feast contentment still brings,
　　If a morsel be spared to the poor.

'Than hey ! for thick bannocks and rich butter sops,
　　Wid iv'ry thing dainty and nice ;
'T' maister says, " Fettle tee, lads, we've good crops,"
　　And neabody needs preezin' twice.

To piggins o' frummety [barley and milk],
　　And bannocks and butter to follow ;
And sops so smeath 'at they slip down like silk,
　　They bang watter poddish clean hollow.

'Than t' breet pewder dishes begin to leuk howe,
　　And mickle mair cannot weel spend ;　　　　[powe,
And youngsters 'll stritch their arms—some scrat their
　　Ilk yan o' them full to t' thropple end.

Harvest o' finish't and o' sydit up,
  Theer steepin' o' hemp and o' line ;
And bleachin' 't on grass, clear o' wet, ev'ry sup,
  Than house it for makkin o' twine.

Tak a pwok up to t' fell when neist thou may gang,
  And efter thou's fund t' sheep o' reet ;
Pyke some ore out—thou'll find in t' rock grykes amang,
  To smit t' wedder sheep wid at neet.

OCTOBER.

Now barns sud be sent to a Whittlegeat man,*
  (As hay time and harvest is ower,)
To larn them to read, write, and count—if he can,
  Or else they'll be daft as a stower.

Their skeulin 'll come to some money by t' spring,
  At a penny a week for ilk heed ;   [string
T' maister's clogs and kelt cwoat they'll mannish to
  Into t' Poor Beuk—famish good thing.

Now settin' o' tar, and soavin' o' sheep,
  Taks up some time and some labour ;
Efter sixteen hours sittin', a soaver may creep
  Off to bed and nit visit his nabor.

Bit o' mayn't be whyet at times like this,
  And befwore o' t' soavin' is done ;
A set o' good soavers wad grummel to miss
  Their lang-used jwokin' and fun.

* This custom became extinct in 1862, at Wasdalehead.

They tire o' lang sittin', and lang for a reass,
　Or a lark, or a moonleet russle ;
And many a youngan gits larn't a fast peass,
　Or a conquerin' chip in a tussle.

Now soavin' nar through and swortin' o' sheep,
　A deal of odd things are to side ;
And lang kidney taties to fork up and keep,
　For taty and point to provide.

For in times we co' good, in them oald-warld days,
　When they'd plenty wi' pinchin' gay hard ;
In scrattin' and seavvin' up o' waifs and strays,
　They niver durst play a wrang card.

Now kye grows uneasy for want o' some fog,
　Through hazel and wythe they'll rush ;
Then leàdd them wi' clammers, and cow beam, and clog,
　You cannot depend on a bush,

Nor a thorn, nor an oald clog-wheel in a gap,
　Nor a teuthless oald harrow in t' dyke ;
And t' bull sud be biggelt or he'll in full slap,
　And care not a wink for dog " Tyke."

NOVEMBER.

Now t' kye o' ty't up wi' wooden D bands,
　And t' coaves ty't wi' plettit hemp string ;
T' woman-fwok poos them hay wi' their hands,
　And nurses them through till spring.

'T" young fwoks 'll gang till a cannel-seave syke,
  And pick a shaff strangans for leets;
Than hotter to heàmm, through bog and wet dyke,
  To peel them and dip them at' neets.

They turn in at neets wi' their clogs o' skarn,
  And clean them a bit yance in a week;
They'd rayder spin hanks o' rough sheep-langel garn,
  And mak t' woo-wheel to whirr and to squeak.

As threshin' time's here, we fit up a flail,
  Wi' handstaff, and soople' and cappin;
And hingin', and hing it on t' wo' on a nail,
  Till wantit for threshin' and wappin'.

Martinmas endit and teram time done,
  In a laal bit o' huntin' what harm
If yan steal off some mworn for a good day's run,
  While t' weather's just canny and warm?

Than up and be off for a day-brek quest,
  Wid a merry and lively chang;
It thrills through yan's brisket as if yan was blest
  Wid good things, and niver ought wrang.

Harkaway! see she's off! o'er hill and through whol
  We spank till we're gaily nar done;
Than hingan a lip like a motherless fwol,
  Sledder heàmmward, but nit in a run.

And next down wi' t' listers and out wid a lowe,
  And away into t' beck efter dark;
A salmon or two will be welcome I trow,
  Tho' listerin's canny coald wark.

A cut o' dry't salmon's a teastily thing,
    When flesh meat cannot be hed ;
It's a savory change and will appetite bring,
    For poddish and taties and bread.

DECEMBER.

They dress up some wots for a melder o' meal,
    And dry't in a kiln in t' kiln croft ;
Than to t' bond-sucken mill tak't to oald Robin Peel,
    And a man mun keep watch at t' mill toft

To stiddy his mouter-dish—help him to sift it,
    And see it's o' tidily done ;
And gedder up offal, and heàmmward to skift it,
    And hev sooins as sure as a gun.

Fwok ree's a lock wheat in a sieve, if they hev't,
    And *that* was their deetin' machine ;
Or they teuk't onta t' deetin' hill, whither they gev't
    O' t' wind they could gedder on t' green.

A masselton batch will be sent off to t' mill,
    For Sunday and Kersenmas breed ;
And for pies, a laal pwok o' some bettermer still,
    For that's thought a varra good deed.

They've havver meal poddish ; and havver meal breed,
    As thin as a sixpence they rowl't ;
They beàkk't on a girdle ; and onta t' wo' heed,
    T' rattans on t' rannel tree, bold

Wad slyly leuk down, watchan o' 'at they dee,
  And waitin' impatient for neet ;
When they pop down as seun as o's whyet they see,
  To clean up t' strow't meal for their treat.

And now you've a swatch o' them good oald days,
  'At fwok brags on as hevvin lang sen ;
And you know summat now o' their wark and their ways,
  Wad ye swap eb'm hands, good men ?

CROSSYAT'S BOGGLE.

(Lamplugh) which always fore-set folk.

Tom Speddy 'd been on at a Club-neet at' Cross,
  Whoar he drank and he hakkert and sang ;
Till it soundit as if he was singan through moss,
  And than towarts heàmm he wad gang.
        Now Tom in his cups,
        Efter three or four sups,
        Or pints as they co' them,
        By neàm we o' know them,
    Was as bold as a lang-horn't bull ;
        And was riddy to feight
        Any man of his weight,
        Or a feut mair height,
    (He'd hed many hard whacks on his skull.)
        Bit a few pints mair
        Teuk his courage down sair,
And then he was nobbet like other fwok ;
And at startin' frae t' Cross he bethought o' t' skeùl beck,
Whoar a girt white boggle, without heed or neck,
Was said in oald times to sair bother fwok.
Seah Tom set to thinkin', and thought narly reet,
It was nin varra canny if boddert that neet,

Wid a thing he could nowder mak end-lang nor side on't,
And at last he considert to keep gaily wide on't.
　　　He could hardly walk street
　　　In that fine summer neet,
So down by Murton Whol he stakkert,
　　To gang a mile about,
And muttert tull his sel and hakkert,
　　Fairly clear o' doubt
Or fear of any evil thing ;
　　And as he wandert on his way,
Just about to try to sing,
　　To keep his spirits frae decay,
And gittan on to Crossyat's beck,
　　A white thing flasht his een across,
And sat and screecht on t' watter heck,
　　And pot Tom fairly till a loss ;
For up it gat and flew ageann,
And let awhile on t' wo' end steann,
And than it screecht, and hisst, and skirlt,
As round his heed it whuft and whirlt,
Ilk way he turn't it still foorset him,
As if to heàmm it waddent let him
　　Gang that neet.
And than it flasht up in a tree—
(That girt oald esh so broad and hee
　　And thick and street,
At Crossyat's neùk it stood and grew,
And into it this boggle flew),
And hovert ower a pyet nest ;
And as Tom's courage it would test,
A screech it gave bangt o' the rest !
　　Wi' sek a hissin' up that tree,
　　By witch, or warse, or warlocks three,
　　Or hagworms any quantity !
　　Tom fear't if they war o' set free
　　That down and at him they wad be ;

And than beside him, nar his feet,
Sek awful greàns that awful neet !
They gar't his varra skin to creep,
    And caused his steps to plet and vary ;
He wisht he'd been at heàmm asleep
    In t' Bird Dyke loft beside oald Mary.
His seet was mebby nit so clear
As it had been some former year.
And what was that low liggan thear ?
He thought it mun be summat whick,
For it appear't to fidge and kick ;
And than for sure, some irons rattelt,
As if ageann t' oald tree it battelt,
It put him in a mortal flay !
He cuddent run—he dursent stay ;
For if it sud turn out oald Nick
Was gaan to play some impish trick,
When imps so many flapt about him,
They seaff wad catch, and scrat, and clout him.
Just than *another* thing foorset him
A man stark neakt com on and met him,
Neakt, but his sark and white beard lang ;
He seemt beàtth to' and broad and strang.
Tom shakt and whiddert in his shun,
For he was lost, sure as a gun,
It's lang sen Tom gat sek a flay,
It fairly dreuv his drink away.
Bit seun he fand some smo' relief,
And mebby meddent come to grief,
For t' man was nobbet oald John Wood.*
That whietly beside him stood.
Seah Tom buckt up and axt him, " What
" He thought o' sek a thing as that ? "

* A harmless lunatic, accustomed to wander about at night without any
covering but a shirt. While the West Pier was being built at Whitehaven
he occasionally went there in the night, and could report progress to one or
two who were in his confidence.

Says John, "It's drucken oald Scotch Jock."
"Dust' say seah?   Ey, it is begock."
And Jock it was, and ravan drunk,
Batteran at that esh tree trunk
Wid ham'r and trowan in ya hand
Jinglan ; yet he cuddent stand ;
Bit he could grunt, and rave, and greànn,
And kick and strike at tree or steànn ;
As mad as any mastiff dog
When worrying sheep, or lamb, or hog.
Now Tom gain't pluck and leukt around,
And seún he larnt, that screechan sound
And hagworm-hiss abeùn his heed
Sprang frae a hulert and her breed,
A hungry nestful up that tree,
And mebby nar as flayt as he.
He bad "good neet" to Murton John,
And left Scotch Jock to snoozle on.
Ageànn he leukt, and seùn he saw
Another white thing on a wo'.
Says Tom, "This is a flaysom neet,
" For turn whilk way I will, I meet
" Some gruntan thing or boggle white."
But Tom was gittan sober quite,
And went to see this new white thing,
And hakkert " Eh, eh, eh, by jing !
" I thought it mud be summat queer,
" It's Jwony Braithet oald white meer,
" Just rais'd her heed on t' top o' t' wo',"
And that was t' last white thing Tom saw.

VERY UNFORGIVING.

A FARMER on his deathbed was visited by a lady, to
whom he complained that he had not been fairly

treated by many individuals, especially by his land-lord, who, he alleged, had formerly, in some way or other, caused him to lose forty pounds. The lady expressed a hope that *now* he would forgive all who might have injured him as he would hope to be for-given, when he offered this compromise; "I tell you what! I'll forgie them o' but N——, but I'll not for-gie him, nut widout he'll pay me my forty pund."

TAKING THINGS EASY.

An elderly farmer's wife stooping to feed some favour-ite chickens was attacked in the rear by a mischievous heifer, and knocked over without very much violence or harm; when a lad who witnessed the attack, and rashly concluded that the result could not be other-wise than fatal, rushed into the presence of her family to break the bad news by exclaiming, "If you please, t' mistress is kilt; theer a cow dumpt her down, and she's kilt."

CHANGE OF TIMES.

In the good old times of three or four generations back, during the American war, an Eaglesfield farmer took his butter to market, where it yielded the un-precedented high price of *three pence* a pound. Re-turning home in high feather, he assured a neighbour that "it was n't sellan', it was fairly coinan' brass."

MEASURING DISTANCE.

A farmer, whose memory went back to the time when nearly every village had its gate opening upon the common at the end of the village, desiring to express distance in a forcible manner, said, "It's as far off as frae here to Lunnon fell yeàtt."

MOST ASSUREDLY.

The yeomen of Burgh-on-the-Sands, or, as they are usually styled, the "Lairds o' Bruff Barony," were noted for their elevated ideas of their own importance and contempt for their less fortunate brethren who happen not to own the soil they till. At a parish meeting a large farmer venturing an observation was immediately stopped with, "Thee sit down and hod thy gob. What the de'il can thou know about it, man? What, thou hes nea land!"

ALWAYS BEHIND.

An old woman said of her slow-going son, who was remarkable for being behind hand in everything and never to be found when wanted, "Our John is just like a cow tail, he's always ahint."

TYRANNICAL.

At a vestry meeting in the Western Division of the county, a modest, but unfortunate shoemaker who essayed a few remarks, had to retire into silence and obscurity by a stentorian voice calling out—"Thee hod thy noise. Thou maks shun o' rotten ledder!"

A STRANGE LOAD.

Two farmers differed on the subject of a heap of rubbish which one of them suggested that the other might cart away. "Car't away! car the divvel away!" was the reply. "Nay, nay," said the first, "if you car't the divvel away,' what! t' parson wad hev nought to dea."

ON AND OFF THE RANNEL BALK.

In the early part of the nineteenth century N—— I—— took a farm near Uldale, on which he went to reside.

He lent a cart saddle to a neighbour, and on a winter Saturday night a servant was sent to return it. I—— and his wife had not come home from Keswick market when the man arrived, and, finding only the servant girl, he stayed and chatted with her till they were surprised by the rattle of the market cart coming over the pavement and up to the door. The young man was fairly in a trap for the house had only one door and he could not get out without being discovered and he did not relish that. With ready instinct the girl handed him a stool and told him to get upon the rannel balk in the open chimney and take the saddle with him. This he accomplished while the girl did her best to detain her mistress outside and the master was unyoking and feeding the horse. By that

time the marketing was brought in and tea was next
had near the fire. The young man on the balk was
amused with the dialogue at the tea-table, the more
so when he saw the farmer was a little elevated with
the Keswick ale and the good results of the market,
and when he arose from his chair saying he would
salute his wife with a kiss, the young man leaned a
little to one side to have a better view, when down he
tumbled, soot and saddle and all upon the hearth.   In
no little astonishment the master called out, "Whoar
cuz thoo frae?"   "Aa'v' brought yer car saddle back
an' thank ye."

HORSE AND CART BREAKING.

A GRAYSOUTHEN man described the doings of a young
horse during its first lesson in drawing a cart, and
said—"It seem't gaily whyet for a laal bit, bit it seùnn
began to keàvv an' shak t' heed on 't, and than it began to caper an' plunge, an' it leapp an' kick't an' swang
t' girt tail on 't, an' skew't sell on 't about till it brak
o' t' ranlin staps an splat yan o' t' car stangs, an' at
last of o' it brak t' car keel!"

SCRAPS OF FUN PERTAINING TO WIT.

When a parcel of jokes are put in print and investigated it is rather surprising to find that so few are the offspring of wit, and so many may be classed as arising from blundering simplicity. But all have a tendency to bring out in some degree the character of the people among whom they originate. The line of demarcation may not be easy to define in all cases, but an approximation is attempted.

There are others which cannot be classed with either the witty or the blundering, but must hold a neutral, or at least a distinct position. Perhaps it may be difficult to find real wit in some which are introduced into this list; but they will have a useful tendency, if only to create a little amusement; and, if at any time they are the means of promoting a hearty laugh, that act is so beneficial to so many temperaments in this vale of dulness and sorrow, that its healthful influence on the system is widely and almost universally acknowledged.

TAILORING.

An ancestor of the Wybergh's, of Isel Hall, had a pair of worsted cord pantaloons, so fashionable at the beginning of the nineteenth century, taken to him by the tailor who waited to know if the fitting was right. Mr. Wybergh, being a well-made man and very particular in having his clothes to fit well, complained of some part about the hips not being satisfactory. The tailor, who was a bit of a droll and knew his employer relished a joke, drew his hand over the part objected to, saying, " Mr. Wyber aa meàdd yer britches thinkin' you war a round-built man, but aa finnd ye're square built, and aa mun tak them heàmm and put guseets i' them."

THE RULING PASSION.

THE late Mr. Joshua Bird, of Armathwaite, was so ill for a time that his life was despaired of; but eventually he recovered health and spirits. When beginning to recruit, a friend called, inquired after his health, and what he thought when so nearly gone. His joking humour had returned, and with no intentional irreverence, he replied, " Ey, thou sees I was varra nar gàan, and was rayder mayzelt, for I duddent ken a fit o' t' rwoad."

When the same Mr. Bird, who was very bald, was giving evidence at Carlisle Assizes, the eminent counsel, Scarlett, afterwards Lord Abinger, was cross-examining him on a fishing case; after some complimentary questions on his knowledge of fishing, which were calculated to lead him astray, he said he was rather a pretty Bird, but could not be considered a finished one, unless he had a toppin. Mr. Bird quickly replied, " Ey, I'll be gaily nar finished when I git a Scarlett toppin on."

The reply got him very quietly through his examination, with the laugh of the court in his favour.

PASTURE FOR A COW.

THE late Sir James Lowther was highly indignant with the people of Whitehaven on one occasion, and threatened to reduce the trade of the town till its streets should grow green with grass. In the next generation some of the townsmen became dissatisfied with the doings of William Earl of Lonsdale, and prophesied that the trade would go to ruin and the streets grow green with grass. The late Mr. William Duggan, a thriving Irish draper, was present, and instantly bolted out, saying—"And bedad, then, I'll kape a cow."

THE FIRST WORD.

WHEN Distington Hall was built and newly roofed, the rooms being cleared, Captain Fisher's gamekeeper had the curiosity to look through the building. While John (Young) was wandering and wondering at the dimensions of one of the largest drawing-rooms in the county, he unexpectedly encountered the Captain; and having some doubts of being welcome there, got the first words and exclaimed, "Cush, maister! what a famish pleàss for a pigeon shootin'!"

A JUDGE'S JOKE.

A WHITEHAVEN paper says, a witness was asked by a deputy judge, " Did you go to the party yourself? " Witness : " Yes, sir." Judge : " And what did he say to you? " Witness : " He told me to go to h—l, sir."

"And so," said the judge—quietly taking a pinch of snuff—with a roguish smile, "you came to the County Court."

VERY LACONIC.

THE late Dr. Dickinson, of Workington, attended the late William Browne, Esq., of Tallantire Hall, for some affection about the throat which required the use of the lancet. When the proper time came, Mr. Browne wrote him thus: "Dear Doctor, come and cut my throat."

A LONG WAIT.

AN Irishman is seldom short of a reply, either witty or otherwise. In the neighbourhood of Penrith a gentleman noticed an Irishman professing to feed a goat from a deep jug, and observed to the man, "Pat, I'm afraid your vessel is too deep for the goat." "Oh, be jabers! mebby yer honour's wrong there, sor. His nose is too short, and he'll have long to wait till it grows."

SHARP AND TRUE.

THE late Mr. John Braithwaite, of Lamplugh, was an inveterate rhymster. One day meeting a servant girl, she asked if he would be pleased to let her hear one of his rhymes. He walked on a few yards without speaking—then turned and said,

"This warld's come to sek a pass,
Yan can't tell t' mistress frae t' sarvent lass."

CAUTIONARY.

About the year 1820, when very narrow brimmed hats were in fashion, and gentlemen wore three or four neckcloths at all seasons, a stranger was pacing before the Globe Hotel, at Cockermouth, waiting the departure of the coach, and John Robinson, of Graysouthen, was standing near, closely scanning the gentleman as he strutted several times past the door in full feather. Not liking to be so scrutinised, and being rather chafed by the delay, he stopped before John and angrily demanded why he stared so earnestly at him. John quietly and readily answered, " I was just thinking that if a girt pash o' rain was to fo', you wad tak in watter varra fast about t' casin,"—or under the eaves of his hat.

WILLY WALKER, OF HACKTHORP.

Willy was walking near the side of the road when a man came riding furiously behind him, and before Willy could get out of the way he was thrown down by the horse against the bank and laid flat on his back, but not injured. Instead of scolding the man he called loudly after him, " Is ta coming this way back, thinks ta ? "

Willy thought he had better be going before the man returned or he might be roughly tumbled a second time.

PRETTY FAR NORTH.

Mr. North, of Uldale Hall, having stayed late one night at Keswick, was returning by the toll gate at which he had paid on coming in the morning. He found the gate closed, and no keeper visible. On calling "gate" the man appeared in his night dress, asking, "Who's there?" "Robert North, of Uldale Hall," was the reply. The man then demanded twopence for toll, as twelve o'clock had struck. The passenger remonstrated without effect, but paid the money and rode off so far as to give the man time to get into bed. Mr. North was fond of a joke, and being rather nettled at having, as he thought, to pay twice in the same day, returned and called "gate." The man again asked, "Who's there?" "Robert North, of Uldale Hall." This was several times repeated, till the man grew angry and threw open the gate, saying, "Robert North may ride o' neet if he likes, and to hell efter." Mr. North thinking he had enjoyed the joke long enough, and given the man sufficient annoyance, rode home.

MINE AND THINE.

The late Isaac D——, of Whitehaven, went to buy some fat cattle from Mark B——, and to conciliate him with a view to promote a bargain, took him a quarter of a pound of smoking tobacco as a present. Mark puffed away at the chimney corner and enjoyed the treat, but no bargain could be effected. At length Isaac requested him to hand over the paper of tobacco that he might join him in a pipe, when Mark gruffly replied, "Finnd thy oan bacca—this is mine."

DAFT JOE RIGG.

As an instance of the shrewdness which occasionally

crops up among people of weak intellect the following
is given :—

Joe Rigg, of Workington, an able-bodied pauper,
had often been sent to the Union Workhouse when in
want; but the sweets of liberty were stronger, in his
idea, than the fear of want, and he had always left the
House after short sojourns, to tax his acquaintances
at home. He could read, and some one handed him
a list of the Workington Poor, wherein he read,
“Joseph Rigg, weak minded.” “Weak minded!
What does that mean?” he asked. “Daft,” was the
answer. “Ey, but I was niver so daft as to work.”

DETERMINED ON IT.

A young Graysouthen collier asked his mother’s leave
to marry a young woman whom he named. The
mother advised him not to marry, saying he would
starve if he married, and there would be two of them,
and might be more. “Wey, mudder, two can starve
as weel as yan, and we’ll dee ’t.” And they did, but
did not starve.

REBUKE AND REJOINDER.

A predecessor of the present Sir Wilfred Lawson,
Bart., M.P., some two or three generations ago, kept
a pack of hounds, and a droll character for a huntsman. He also had his ale brewed at home, and was
said to be rather sparing of malt. One morning the
master looked in on the man and snappishly said,
“What are you doing here, Tom? Why don’t you

turn out with the hounds?"   "I am warming some ale, Sir Wilfred."   "The devil's in the belly that won't warm the ale," exclaimed the Baronet.   "I say the devil's in the ale that won't warm the belly," responded Tom.   He turned out with the hounds, soon after overhearing the affair good-humouredly related to the field, and was often quizzed on it afterwards.

MAD OR NOT MAD?

During a period when dogs were required to be muzzled or chained to avoid hydrophobia, a well-dressed youth of delicate appearance, and wearing a respirator, stood looking at the pictures exhibited in a printseller's window in Workington, when two or three ragged boys came staring and wondering why his mouth should be covered.   After a little silence, one of them, who thought he had solved the mystery, took courage to express his opinion, saying, "Thou bites."   "No, I don't bite."   "Wey, what ista muzzled for, than?"

POLITENESS UNDER DIFFICULTIES.

Some time ago a West Cumberland magnate on riding out met a boy leading two calves—one in each hand, and both tied to his girdle.   The gentleman had been, deservedly, accustomed to receive honours from all who knew him, and prized the honours accorded by his neighbours.   The calves were frisky and the lad, finding he could not pay his respects properly, pre-tended to be so busy keeping his calves in order that he could not look up to see who was passing. On seeing no signs of recognition, the Squire called out, "Why don't you take off your hat to me, boy?" "If you please, sir, if you'll hod teaà cofe, amess I will."

JOHN DRURY.

MANY yet living in Whitehaven will remember a burly, elderly man named John Drury. By the misconduct of his wife John's mind had been thrown off its balance, and he was in the constant habit as he traversed the streets of talking to himself in a rather loud tone about his private grievances and wrongs. As this became more marked the magistrates deemed it their duty to have him before them to ascertain if it might be proper to put a stop to his public eccentric doings. One of them kindly suggested that he would be more comfortable in the workhouse than in wandering about, as some accident might happen to him, as he was evidently a little *beside himself.* John sharply replied that his mind was not disturbed in any way. Upon this a magistrate asked, "Then what makes you talk to yourself so much?"

Casting a quick glance of his grey eye at his reverence, John smartly replied—"Oh, I always, all my life, liked to have a crack with a sensible man!" John's liberty was not interfered with.

LUXURY DEFINED.

A GRAYSOUTHEN collier having taken too much beer, fell over a roadside wall and injured himself, lying for some time insensible. When rather come round he

was discovered by a comrade, and cried out, " O Kit,
I is bad, man ; git me a cwol to lig my head on."
" Nay, nay, Jim, my lad, thear nea luxuries to be hed
heer."

A LEFT-HANDED READER.

DOROTHY LAWRENCE, of Workington, received a letter
from her son who was on a long voyage at sea and had
not been heard of for many months.   Being unable to
read. she took the letter among her acquaintances and
heard it read so often that she remembered it all.
Unwilling to be thought ignorant, she one day took
the letter to a friend and held it before her pretending
to read it.   The friend noticed the position of the
letter, and said, " Dorsy, woman, thou hods t' letter
t' wrang side up!"   " Hod ty tongue, thou windy
feùll.   Duzzent thou know I'se left handit?"

ARCHITECTURE.

A WORKINGTON gentleman went to a large old inn in
a neighbouring town for a night's lodging.   The house,
as many are in Cumberland, had been enlarged by
adding some adjoining houses to it.   It had sundry
lobbies and turnings, and the levels of the floors were
broken by two or three steps up or two or three down
in different parts.   While the gentleman was being
conducted to his bedroom, he remarked the uneven
levels and many turnings, and inquired who was the
architect.   The servant slyly replied, " O sir! they
built it first and architectit it efter."

TIT FOR TAT.

A READY-witted Cumbrian perambulating the streets of London, observed a large building which excited his curiosity to know its name and uses, there being no sign-board or name visible to him. The entrance being open he walked in. He found an inner door open and a solitary clerk sitting at his desk, and said, "If you please, what div ye sell here?" "Logger-heads," said the Cockney. "Wey, ye mun hev hed a brisk trade for them, when you've nobbet yan left."

THE CHOLERA.

IN 1832, the year of the first attack of cholera, the wife of William Weir, of Workington (best known as Fish Will) was seized with the disease and died; and Will was so ill that he was not expected to recover. Nathan Walker, a joiner, was brought to prepare the wife's coffin, and said, he "med as weel measure Will an' o', as it would spare a journey, for Will was sure to dee." Will was not so far gone but he heard and remembered Nathan's remark after his recovery. After a few years something went wrong with the joiner and he hung himself, when Will was summoned on the jury and said he was then quite satisfied—he had had his revenge on Nathan. Nathan kept an inn and had an eye to business to the last, for it was found he had written in chalk in his bedroom—"Gury (jury) in my house."

WILL AND THE CONSTABLE.

FISH WILL being committed to prison for an assault, was started on the coach in custody of William Bell,

a parish constable. The prisoner had money in his
pocket, and knowing Bell's liking for drink, he treated
the constable so often on the way that the liquor took
effect, and Will seized the opportunity to abstract the
warrant from Bell's pocket. On reaching Carlisle, he
boldly conducted the drunken bailiff to the gaol, and
knocked for admittance. On the door being opened,
he steadied Bell within, produced the warrant, and
saying, "Se ye, I've brought him at last," out he walked
with his receipt, leaving Bell where he himself should
have been.

POPPY OR PUPPY?

The late Robert Elliot, gardener at Rosehill, was one
day supplying a party of visitors with cut flowers, when
one of the younger gentlemen called out in a super-
cilious manner—"Elliot, cut me a flower." "Would
you like a poppy, sir?" was the dry response of the
old Scot, to the great amusement of the other guests.

BITTER-SWEET.

When J. C. Curwen, Esq., took to farming he grew
large crops of mangold-wurzel, a plant that few here
had ever seen. A lady visitor, admiring the large red
roots, asked him what they were. "Mangold-wurzel,
mam." "What do they taste like?" "They are
bitter-sweet, like matrimony."

SAMMY ROOK.

A lazy, idle fellow, who was fond of dress and good

living, and who, from being an inveterate smoker, had earned for himself the sobriquet of "Smeuky" Graham, once asked Sammy if he could make a rhyme about him. The question elicited the following prophetic impromptu couplet :—

> " Thou cleads thy back, and pangs thy weamm,
> But mark the end of ' Smeuky Greamm.' "

Graham eventually became a pauper.

TOM FOOL O' MUNCASTER.

In an age when it was the fashion both at court and elsewhere for the higher families to keep a household fool for the amusement of their visitors and themselves, the Lord of Muncaster had a noted one, who, like many a better fellow, was apt to resent an insult when he thought it was carried too far.

During those days when each feudal lord held jurisdiction over his manors, evil deeds were done and punished or passed over at the will of the lord.

Tom was a favourite with his master, and one hot day he found the castle joiner in his workshop taking a nap after dinner, with his head resting on a block of wood for a pillow. Calling to mind the many instances of the joiner having made more sport of him than was agreeable, he took an axe and chopped off the joiner's head, hiding it among the shavings. He then capered into the hall in great glee, saying—" When the joiner wakes he will have some trouble to find his head." It is said of that far-off time, that a good joiner was easier to find than a good fool, and Tom's exploit was overlooked.

Among the numerous visitors who met at Muncaster

Castle in Tom's day, was a gentleman blessed with a large nose, who plagued Tom unmercifully. Tom thought it prudent not to come the joiner over a gentleman, but he was at no loss for revenge, and one morning spread an offensive substance on the top rail of the stair leading from the gentleman's room. In coming down stairs the visitor drew his hand along the anointed rail, and found himself the victim of a dirty trick. An immediate and angry inquiry was made as to who the delinquent was, but no one would admit knowing anything of the matter. "It must be the fool you keep," said the indignant gentleman; so Tom was brought forward and asked if he put the dirt on the stair rail? "Yes," said Tom, "but the man with the big nose had a hand in it."

ROB O' THE SHOP.

"Rob o' the Shop," as a clever and comical blacksmith of one of the north-eastern parishes was usually called, had a liking for a ramble among his customers when their accounts became due. He also had a liking for a good glass of whisky. His friends knew his failing and were careful to serve him with as small a measure as decency would permit; but the hospitality of the district would not allow the omission of the treat. At one of his calls the good woman was so thoughtful of his good as to stint his customary glass to the very lowest limit. On receiving it he turned it first to one side and then to the other, and, as his sayings were often witty and always in good humour, he remarked — "Ay mistress! ye sartenly think āā hae varra thick lips; for a fellow wi' thin 'ans coul'l niver reach down to sook this drop up."

MISCELLANEOUS ANECDOTES.

BURYING AN IRISHMAN.

BEFORE the days of the new Poor Law, an overseer of Carlisle had so many entries charged in his books for "burying an Irishman" that the ratepayers began to doubt the correctness of the accounts. On these items being disposed of, a saying got abroad in the city that when a charge was suspected it must have been for "burying an Irishman."

A FRIEND INDEED.

THE late Mr. W—— M——, of Whitehaven, related a story of being awakened one night by his wife, who thought she heard a strange noise in or about the room, with—"William, didst thou hear anything?" "No, Mary; what is it?" "Thou must get up, William, and find out what it is." He got up, and struck a light in time to see a pair of feet and legs, and then the rest of a man, sooty enough of course, come down the chimney. In some astonishment, Mr. M—— said, "Friend, what does thou want here?" "Oh, Mr. M——, I do beg a thousand pardons. I've come down the wrong chimney to see my sweetheart. Please let me go quietly out." Mr. M—— conducted him quietly out, with, "Now, go thy way, and come no more here."

GOING TO DIE.

John Stamper, a bachelor farmer, near Penrith, fell into reduced circumstances and took lodgings with Bella Ellison. His misfortunes preyed upon his mind and he fancied he was going to die, but was generally ready for his victuals. One day he told Bella, in a feeble voice, he was sure he was near his end and she might call in some neighbours to see him die. Bella was a good nurse in her way, and of more honesty than civility. She tried to persuade John he was strong enough to live over winter and come out in the spring, and she thought it better not to make fools of their kind neighbours, as he " wad dee nin that time." John sprang up in his bed and roared out in a strong voice, " If thou duzzent gang, Bella, I'll gang mysel, and tell them seah ! "

On another occasion he fancied himself very weak and must die ; when Bella, not in the best of humours, struck in with, " Wey, set a time and keep't than, for you're still gaan to dee and niver does dee."

NO LAW FOR DONKEYS.

A lottery for a donkey and some smaller prizes came off at Penrith, when Tommy Bradshaw, labourer, drew the head prize. By some cajolery the concocters of the lottery got the drawing upset and re-drawn when Tommy was not the winner. In great anger Tommy applied to the leading solicitor to prosecute the parties for the recovery of his prize. The man of law was highly amused at the request, and searched, or pretended to search, a great many law books without success, and finally dismissed Tommy, saying, with great seriousness, " There was really no law for donkeys." Tommy was often quizzed and asked if Mr. J—— was going to do anything for him, and seemed as much delighted as if he had got his prize, saying, " Mr. J—— telt me theer was nea law for a donkey, but if it hed been a horse he *wad* ha' warm't them."

A CROCODILE.

A WORKINGTON solicitor relates the following as having taken place in his office :—

Client—" Mr. T——, wad you tell me summat about this will? It hez a crocodil til't."

Sol.—" A what, my good woman?"

Client—" Wey a crocodil. You see, sir, I mebby doon't tell ye t' reet neàmm on't, but it's summat at t' end on't."

Sol.—" Oh, I see! It is a codicil."

Client.—" Ey, that's it awivver."

PORTRAIT PAINTING.

" NEVER mind the likeness ; make us a nice picture," was the instruction given by a young lady at Cockermouth to Sammy Crosthwaite, the portrait painter.

O' MAKS.

DIFFERENT versions of this story are given, and without vouching for the correctness of any, the following will be found as near the truth as any of them.

A certain judge recruiting his spent energies among the pleasant Cumberland vales, and, sauntering along the banks of a noted trout stream, came suddenly into close proximity with a countryman plying the craft of angler. The man was so intent on his occupation that he did not look up to see who accosted him with, " What kind of fish do you angle for here?" "O' maks," (all kinds) was the prompt reply; and the judge walked on, after asking if they were good eating, and being answered with—" Ey, t' best in England." On going to his hotel the judge ordered dinner; and, willing to perpetuate the joke, asked if he could have some of the fish called o' maks, that a man he had passed was angling for. The puzzled landlady declared she did not know any fish of that name, but would ask her husband who was just coming in from fishing. The man was sent in, and was not a little confounded on finding he was required to give a more explicit answer to the judge's first inquiry, but got out of it by saying, he " fished for o' maks, but hed gitten nea mak but yan, and they were varra fine trouts." With some amusement at the man's ingenuity, a dish of trout was ordered to be cooked, and enjoyed accordingly.

⁓⊶≫⊰⊱⊷⁓

THE SILVER BUCKLES.

At the time when silver buckles were worn as shoe-fasteners, a girl who had procured a pair went to a party with her new buckles on, and to her great disappointment no one noticed them. At length, being seated near the fire, she put her feet upon the fender by way of courting observation. Still no notice seemed to be taken of them; but. determined on another effort, she said, drawing her feet hastily back, " Silver buckles mun be het things !" A general laugh was the only result of her persevering vanity.

LIFT ME GENTLY.

A SCULPTOR and architect in Carlisle was successful in business, but gave way to drinking. On one occasion he was found by some weavers, late in the evening, extended on the footpath, and drunk. They were about to assist him to rise ; but he, recognising one whom he knew, called out, " Hands off ! I'll not be lifted by a lot of weavers." They left him, and were succeeded by two well-dressed men who volunteered their help. The drunken man could make out that the two were more respectable in appearance than the weavers, and accepted their aid, saying, " Lift me gently, my good fellows, I'm a ten thousand pound man."

SAMMY ROOK.

IN the early part of the nineteenth century, Wigton possessed an eccentric character named Sammy Rook, who was Jack-of-all-trades,—bricklayer, painter, fisherman, rhymster, &c. ; and when work was scarce he had an extraordinary genius for making two jobs out of one. He was once employed by the landlady of the Lion and the Lamb Inn to paint her signboard. He asked if she would go to the expense of a chain for the lion, but she thought it quite unnecessary, moreover the cost would be less. Sammy resorted to the oft-told expedient of using only water colours for the lion ; consequently after a stormy night the animal was nowhere.　The lady in distress went to Sammy's door and called out, "Sammy, t' lion's run away." "Aa telt ye seah, and ye waddent let me chain him. A wild beast sud olas be tied up."

Sammy was more fortunate than Selathiel Court and others under similar circumstances, for he got the job of chaining the lion.

On another occasion Sammy was employed to set a grate for an old woman, who cautioned him especially to give it plenty of draught.　When the work was finished a fire was lit, and the old woman put her knitting down on the hob and went to the door to see the smoke ascend, when Sammy surreptitiously threw the knitting out of the window.　The woman thinking it had been drawn up the chimney, exclaimed, " Loavin days, Sammy, ye've gien it ower mickle draft, yan can trust nought on 't hud for't.　It wad draw t' teapot up t' chimlay, and ye mun poo't down and set it ower ageann."

Sammy once set a grate with black peats and mortar in order to get another job.

Old Mr. Lightfoot, an attorney, who was of a busy, meddlesome turn, and no favourite of Sammy's, was once passing over Wiza bridge when Sam was plying his rod in the stream.　" Well, Samuel, what are you fishing for there ? "　Sammy had a stammering in his speech, and replied, "d—d—d deevils."　" Indeed ! those must be curious fish.　What do you bait with ? " " T—t—t— turneys," was Sam's reply.

* * *

DITTO.

At a vestry meeting of the ratepayers of the township of Hensingham, the accounts were being read over, and the word "ditto" having occurred a number of times among the disbursements, a person present remarked that he now knew the cause of the rates being so high,—"It's them d—d dittos. Cannot we do with fewer of *them?*"

OLD MOSES.

BEFORE the establishment of rural foot-postmen, Moses Jenkinson travelled as daily messenger between Cockermouth and Eaglesfield. One day he had a bridal cap to take to Eaglesfield, and to carry it safely without crushing its ornaments he very considerately took the strings in his teeth, and walked the three miles with it dangling over his breast. Moses was an elderly man and chewed tobacco, as was then the fashion. When he took charge of the cap he forgot to take out his quid. Still he was careful of his treasure, and tried to spit over it as he walked. On delivery it was found, to his horror and the dismay of the bride, so much besmeared with tobacco juice as to be totally unfit for the high occasion. In deep sorrow Moses says, "Wey, wey, I dud' o' I could, and who could dea mair!"

BETTY WILSON AT CHURCH.

A NEWSPAPER paragraph of 1867 stated, that a decent looking country-woman, with two children, walked into a church near Penrith, one Sunday morning, just in time to hear the clergyman give out the text, "Jesus I know, and Paul I know, but who are ye?" In great amazement the woman said, "Wya, Sir, I's Betty

Wilson frae Langsleddale, an' this is awer Tommy, an'
this is awer lile Mary, an' we's gangan to see my
brother Jwony; an' I thàwt I'd just step in an' see
what ye war aa makkan here."

I DINNA KEN MY AIN HOUSE.

CUTHBERT HALL, an old resident in Workington, was
originally from Newcastle, who brought and retained
his provincial dialect; also a propensity to occasionally get drunk.   In one of his excesses he lost his
reckoning of locality, and applied to a brother collier
from the same quarter, whom he met, to get the information.   "Aa say. man; div ye ken whoa Cuddy
Haa leevs?"   "Wey, smash mey brains if ye aa' n't
Cuddy Haa yer sel, man!"   "Aa ken thaat weel, bit
aa divent ken whoa he leevs."

READY CONSOLATION.

A MR. H—— died at Workington a few years ago,
and his widow, as in duty bound, lamented him very
much, until a neighbouring woman went in to condole
with her.   The bereaved one took the visit very kindly,
and invited her neighbour up stairs to see the corpse.
On uncovering the face she sorrowfully said, "Ey,
theer he ligs, poor fellow! He was a varra decent
man, and a rare dancer."   By invitation the visit was
repeated next day, when the desolate one found great
consolation in a demure game of pool with her friendly
neighbour.

DR. MILLER.

THE late Dr. Miller, the eminent meteorologist, had some thirty rain gauges distributed over the lake district, one of which was placed on the summit of Scawfel and was maliciously destroyed by some students. The act was thus described by his informant : " They mash't t' tunmill heed in wi' cobble steànns, and than they proddle't t' boddam out wi' their kebby sticks."

Another of Dr. Miller's mountain gauges was missing, and he wrote to a farmer acquaintance stating his loss and asking him to make inquiries about it. The man, having mistaken the word gauge for goose, replied to Mr. Miller that he had made diligent search, but could not " hear tell of any stray geuss hevvin been seen or fund on their fell."

COACH WHEELS.

SOME years ago two ignorant country lads (just over the Westmoreland border) beheld for the first time a four-wheeled vehicle in the shape of a post chaise. What astonished them most was that the wheels were not all of the same size. One of them said to the other, " I'll tell tha what. I'll bet tha' a shillin' t' girt wheel owertaks t' laal an afoor she gits tul t' guide post." " Done," said the other. They ran after the carriage till it reached the guide post, which happened to be at the foot of a hill, and there found the positions of the wheels unchanged. .

The loser protested that he " waddent hae lost t' shillin' if t' fella heddent gitten down at t' hill top and fassent t' girt wheel wid a chain."

OYSTERS.

A Cumbrian residing in London sent home to his brother a Christmas present of oysters and many other good things. Meeting him afterwards, he inquired how he liked them. "Oh, weel enough, but they war mortal hard to git at." "How did you open them?" said the giver. "Wey, I carried them out into t' foald and bray't them on t' wo' wid a cobble."

AFFINITY OF SPEECH.

A happy recognition once took place between two men who as boys, very many years before, had been playmates in a quiet Cumberland village. One of them was a passenger on board a merchant ship in some far distant ocean, and happened to be on deck on a still night, when he heard a sailor who was stretched on his back on the deck, dreamily thinking of home and the loved ones far away, mutter, "Cush ! that foretopsail yard comes and gangs, and jeyks like Pardshaw-lee yat." The sound of the old familiar name of the gate at the entrance to the common at his native place at once led to very unexpected mutual explanations and congratulations between the two.

ACADEMICAL.

A very illiterate old man named Telford kept school at Graysouthen. When a pupil came to a hard word

which he knew no more how to pronounce than did
his master, the latter would say, "Co't summat and
gang on."

HARD TO CONVINCE.

DURING the memorable hotly-contested county election of 1768, an active agent of the Tory party was
treating some of his political friends in a country ale-
house. After the tankards had been renewed again
and again, still the thirsty souls called for more. The
landlady came to say they had entirely exhausted the
supplies, and that the barrel was dry. "I will n't
believe tha," said one roysterer, "not without thou'll
gang and poo t' spiddick (spigot) out and fetch't here."

TEETOTAL MEDICINE.

A WHITEHAVEN tradesman, who had long been a leader
among teetotallers, was seized with illness ; and growing worse, called in a doctor. Suspecting his patient's
hidden proclivities, after due inquiries and close examination the doctor said he would send suitable
medicines, and along with them a certain quantity of
brandy was to be taken. The sick man strongly
objected to alcohol in any shape ; and, having been
so long a total abstainer, asked what people would
say or think of him whose example and advice, he
hoped, had been the means of saving and reclaiming
so many who might have been lost. The doctor insisted he should take it, saying, as he had saved so
many he must now think of saving his own life, and
take the medicines indispensably necessary for that

purpose, and he would order a supply of brandy to be sent him. As if afraid of consequences, the patient gave in and said, " Well, doctor, if it is to be so, it must ; but *mind it be good.*"

JOB'S MOTHER.

A very passionate and certainly blamable mother threw a tea-cup at her boy. His grown-up sister endeavoured to pacify him, saying it was their duty to bear with patience such outbursts of temper, and reminding him of the example set before them by Job, about whom she had lately been reading to him, when the little fellow observed, " Ey, but Job's mudder niver scop't him on t' heed wi' tea-cups."

The following is from the Wigton Advertiser of September, 1860.

MERELY A TRIFLING DIFFERENCE.

Some little time ago, in a country parish in the North of Cumberland, the inhabitants took it into their heads to have a harmonium for their parish church, which was accordingly ordered, and duly announced as being ready at the nearest railway station awaiting its transport to its destination, which was to be by means of a farmer's cart who had kindly offered to take it up to the village, at the same time that he carried home a " Patent Time Saving " washing machine, which the farmer's wife had persuaded the good man to invest in to get up their household linen. Safely deposited

in his carts, the two "new-fangled things" got home;
but lo! "Which is t' thing et weshes t' cleas?" and
which "t' new organ fiddle?" Neither had ever been
seen at work by the astonished churchwarden, and
"for t' varra leyf on 'em" he could not tell "whilk
was whilk." At last, however, the larger of the two
was pitched upon as being more like the harmonium,
and was set in its appointed place in the church, the
other being deposited in the wash-house ready for the
next wash. We need scarcely go any further, but may
leave it to our readers to imagine the astonishment of
the schoolmaster on being taken down in the evening
to "give a tune or two" to the village choir and a
select circle on what turned out to be a washing
machine.

JOE HENRY.

A GENERATION ago a half-witted compound of knave
and fool had a weekly allowance from the parishioners
of Gilcrux, and the smithy was his usual lounge. He
sat on the window sill in the summer, and when colder
weather came on he and his ragged habiliments were
allowed by the good-natured smith to occupy the form
on the hearth provided for customers.

Joe had been presented with a tattered scarlet coat,
and was not a little proud of it. He was enjoying the
warmth of the smithy fire when a neighbour came in,
and asked if he had taken to hunting that winter,
having got a scarlet coat. "Nay," says he, "huntin's
nobbet a ratchan kind o' business, and it taks o' t'
meat out of a body's belly."

It was once asked why he did not work for his living like other people. He readily answered, "Let
them work at's gitten nea forton o' their oan. I was

bworn to *my* forton, and it comes to me ivry week,
and that's mair ner any on ye can say."

AN UNINTENTIONAL RHYMSTER.

IN the north-eastern part of the county a young farmer
aspired to be a poet, and on a rainy morning retired
to an upstairs room, telling his mother he was going
to write poetry and wished not to be disturbed till
dinner time.   The mother did not relish his proposal,
but as it was wet and not a busy season, she for once
felt disposed to indulge his fancy, and would call him
when dinner was ready!   On being duly called, he
answered, saying he would be down shortly.   Time
passed on, and not coming down, the old lady went
up in no very good humour at his delay, telling him
the family had done dinner, and asking him what he
had got done.   He said he had written

"A dwelling-house, a barn, and byer,"

and was fairly puzzled for a suitable rhyme to it.

Her patience being exhausted with the small amount
of the forenoon's work, she angrily and unhesitatingly
exclaimed: "The muckle deevil set it o' afire," at
once finishing the couplet, and ordered him down to
his dinner.

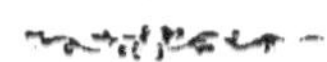

LONGS AND SHORTS.

MANY years subsequent to the general transition
period from short-knee breeches to trousers, two old
acquaintances met at a railway station.   Both were

old men, and both stuck by " shorts."   One was somewhat of the typical John Bull build, whilst the other
was more of the " lean and slippered pantaloon."

After exchanging the usual salutations, the lean
man observed, " What, I see thou's like me John, thou
still wears t' oald-farrant mak o' brutches."

John, who was deaf, and had a loud ringing voice—
" Ey, bit if I was thee, I wad wear lang breeks."

Lean man—" What for, min ? "

John—" Wey, because thou's gitten sec a par o'
shanks !   I've seen many a heeron-sew [heron] on our
fell edge wid a better pair ! "

ADVICE.

" Theer nought like gittan hod ov a gay heavy tail't
an," said an old man in giving advice to a young friend
on the subject of matrimony.   " Fwok talks about love.
Wey, issent it just as easy to love a lass wid a lock o'
brass as yan et hes nin ? "

A COMPLIMENT TO FELL-SIDERS.

The following advice from an industrious master
mason to his son was lately overheard :—" Aa wish,
wi' o' my heart, thou wad git weddit, Mat ; but divvent
git hod o' yan o' thur feckless dris't up things about
here, bit gang thy ways up amang t' fells and lait a
lass 'at's fit to mak a wife on."

TRUTH BEFORE POLITENESS.

A MAN of not very bright intellect received many
kindnesses from the first Lord Lonsdale. On one
occasion he rang the bell at Whitehaven Castle, and
inquired, "Is William in?" The footman asked,
"William! what William?" "Wey, William, Earl of
Lonsdale, to be sure," said he; "dus ta nut ken thy
maister's neàmm?"

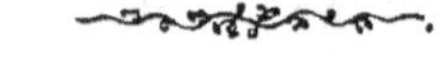

ENTERPRISING, BUT NOT CREDITABLE.

A COLLIER, who had risen from the ranks to a position
of considerable trust and emolument, was asked how
he had managed to attain his standing. He thus
explained the process: "Wey, I'll just tell you how
it was. Whenever I fand a man 'at I thought knew
mair about a colliery ner what I dud, I just tuk him
till a public-house and gev him two or three glasses,
and than I wrought out on him o' 'at iver he hed in
him. And that's t' way I raised mysel up frae t' varra
dregs to t' position I now stand in."

DESCRIPTIVE.

THE following, illustrative of the genuine Cumberland
dialect, is told by an elderly lady who, in her youth,
heard a Cumbrian, just returned from London, describe
to another who was about to go there, the locality of
some house in St. Paul's Churchyard, in these words:
"It's ebm fornenst t' girt Kirk, and down in t' low
neukk o' t' garth."

FORCED TO GIVE IN.

A COMMERCIAL traveller, noted for his beer-drinking powers, once met with his match in that undesirable accomplishment in a village blacksmith, whom he was treating at the ale-house over the settling of an account. When they had consumed nine quarts, he asked for the reckoning; but the son of Vulcan exclaimed with the most unfeigned surprise, "What, you're sartenly not done yet, Mr. Robison!"

A WHAPPER.

A MAN, who had been engaged in catching lobsters, said that he "rov t' clea off yan that was as big as a taty swill!" (A large basket used for gathering potatoes in.)

ANOTHER.

AN old man at Graysouthen, whose office it was to toll a hand-bell through the village to give notice to the inhabitants on the occasion of funerals, was notorious for the large-sized clogs he wore. One day he suddenly stopped his bell, and remarking, "Sarten-lye, theer mun be summat i' my clog;" pulled it off, turned it upside down, and out rolled a casley, that is, a peg-top.

ELECTRIC FORCE.

MANY years ago, a ship on its way from Whitehaven to Dublin, was disabled in a storm ; when all hope of safety was at an end, the officers and passengers assembled in the cabin for the solemn purpose of prayer and meditation ; and, when after a short period of silence, the rudderless vessel made a tremendous lurch, one of the latter calmly observed, " I doubt, indeed, she 'ill toup, lads ! "　This remark so tickled the captain that he became infused with fresh energy, which communicating itself to his nearly worn-out crew carried the ship into port.

CONSOLATION.

WHAT description of a cadaverous individual suffering under a complication of face-ache, neuralgia, and boils, can be more graphic than that with which a jolly John Bull-like man addressed his less fortunate neighbour ? " Noo, what's t' matter wid thee ?　Thou leuks as yalla as a fellside teadd, and thy chafts is o' covered ower wid girt blebs, fit to freeten a body."

A DISTINCTION.

VERY many years ago two intimate friends went to London together.　One was of gentlemanly manners and bearing, the other more homely, who only spoke the broad vernacular of Cumberland.　Going into a barber's shop to get shaved, they were taken for mas-

ter and servant.   When the operations were concluded,
the homely one asking what was to pay was informed,
" A penny for you, and sixpence for the gentleman."

ELEGANCE.

An Allonby yeoman relating what he saw when dining
at the house of some great man, said, " Barn, they hed
mahogany dooers, an' whushins till their chair backs,
and stuff for dinner 'at they co't blue manj !"

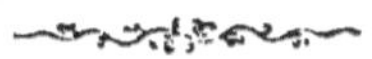

STARTLING.

Two neighbours going by way of Rottington to St.
Bees Church had to cross a swollen stream where
large stones were placed as steps.   These being partly
covered by the flood one of the pair said he thought
he could manage to get across without being much
wet.   The other replied, " Thou may gang to hell thy
own way, I'll gang round by t' brig."

AMIABLE OR BLAMABLE.

A CUMBERLAND worthy, extolling the affection and
amiability of his wife, said they had been " weddit
abeun twenty year, and he hed cun heämm at o' times
o' neet frae sun-down to cock-crow, and in o' maks o'
conditions frae teetotal to total nincompoopsy, and still
niver a wrang word come frae her."

LOWTHER SECURITY.

There was, and perhaps still is, an itinerant family of pot-sellers and dealers in old iron who happen to have the same surname as the noble Earl who fills the office of Lord-Lieutenant of the county. One of its members purchased a number of houses at a public sale at Wigton. The auctioneer, struck with his shabby dress and mean appearance, asked if he was prepared to give security for the payment. Slowly rising, he drew from his pocket a stocking well-stored with gold, and, deliberately shaking it at arms' length, exclaimed, with as much dignity as he could assume, "There's a Lowder's [Lowther's] security."

DECEIVED.

At a political banquet at which Sir James Graham was present, one of his tenants catching the eye of the baronet seized a tall glass of coloured jelly which he mistook for wine, shouted, "To your good health, Mister Sir Jems," and tried to toss it off, amid the laughter of the company and his own confusion.

DR. DALTON AND THE KING.

The celebrated chemist, Dr. John Dalton, who was born at Eaglesfield, never forgot to use his native dialect when, as he loved to do, he revisited the scenes of his youth, and the friends of his early years.

On one of these occasions he was narrating to one

with whom he kept up a long intimacy and correspondence an interview he had with King William IV., when that monarch offered him the honour of knighthood, which the philosopher refused, chiefly on the ground that he could kneel only to his Maker. When presented the king said to him, "Well, Mr. Dalton, how are you getting on at Manchester?" [his residence.] The Doctor answered in his homely way, "Oh, I don't know; just middlin' I think." On his friend expressing surprise at the curtness of his reply, he said, "Wey, John, what can yan say to sek fwok?"

FINGER GLASSES.

A RAW youth, who was being trained as a sort of page in a family in West Cumberland, desiring to know if finger glasses were to be put on the table at an approaching dinner party, went to his mistress and said, "If you please, mam, is t' company gaan to wesh thersels to-day?"

HOUSE OR BARN.

AT a meeting convened for considering the repairs required in a fine old parish church, the Rector explained among other things, that it was proposed to remove a modern flat ceiling, and restore the ancient oaken rafters of the high pitched roof. To this project a lusty 'statesman dissented, adding, "T' church is coald eneuf as it is, and dus ta mean to tell me 'at it is n't snugger sleepin' in a ceiled house, ner what it is in a leaàth oppen clean up to t' reuff?"

ALL DOWNHILL.

Tommy D——, of Keswick, had a quarrel with his wife at the head of the staircase. After much altercation his passion got the better of him and he contrived to tumble her down the stairs. Whilst she went rolling towards the bottom Tommy looked on and coolly said, "Tak time oald lass—it's o' in-bank."

TOMMY DUNN.

Tommy at Green Row School had sent his watch to Wigton to be cleaned, and as the holidays approached he wrote for it—"Please send Tommy Dunn's watch done or undone.—Yours, Tommy Dunn." We say, shortly done, and well done, Tommy Dunn!

ASS OR ASH.

A gentleman near Maryport wanted to purchase a donkey for his young children to learn to ride upon. Meeting a boy with a good looking ass drawing a cart laden with coal he called out, "Stop, you boy. Whose ass is that?" "It's nut ass 'at o,' it's smo' cwol."

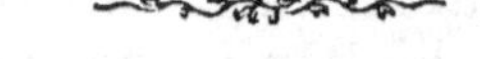

A POUND TOO LIGHT.

An acquaintance met Gerard Armstrong and inquired after the health of his mother, who was a very old

woman.   He replied, "The āāl body's gay an' weel
for her yage, bit she's a pund leeght."   "What's that,
Jarrat?"   "She's a pund leeght aa tell tha."   "An'
how can that be?"   "The āāl body's teànn to sayin'
her bits o' prayers, an' aa owerhard her ya neight
amang her bits o' prayers sayan she'd been weigh'd
an' fund wantin'."

D. A. M.

A YOUNG lady of Whitehaven called on a seal engraver
and wished to have a monogram of the initial letters of
her name.   "What are the letters, mam?"   "D.A.M."

The engraver was at once struck with the word they
formed, and asked, "Could you not omit the middle
letter or alter the arrangement in some way a little?"
"No; that is my name and I cannot alter it."

EGG SKELLFUL OF STEAM.

THE *Union* steamer from Liverpool was driven past
Whitehaven in the night and took refuge in Workington harbour.   At early morn a lady passenger on
landing met the commander, Captain John Glaister,
hastening towards his vessel in a not very gracious
mood.   On asking if he was going to sea again—
"Gang to sea!" he snappishly replied, "hoo can we
gang noo?   Theer is n't a egg skellful o' steam!"

CHEAP AND GOOD.

A LADY relative called to see John B——, of R——,
on his death-bed, and, after due inquiries, asked,

"What age are you, John?"　"I's sebbenty-two."
"And what age is Mary?"　"She's two year younger,
an' as teuf as pin wire.　She nobbet cost me hoaf a
crown (marriage fee), an' she wears like a bit o' broad
cleàtth."

DOING THE TOLL-BAR KEEPERS.

A YOUNG man of Aspatria was accustomed to ride to
Edderside a courting, and, according to the ways of
the district, he often stayed till midnight or after.

On that road there are two toll gates about a mile
apart; and the keepers, judging his errand, for a time
kindly got out of bed to open their gates without
charge, and to pass their jokes; but there is a limit to
the patience of even a toll-bar keeper, and instead of
jokes sharp words began to occur, and toll was
demanded as incurred on another day.　The young
man knew his liability, and submitted with a grumble
till a cold and stormy night came.　Then (in imita-
tion of " Robert North " mentioned in a former place)
on returning he reined up his horse in the middle of
the road at the first bar and called "Gate!"　The
keeper turned out in his shirt only; opened the gate
and received his penny in the storm.　The like occurred at the second gate, and neither keeper blessed
him!　For a few journeys after he managed to cut
his courting shorter and to return before midnight, so
having nothing to pay.　But another stormy night
came when he was out, and he stayed (of course for
shelter) till after midnight, when the keepers, finding
themselves defeated, good-humouredly begged him to
get married soon, for they did not like such night dis-
turbances and were fairly beat.

THE VIRTUE OF SILENCE.

Business once led the late John Ritson, of Wasdale-head, and his son (the noted Will)—both drolls, into Loweswater, and on arriving at the Churchstile Inn, refreshment was found desirable. Till lately it was no uncommon thing in many of the families in the fell dales for the individuals to address each other with the Scriptural *thou* instead of the modern *you.* When the good things were set on the table Will helped himself and proceeded to charge his father's glass, saying, "Thou mun say when, fadder."

Old John was silent, and Will filled the glass till it began to run over, saying, "Thou niver said *when,* fadder." "Nea, Will. A lucky man may mak his fort'n by hoddan his tongue."

THE TWO SWANS.

When Jemmy Bohanan (Buchanan) kept the much frequented Angler's Inn at Ennerdale Lake, Mr. and Mrs. S—— and party came one day to try lake fishing. Seeing two fine swans on the water Mrs. S—— observed to her husband that it was strange the swans had no cygnets at that season of the year.

Mr. S—— dryly recommended her to ask the landlady about them. Sally was an excellent hostess—always providing plenty of the best and trying to make her visitors comfortable ; she was also one of the bluntest of her class, and scorned to use what she called fine talk, or any but her native dialect. Accordingly she was asked by the lady if the swans had any cygnets. "Cygnets ! what's that ?" "Young ones."

"What, how can they hev young uns?　They're beàtth stegs."

AN OVER FREE TRANSLATION.

Soon after the Bransty Arch was built at the north-east entrance of Whitehaven, a country-man was observed to stare intently at the Lowther coat-of-arms upon it, and appearing to be spelling over the motto, "Can you read it?" said Mr. Joseph Dickinson, the shipbuilder, to him. "No, what is it?" "*Magistratus indicat virum*—the town is all my own," said Mr. D.

HOW MANY GOLD WATCHES HAVE YOU?

"Do you know where Mr. Scaley, the watchmaker, lives?" said a stranger to a good woman in the main street of Egremont. "Ey, I think I sud know, for we've five gold watches in t' house and theer meàsstly some on them theer."

THEY SAY.

Many years ago when the business of the Whitehaven Police Court was conducted in a patriarchal manner without the help of attorneys, the landlady of the Royal Standard was requested to appear "before the gentlemen" to answer for some alleged irregularity in her house.

Magistrate—"They say you keep an idle house, Jenny."

Jenny—"*They* say! Who says so? You don't,

Mr. ——, I know." To another she warmly said,
" *They* say such and such things about you, Mr. ——,
but who minds what *they* say? we know better."
"Stop, Jenny. Mind you do better in future." Exit
Jenny in triumph !

FOR BETTER, FOR WORSE.

A VETERINARY in East Cumberland, named Walker,
became ill and was obliged to keep his bed.

After some weeks of pain and uneasiness he took a
fancy that if his favourite saddle and bridle were
within sight he would be soothed and able to obtain
his former measure of rest and sleep. Finding this
not to have the desired effect he insisted on having
the saddle and bridle on the bed where he could put
his hand upon them. He would gladly have had his
pony in the room, but these fancies gave rise to much
matrimonial bickering, and also renewed some matters
of older standing. After several occurrences of this
nature he one day said to his wife regarding their married life—" Thou might ha' deùnn better, bit I couldn't
ha' deùnn warse."

VERY DECIDED.

A FORMER editor of the *Cumberland Pacquet* had a
little paper war in which a Dumfriesshire gentleman
was concerned. The Scotchman got to be so irritated
that he could not vent his anger sufficiently by pen
and ink, and so resolved on a personal interview and
to take the consequences that might ensue. Having
come to Whitehaven, he made out and entered the

Pacquet office, saying, "I want to see Mester Gebsan —Mester Robert Gebsan I mean." The editor quietly said, "I am Mr. Robert Gibson." After staring a moment the stranger said, "Weel, I cam to say a gret deal to ye, but Lord man! ye're just the vera ugliest falla I iver saa, an' I'll no tal ye what I cam to say."

A SNUBBER PROPER.

A YOUNG village tailor when out of his time went up to London. After some years spent in the metropolis he revisited his native place, in, as he doubtless flattered himself, a high state of polish. How *small* he must have felt, when after greeting one of his old friends (not with " Isaac how is ta ?" as in old times, but) with, "Well, Mr. Dockwray, how are you? I hope I see you well !" He was quietly snubbed with, "Middlin', Tommy, middlin'."

PURE ECONOMY.

WHEN tobacco was sold at a high price on account of the duty upon it, and from some other cause was reported to be likely to become still dearer, John ———, of Dearham, being accustomed to smoke a certain number of pipes daily, resolved to economise without curtailing his regular number. In this humour he engaged a lad to turn a grindstone for him. A neighbour passing them at work observed some old clay pipes laid near them, and John busy pressing the bowl of one upon the stone to grind down its holding capacity. The neighbour inquired what they were doing, and was answered, " Wey, bacca's gittan dearer ivry week, and I *mun* hev seah many pipes i' t' day ; and, thou sees, a pipe 's a pipe if it's iver sa smo."

TWO FLATS AND A SHARP.

A few years ago, Mr. T —— bought a horse from Mr. C —— for eighty pounds, and after a trial of a few weeks took a dislike to it, and requested Mr. C —— to take the horse back and to refund the money. This was declined as forming no part of the contract; so the parties differed, and called in Mr. R ——, a dealer in horses, to advise and try to settle the knotty point. When the three met, the two most interested got warm on the subject, and Mr. T —— said he would rather give thirty pounds than keep the brute. The seller declared he had known enough of the horse, and would rather give twenty pounds than take him back. The whole matter being referred to the mutual friend, he shrewdly observed that they had thrown sufficient light on the affair, and he could now see his way to satisfy both parties, saying, "You, Mr. T ——, must give me the thirty pounds, and you, Mr. C ——, must give me your twenty pounds, and neither of you shall be annoyed with the horse; for I'll take him at the eighty, and relieve you both."

A POWERFUL ARGUMENT.

A pompous swell was driving in a hasty and unguarded manner in the neighbourhood of Carlisle, when an elderly decrepid man endeavoured to get out of the way but was thrown down by the vehicle near his cottage, run over and considerably injured. His wife and son John saw the accident, and ran to the rescue; the woman screaming loudly, and the son determined on violence. The swell not liking appearances, called out, "Stand off there! If I have cracked the old crab, I am willing to pay for him." The wife hastily cried

out, " Stop, John, we'll tak the man's money ; it mends
a deal o' things, it 'll mebby mend thy fadder."

FAIRLY DEFEATED.

MRS. HUTCHINSON, of Whitehaven, died a few years
ago nearly a hundred years of age.　The date of her
birth was not known, and she steadfastly declined to
impart any information on the matter.　Not long
before her last illness her medical adviser, curious to
know her age, thought he could worm it out.　Calling
on her one day he introduced some confidential subjects, and the chat went cosily on, giving him lively
hopes of success.　At last he put the question as to
her age, when the lady said, " Doctor, can you keep a
secret ?"　" Yes, mam, I can."　She quickly replied,
" And so can I."

AN ENGLISH BULL.

A JOINER, of Whitehaven, named ——, was proceeding along the street when two young girls saw him
from an upstairs window and called out, " There is
John ——, the bull maker."　Whether real or assumed,
John was very apt at bull making, and hearing them
he said, " You little jades, I know you well enough,
and if I only had you here, I would quickly pitch you
out of the window."

ANOTHER.

JOHN was once sent for into Queen Street to measure
a corpse and take orders for the coffin.　Forgetting
the number of the house, he ventured to knock at the
door of one on chance, and on an inmate appearing,
said, " If you please is there a dead man lives here ?"

ST. SWITHIN'S DAY.

MANY believe that if rain falls on St. Swithin's day the following six weeks will be more wet than dry, and the contrary if the day is fair. The annexed table, from my carefully kept diary of twenty successive years, proves the falsity of the superstitious belief so far as the district of Workington is concerned.

St. Swithin's Day.		Six weeks following.	
		Days on which rain fell.	Days on which no rain fell.
1855	rain	27	15
1856	rain	22	20
1857	rain	22	20
1858	rain	21	21
1859	fair	19	23
1860	rain	29	13
1861	fair	33	9
1862	rain	32	10
1863	fair	22	20
1864	rain	13	29
1865	rain	23	19
1866	fair	26	16
1867	rain	23	19
1868	fair	23	19
1869	fair	17	25
1870	rain	13	29
1871	rain	20	22
1872	rain	23	19
1873	fair	32	10
1874	fair	21	21

A CLEVER DODGE.

MANY years ago a cottager at Camerton slaughtered a fat swine and hung the carcase up for the night in an outhouse to stiffen. Next morning the pork was missing, and the aid of the constabulary was called in. They having strong belief in the proclivities of a neighbour on the opposite side of the road, called on Israel Cuthbertson in obedience to a search warrant. On entering his house, the only person visible was Israel himself, rocking a cradle and crooning a song. The two constables (there were no police in those days) stated their authority, and said they must search the premises. Israel was a man of some education, and having a polite turn told them to go where they thought proper, only requesting them to make as little noise as possible, for, said he, " My wife is from home ; I am only a poor nurse, and if you waken the child, I may have great difficulty in keeping it quiet." The men searched the house and retired unsuccessful, after looking into every place but the cradle, where there was a carcase of fine pork instead of a living child.

A HARD PULL.

ON two Clifton young women awaking one morning, one of them called out, " Betty, it's time to git up." " O Sally," said the other, " T' bed poos hard. I've been tryan to git up for a gay while, bit it still poos me down ageann."

A PAIR OF PREACHERS.

THE late Rev. Canon H ——, of Carlisle, took some delight in a roughly expressed joke in his native dialect.

Once when an Oxford graduate came out of the Cathedral from hearing a sermon preached by a nephew of the Canon, passing the rev. gentleman, he, the Canon, asked if the graduate had heard his nephew preach? On being answered in the affirmative, he asked how he liked the preaching? He scarcely got any answer, but followed up in his very homely way, "And dudta iver hear a warse?" The graduate, after some hesitation, admitted he did not remember hearing a worse. "Then gang and hear his brother preach at Stanwix Church!" The Carlisle nephew was a notoriously bad preacher, gobbling his words so as to be nearly unintelligible; and the Stanwix nephew, a drony weak-voiced one, and very indolent. The latter had a small window in his church on a level with the pulpit, and through it he could see his servant girl come out of the vicarage at half-past twelve, and wave her apron when dinner was ready; the parson would immediately close his sermon whether finished or not, and dismiss the congregation. He used to close the afternoon service as soon as the mail passed the church, which was timed to be at ten minutes past three. The service done or not it was all the same, he struck up with, "And now to God," &c., and dismissed his hearers.

ON THE TENURE OF LAND IN CUMBERLAND.

Origin of Freeholds under the Feudal System.—"At first, the estates called *feuds* were held only during the will of the lord, and they could not be transferred or disposed of by those who held them during their lives, nor did they descend to their heirs at their deaths. Those persons only who were capable of bearing arms, and who were chosen by the lord, could succeed to them. Infants, women, and monks were therefore excluded as a matter of course. Subsequently the heirs of a deceased tenant were permitted to share his lands amongst them upon payment of what was called a *fine*, or present of armour, horses, or money to the lord. But the division of authority this occasioned was found to weaken the defences of the country, and it became the general rule to admit one heir only, in some parts the eldest, in others the youngest son of the deceased, or some other male relative capable of taking upon himself the conditions of the feud. Gradually. as intelligence and wealth began to increase, and other arts than those of war to be followed, these feuds became the absolute property of the tenants—no longer *vassals* liable to be dispossessed at any moment at the mere caprice of the lord, but *free holders* of the soil, possessing power to sell or bequeath it as they pleased, subject only to known rules of law, which in every succeeding reign were relaxed in their favour."—"*How we are Governed,*" by *Albany Fonblanque, 1858.*

THE nature of a hotch-potch publication is to contain matters of variety, and the privilege is claimed on this occasion to introduce a subject altogether foreign to the other contents, and one that may interest some who may derive little enjoyment from the perusal of the lighter portions; and it is highly proper that all should know something of the conditions on which the possession of the greater part of the landed property of the kingdom was once held, and no inconsiderable portion continues to be held by the present owners. An attempt is offered to explain this subject in a short and familiar way, as it relates to Cumberland.

It has been an uncontroverted maxim in the political economy of all late ages, and a highly commendable one, that few men in tolerable health, and none of a right-minded turn exist, who do not entertain a desire to become the owners of real property, that is, of houses or land—of a house to live in at least, and of more if possible; and every young man ought to look forward and try with his greatest energy, next to his duty to his Creator, to honestly acquire, and to carefully save, as much as will enable him to shelter himself and his family under his own roof, having nothing to pay after the purchase but his taxes, if of freehold tenure.

If the property should happen to be of other tenure, arbitrary or customary, the purchase money should be so much less as is equivalent to the annual payment of customary or lords-rent, with *Customary Tenant.* what are called fines, payable on the death of the lord of the manor, or on the death or change of the owner, or whom he may have nominated as his customary tenant—that is, a person appointed and enrolled in the court books of the manor as nominal trustee, or tenant in trust, for the property, whose duty it is to appear at the Manorial Courts to answer to his name there when called on, to serve on the juries of the court, and to perform certain other suits and services, the chief of which will be presently described, and to pay or cause to be paid the several rents, fines, &c., to which the property may be liable.

On some minds the impression is, that these rents and taxes, suits and services, are an imposition at the will of the lord of the manor, and that *Partnership.* they ought to be contended against and abolished. But on searching out their history, they are found to be as much the property of the other partner (who is lord of the manor) as the residue is the property of the ostensible owner of the estate.

Thus it will be seen that the long-standing partner, the lord of the manor, has a defined right, by no means of his own creating, which does not vary much in value ; and the other partner, who is called the owner, possesses the rest.

At the present day a large majority of owners hold their possessions by freehold tenure, the best of all tenures. But at one time, say eight hundred or a thousand years ago, it was a common saying that there was " no land without a lord," meaning that all land was then of this arbitrary or feudal tenure.

At the time of its origin, the baron, or great man of the district, now and then conditionally rewarded a follower, a friend, or a servant, with a slice from his estate, instead of paying him wages or rewards in that exceedingly scarce commodity, money, of which few of the barons of old could produce as much as several of our retail tradesmen can do any day now.

The land thus granted and accepted was commonly

worth more than the services rendered ; and, by way of equalizing the matter, and of retaining the
Grants. command of the services and assistance of the grantee, he was bound, in this northern part of the kingdom, to be at the call of the baron or lord of the manor in war time, either on foot or with horses, weapons, and provisions, for so many days as the civil broil, the raid across the border, or the dispersion of an enemy was expected to occupy ; also to pay the annual and other suits and services then attached to the grant.

This military service seems to have been the most oppressive custom, if an accepted duty ought to be called oppressive, and glad we may be that it has gone out of use.

When this was in force, and circumstances were thought to require it, the lord of the manor was bound, by his superior, the king,
Military Service. to appear at a certain time and place at the head of his tenants, who were to come at his call, armed and provisioned for war at their own cost of horse and equipment. and often without pay except what the plunder of friend or foe might give them. And no matter what the season might be ; seed time or harvest, sickness or death in the house, out he must march under the banner of the chief or forfeit his estate. But it must be kept in mind that the possessions of the chief were also liable to forfeiture, if the call of the sovereign was neglected or disobeyed, or even if he delayed. For precisely in the same way the lord himself was bound to serve his superior, the sovereign, who had granted the manor to *him.*

On the one hand, services were requited by a grant of land ; and on the other, protection was compensated by services ; and the deserving menial was elevated from a state of actual servitude into the yeoman or statesman, as the landowner of Cumberland is called at the present day.

There was, and still remains, one very important difference in the partnership before mentioned. It is contended that if the fine is *Two years' possession.* not duly paid, the lord can demand, take, and keep possession of the property for two years, or may let it to another; but precedents are not forthcoming.

Some of the services originally imposed were not a little arduous. Others, though important at that time, appear trifling and even ludicrous in modern times.

Others again were of a nature so inconsistent with the morality of after ages, that we are glad they are fallen into disuse, or have been commuted by an annual money payment, or enfranchised by purchase. Not many generations back, the family estate was *Marriage.* always left to the second son, if the first-born of marriage was a male child, on account of the uncertain lineage of the eldest—the lord of the manor claiming, and perhaps exercising, the right to sleep with every bride within his manor, high or low, on the first night of her marriage. And if more marriages than one were intended for the same day, he could command the postponement of all but one. The abolition of this intensely feudal and debasing custom gradually crept northward and has happily died out, in the far highlands at no very distant date. The customs and usages of the Cumberland manors vary considerably; not as to time or period, but as to one manor compared with another.

A variety of customs prevail respecting heriots, which consist in the liability of certain lands to pay to

the lord on the death of the tenant, in addition to the
fine of two years' value, the best living ani-
Heriots.   mal on the premises, from a horse to a tame
rabbbit, if the impost be what is called a
live heriot.   If a dead heriot, it is the best weapon,
article of furniture, or implement of husbandry.   In
some manors only the *live* heriot can be claimed ; and
if none belong to the premises, or to the tenant in
trust, no substitute can be had.   In some again, if no
animal can be had, the clock or some dead chattel of
greatest value must go.

In some manors the most valuable heriot on the
premises, dead or alive, or the best belonging to the
tenant in trust is claimed, whether on the premises or
elsewhere : and within the memory of the writer, a
horse of seventy pounds' value was taken on the death
of the lord from a customary tenant, although the
estate itself was only worth about sixteen pounds a
year, and did not belong to the tenant in trust at all,
nor did he occupy the land.   He was merely a friend
who had consented to allow his name to stand in the
court books of the manor as representative of the true
owner.   In some manors a heriot is only payable when
the tenant in trust leaves a widow, and then as com-
pensation to the lord for the loss of a man's military
service.

On such manors the evasive custom of putting in a
woman as tenant in trust has been resorted to, and
then no widow is left at her death, and no heriot could
be claimed.

Instances of joint manors have occurred where two,
and in some cases three lords have claimed heriots by
custom on the same property.   In
Joint Manors.   such cases it has sometimes happened
that very unseemly proceedings have
taken place.   When a tenant has been reported to be

dying, the stewards of the manors claiming heriots have each placed watchers around the dying man's house, and by means of a treacherous confederate within, one of them has outstripped the rest in the rush for possession of the best animal, at a time when the sorrows of the household should have been sacredly respected.

This custom is happily nearly obsolete. In some manors where horses were obliged to be kept for military service, heriots were not claimed.

Crown Rents. The crown possesses the manorial rights in some few instances within the county. and small rents called crown rents are paid; lands of this tenure mostly claim to be toll-free.

Game. In a few manors the tenants were bound to bring all the game they killed to the lord or bailiff of the manor under a penalty of three shillings and fourpence per head, and were then entitled to claim a specified price for each kind of game.

Birds were held to be game in those days which are not esteemed as such now, and singular discrepancies in value are recorded : for instance, a halfpenny each was to be given for field-fares, throstles, lap-wings, and ouzels; and a penny each for partridges and woodcocks.

Timber. On lands of arbitrary custom some lords are entitled to all the timber except that of fruit trees, and may cut and carry away all but the trees sheltering the buildings, and may take the timber of those too when the tenant consents to have them cut down.

Other lords are entitled only to the oak, or to the oak and whitethorn, the yew, the ash, &c., or to some combination of these ; but not to the timber of different kinds brought from abroad and grown here.

The tenants could not cut any timber without a
license from the lord or his forester, although entitled
to timber for husbandry implements and repairs of
houses.   This will account for the lavish use of
English oak timber in houses of the olden time.   The
tenants used it freely because they could not benefit
by it in any other way.

And if a tree was cut for the tenant's use, he must
plant at least two of the same kind ; but we do not
learn that he was bound to protect their growth, and
in consequence some estates are nearly denuded of
timber.   The oak bark was the property of the lord
of the manor.

In the important manor or barony of Egremont,
the burgesses were obliged to find armed
Egremont. men to protect the castle forty days at
their own charges ; and occasions would
arise when the warder might think the safety of the
princely castle depended more on their aid than on
the winding of his horn.   The people were
Aids. bound to what were termed aids ; that is, customary subscriptions for redeeming the lord and
his heir from captivity ; for knighting one of his sons ;
and towards a marriage portion for one of his daughters.   They were to keep watch and ward when occasion required on the turrets and battlements of the
castle, or elsewhere.   They could not enter the lord's
forest with bow and arrow, however ineffective these
rude and primitive implements might then be in the
capture of game.   They were not allowed to cut off
the feet of their dogs within the borough, such
Dogs. being useful in its defence.   This restriction
points to a custom then obtaining that the
dogs kept for defence within the limits of the forest,
but outside the borough, were required to have one
or more feet lopped off to prevent their chasing the

game ; this did not injure them much for the defence of the dwellings.   At one time it was intimated to the Egremont tenants that they would be permitted to come into the borough on market days without their bows and arrows, and this implied an order not to kill

Seduction. the game.   A fine of three shillings was payable to the lord for seducing a woman belonging to the borough ; but if a rustic outside the borough, no fine was levied, unless under promise of marriage.   The tenants of Egremont and

Fairs. Muncaster were bound to attend their respective fairs at Egremont and Ravenglass, to protect the trade and merchandise against pirates or a foreign enemy, and were entitled to go into the town field at each place to cut a swathe of grass for their horses.   These services entitled the people to the protection of the lord and of his retainers as one large family ; and the payments, suits, and services, whether obligatory according to the tenure, or volun- tary as in hunting and other sports, were commonly followed by unbounded hospitality and high revels in

Mete Corn. the hall of the castle.   A custom also prevailed of bestowing rewards of what was called mete or measured corn to the tenants as encouragement for labour.   The burgesses of Egremont could then send two members to Parliament, but this privilege they do not seem to have held in much esteem, as they petitioned to be disfranchised on account of the expenses.   This matter might be viewed in a different light in the present century !

Credit. The lord of Egremont was only entitled to forty days' credit, "and no more," for goods he purchased within the manor.   It may easily be thought that "good old times," such as these, might suit our ancestors better than we can imagine they would suit ourselves.

Many singular customs have existed in various manors, some of which have been redeemed or suffered gradually to fall into disuse. But at
Customs. the time of their existence, the tenants were punishable for disobedience to or non-observance of these customs, by being compelled to expend the whole produce of the tenement or farm within the same for its improvement, that it might yield a larger fine to the lord on the next occasion.

Some lords exacted small fines from the
Lodgers. tenants for admitting lodgers ; for keeping
Goats. goats or a breeding sow ; for allowing swine
Swine. to go without bows on their necks, to pre-
vent them from creeping through hedges into corn-fields in harvest.

In the manor of Workington twopence was charged for every meat swine or swine intended for slaughter within the year, and all swine kept in Priestgate and Workington were ordered to be double rung. and bowed before the first day of November.

Some tenants were restricted from letting or mort-
gaging their properties for more than
Mortgages. three years without consent ; and some were bound to pay so far as five per cent. on the amount of mortgage for liberty to raise money in that way.

Possession is given to purchasers and mortgagees at the manor court of Abbey Holme by the steward
of the court handing a white rod to the
Possession. seller or mortgagor, who passes it to the purchaser or mortgagee, and by him it is returned to the custodian of the court. In some manors a sod is cut by the new owner to denote taking possession ; or a leaf, or a handful of grass, or anything severed from the ground is passed in the same way.

In the manor of Wythburn a large stone may still be seen in a field on the west side of Thirlmere Lake, upon which contracts were made, deeds and wills signed, possession given, money lent or returned, records made, and divers business transactions, manorial, parochial, social, and domestic performed, which now require more formal observance.

Whatever was done on these occasions, with or without stamp, and frequently without pen and ink, or witnesses, or written memorandum at all, was held as obligatory as if done in the most formal manner; and probably as few instances of non-observance followed this primitive and Scriptural form of contract as are known in the modern time of legal exactness.

At one time the lord of the manor granted licenses for keeping public-houses, and the sum *Brew Farm.* paid him was called a Brew-farm rent; and above the door of a farm-house of old date at Isel there are still the figures of the ale-jug and drinking cup cut in the stone lintel, as a sign that it was once a brew-farm or public-house.

Some estates are held by the payment of a rose at Christmas. An estate in Setmurthy is held on *Rose.* this tenure, and the rose is actually paid at the Christmas audit at Cockermouth Castle. A few years since, when the cultivation of roses was not so well attended to, and the flower was a rarity at that season, a penny was paid annually in lieu of the rose.

An estate, here and there, is held by payment of a pepper-corn; and an estate is known to the *Pepper.* writer which pays a pound of pepper-corns annually. The adjoining property pays two-pence-halfpenny towards another half-pound of pepper-corns, and the former estate makes up the remainder of the cost.

Our remote ancestors knew the piquant relish of

pepper and spices, and they used the little stone-mortars seen about old farm houses for pounding or crushing the pepper-corns before mills came into use. The hollow of some of these mortars is not much larger than a common breakfast cup, and the outside form is usually square, while some are ornamented with carved work.

Spurs.
Gloves.
Goose.
Spelk hens.
A pair of gilt spurs is no uncommon payment still, and so is a pair of gloves. Some farms pay a Michaelmas goose; and some one or more hens. Some pay a hen for liberty to cut spelks or pegs in the lord's woods for pegging down the thatch of their roofs, and these are called spelk-hens.

A stipulated quantity of corn is paid by some called

Corn.
Metlam corn; and is, or was lately, collected by the lord's officers, being measured by them in a certain measure called a Metlam peck. The wood-warden was entitled to an annual quantity of oats, called Forester's corn.

There are, or were, many other singular payments, but the foregoing may convey a general idea of the rest.

The customs and services not yet recounted are very various, and not a little curious; they show what devices have been resorted to for securing equivalents for money when that commodity was almost a stranger in the land.

At the present day Boon services are payable by

Boons.
the tenants of many manors, by half-day, whole day, or many days' labour for the lord, according to the value of the farm originally granted.

Some Boon-services were paid in ploughing, some in harrowing, others in mowing or shearing, cutting peats, dressing meadows, cutting brackens for litter, or rushes for carpeting the hall on banquet days, carting coals or peats, cutting and splitting fire-wood, embanking rivers, cleansing sowes or ditches, repairing the lord's park wall, catching eels or fish, and various other services. With some of these the workmen had to provide victuals for themselves and provender for their horses. Others had dinners provided for them. Some had a cake each of regulated sizes for men, women, and boys, provided they made their appearance at a certain time and place; otherwise the cake was forfeited but the work still exacted.

Before rural post-offices and post-messengers were established, there was a manorial custom prevalent in some parts of Northumberland called *Catch Boon.* "Catch Boon." Under this custom the lord of the manor could send a servant out directing him to *catch*, or impress, any one of the customary tenants of the manor and order him to carry a message from his lord to a distance not exceeding ten or twelve miles, according to the custom of the manor, the messenger being provided at starting with a prescribed dole of provisions. On his return, he would be entitled to a certificate exempting him from "Catch Boon" service for one year, except in cases of invasion by an enemy.

The tenants of Holm Cultram were entitled for three days' ploughing, to the very liberal allowance of seventeen white herrings, and of *Holm Cultram.* six red; to a quarter of a "killin," as it was called, probably a quarter of mutton at the killing of a sheep; a quarter of a salmon; three wheat loaves; three loaves of some other kind of bread, called yeoman's bread, most likely of barley or rye; and three gallons of ale. This seems a large allowance for a ploughman for three days, keen as his appetite is reputed to be, but it must be remembered that nothing is mentioned for the pair of horses, and probably four oxen drawing the plough as was then customary, along with three or four men and boys to drive or guide the half-broken animals, and to assist in holding down the plough beam, and to turn the furrows with a spade, which the defective plough of the day would slide over and miss. For every shear-bond, that is, every farm bound to assist his lord in harvest, for three days' work, three loaves (no size mentioned), six white herrings, and three pints of ale. A meagre provision indeed, compared with harvest allowances of the present day !

Some tenants near Penrith were bound to bring a number of pack-horse loads of salt annually from St. Bees. If the season happened to be rainy, *Salt.* they must either rest on their journey home at their own cost during rain, or run the risk of arriving with empty sacks and being sent back in dryer weather. But if they were lucky enough to miss the exciseman, and were able to get their private kegs of Hollands, or smuggled brandy, or tobacco, safe home in the ends of their sacks, they would hardly object to a second journey, let the weather blow rain or fair.

A small rent, called Greenhue Rent, is paid in some manors for liberty to cut green wood or *Greenhue.* brushwood in the forests for fences, hurdles, or stakes, and for cropping the ash trees when in full leaf to feed milk cows with.

A door-toll rent was also paid, but for *Door-Toll.* what purpose the writer has not ascertained.

In troubled times officers were appointed by the lords of manors whose duties were to blow *Cornage.* horns on the appearance of an enemy. To pay those officers small rents called Cornage Rents were paid by the tenants.

Some lords could command the services of their tenants to repair the manorial mills and dams and to fetch stones if necessary.

At Keswick the tenants coming to market had a right to cut grass with a sickle for their *Grass.* horses, only on market days, on a certain *Swill-* piece of swampy land called the Cass, set *Wood.* apart for that purpose, and for growing Swill- wood, which they might also cut for home use but not for sale.

So scarce and valuable were peats for fuel in that manor (the manor of Derwentwater), that the tenants were not allowed to keep two fires burning in *Fuel.* the same house or *toft* without license, what- ever the requirements of sickness or feasting might be. And so important was economy held to be in that department, and its non-observance so fla- grant a misdeed, that fines of ten shillings each are recorded in the court-books as having been levied on the offenders. The ten-shilling fine of that day might be equal to about seven pounds at the present time.

Commonly one farm in each manor was bound to provide and keep a stallion, another *Male Animals.* a bull, and another a boar for the free use of the tenants of that manor. There was no obligation to provide good male animals to improve the breed and to prevent the *Stallions.* annoyance of these free services. It was usual to keep the very worst of stallions, if it only was useful in working on the farm.

In some manors the lord allowed a piece of land towards the support of those free-serviced animals, and the writer of this lately got rid of the liability to keep a stallion, which no one made use of, by an agreement to restore the stallion field which was of little value but for planting.

When Richard de Lucy granted Mosser to Adam, of Mosser, and his heirs, he received a hart and a hind; a boar and a sow; and an eyrie of hawks, when they shall be there, along with knight's service, &c.

Some lords of manors are bound to keep a stallion, a bull, boar, or game cock, for the use of the tenants.

Some customs bind the tenants to find and keep bulls in annual turns. From this had arisen the term *Bulls.* of "Town Bull," or "Turn Bull," an animal always famed for his powers of oratory, and not always of a peaceful character. In Loweswater there is a large pasture held in stints or grasses, and several of the farms have each a right to send so many cattle in summer and sheep in winter. These owners are bound in their annual turns to provide a bull for the use of the rest, according to the number of stints they occupy. It is open to each owner in his turn to put in the worst bull he can find, and the rest have no redress.

The romantic and primitive township of Troutbeck, in Westmoreland, is divided into three parts, which *Troutbeck.* are called hundreds, each hundred having a large stinted pasture, and each pasture requiring a joint-stock bull annually; these were called *hundred* bulls, or bulls to serve the hundreds. Some years ago a person was deputed from Troutbeck to a Yorkshire fair to purchase the three bulls for that year. He quietly went to work and bought his number, then made it known that he came with a commission to buy *three-hundred* bulls. Before long the fair ground was thronged with nearly all the bulls that could be hurriedly brought for his choice. The bull buyer thought he was "doing" the Yorkshire men, but soon the uproar of voices and war of horns very plainly intimated that it was not prudent for him to enjoy his joke any longer, and he left as quickly as he could to avoid more unpleasant results.

When water power for driving machinery was in small request and the population less numerous, salmon were much more plentiful in the streams, and they formed an important item in the provisioning of the country. At that time the tenants of the manors of Ennerdale and Kinniside claimed and took good care to enjoy a free stream from the *Free Streams.* lake to the sea. So jealous of these rights were they that they periodically assembled on horseback to ride down the stream of the river Ehen, accompanied by a numerous retinue on foot. If any obstructions were found—in the shape of weirs for mills or otherwise—detrimental to the free ascent of the fish, whether erected by the lord of the manor or others, they were quickly doomed to a ready-handed destruction. On such occasions provisions and drink were either levied from willing contributors, or provided and partaken of at certain places; and mischievous pranks, often of a very moist character, were slyly or openly practised as opportunity offered (and no doubt they were as duly expected) on every member of the cavalcade.

History does not record the existence of professed teetotallers in those days; and probably never a river-riding there ended without some fights and all being made drunk, by compulsion if not by choice; and often quarrels which originated in frolic were settled in earnest, or were tacitly adjourned and remembered, to be decided by warfare at the next river-riding. These customs have gradually fallen into disuse, and the river is doing better service in driving machinery which gives employment to hundreds of people in more profitable ways than preserving open streams or killing salmon.

There is an extensive variety of quaint, and to our ears, uncouth terms belonging to feudal times and feudal tenures which it is the business of the lawyer and delight of the antiquary alone to preserve and understand. These terms are fast becoming obsolete, we hope not to be revived in practice.

Many other interesting and some amusing customs might be recorded here, but even patience has its limits, and it may be better to conclude so dry a subject.

NOTE.—The Earl of Derby claimed the royalty of part of a field in the parish of Dalton, near Lindal, for an extent sufficient to graze three langled sheep, and it was set out on the east side of the field, about sixty feet wide, and comprises about two acres, which is found to contain a very large body of valuable iron ore.

THE END.

CALLANDER & DIXON, PRINTERS, 3 MARKET PLACE, WHITEHAVEN.

9 783743 349971